LIGHTING
FIRES

LIGHTING FIRES

How the Passionate Teacher
Engages Adolescent Writers

Joseph I. Tsujimoto

Boynton/Cook Publishers
HEINEMANN
Portsmouth, NH

Boynton/Cook Publishers, Inc.
A subsidiary of Reed Elsevier Inc.
361 Hanover Street
Portsmouth, NH 03801-3912
www.boyntoncook.com

Offices and agents throughout the world

The author and publisher wish to thank those who have generously given permission to reprint borrowed material:

"The Affective Teacher" by Joseph Tsujimoto first appeared in *The Teacher's Journal*, Vol. III, 1990. Published by Brown University, Education Department, Providence, RI. Copyright by Joseph Tsujimoto.

"Mantis" by Joseph Tsujimoto first appeared in *Hawaii Review*, Winter 1989/1990, Vol. 14, No. 1. Copyright by Joseph Tsujimoto.

"Four Temple Gates" haiku by Bashō is reprinted from *From Beneath a Single Moon: Buddhism in Contemporary Poetry* edited by Kent Johnson and Craig Paulenich. Copyright © 1991 by Kent Johnson. Reprinted by arrangement with Shambhala Publications, Inc., Boston. www.shambhala.com.

"Old Kimono" is reprinted from *Bananaheart and Other Stories* by Maria M. Hara. Published by Bamboo Ridge Press, 1994. Used by permission of the author.

"Sand Castles" by Wayne Kaneshiro. Copyright © 1982 by Wayne Kaneshiro. Used by permission of the author.

"The Grandmother" is reprinted from *A Small Obligation and Other Stories of Hilo* by Susan Nunes. Published by Bamboo Ridge Press, 1982. Used by permission of the author.

Library of Congress Cataloging-in-Publication Data
Tsujimoto, Joseph I., 1946–
    Lighting Fires : how the passionate teacher engages adolescent writers / Joseph I. Tsujimoto.
      p. cm.
    Includes bibliographical references.
    ISBN 0-86709-504-0
    1. Creative writing (Middle school)—Hawaii—Honolulu—Case studies. 2. English language—Composition and exercises—Study and teaching (Middle school)—Hawaii—Honolulu—Case studies. 3. Tsujimoto, Joseph I., 1946– I. Title.
    LB1631 .T78 2000
    808'.042'071296931—dc21   00–049406

Consulting editor: Tom Newkirk
Production: Lynne Reed
Cover design: Night & Day Design
Cover photographs: Tami Dawson/Photo Resource Hawaii
Manufacturing: Louise Richardson

Printed in the United States of America on acid-free paper

05 04 03 02 01 RRD 1 2 3 4 5

For Sharon

There is an art in lighting a fire.

—James Joyce, A Portrait of the
Artist As a Young Man

*Sometimes our light goes out but is blown
into flame by another human being. Each
of us owes deepest thanks to those who
have rekindled our spirits.*

—Albert Schweitzer

Contents

Acknowledgments

I would like to thank Punahou School for supporting my efforts through a half-year sabbatical, though the fiction I intended to work on (and still intend to complete) was superseded by this book.

I want to thank my brother Richard and his wife Alice for accommodating my long stay in their Brooklyn home, which gave me the space and solitude—at the expense of their privacy and freedom—to complete a good portion of the first draft. I also want to thank Stanley and Miriam Monk for the loan of their summer house in Thompson's Point, Vermont, overlooking Lake Champlain, which, together with the sudden changes in the weather and the red squirrels, the chipmunks, the rabbits, the gulls, the blue jays, and the hummingbirds—provided a retreat both peaceful and refreshing; where I was able to complete the first draft.

Thanks also to the University of Vermont for allowing me the use of its computer lab, and to Ben Schacher, the student lab consultant, who helped me manage the mysterious machines.

And I must thank my four colleagues: Sheryl Dare, whose grasp of my intentions was stronger than my own; Cathy Kawano-Ching, whose feedback was meticulous and invaluable; Terry Woody, who would not countenance my penchant for parenthetical comments; and Steve Waggonseller, who rubbed my back and urged me on. All took time from their busy work schedules to help me see my work from the perspective of my audience, preparing me for the revision I had to complete.

Which brings me to teacher/writer/editor Tom Newkirk, whom I worked with through e-mail, whose enthusiasm and insightful queries ushered me on to the end. Perhaps someday we can work together again.

And, of course, I want to thank my wife, Sharon, for providing us, always, a home-away-from-home and for advising me about what to add, cut, revise, and refine in the manuscript, which she helped to edit and type.

Finally, I want to thank the students who allowed me the use of their exemplary work, without which this book would not be possible. Their writings closed whatever arguments I began. Whether they know it or not, they have contributed much to my development as a teacher.

As I walked into class that first day of the year, I remember Mr. Tsujimoto sitting at his desk and doing nothing more. What he looked like was no surprise to me. I'd seen him before. I was still worried about class, though. All the rumors roared through my head. But I figured English couldn't be as bad as some of the stories I had heard.

Finally, class began and the teacher spoke. The distinct voice spoke of New York. He acted Italian, though he was Japanese. He then talked about his class, then moved into poetry.

—*Jason Morrison (Grade 8)*

There was a time when poetry was like liver and onions. The sight of it made me feel sick, the smell of it churned my stomach, even the idea of it made me quiver. The first time Mr. Tsujimoto said the word "poetry," I felt like I was going to throw up.

—*Andrew Yeh (Grade 7)*

I could feel the tension. I was getting some pretty negative vibes. The teacher was a short, chubby man. He had sunglasses sitting on his head, which we learned would never ever come off, only when we listened to some pretty lame music and he lowered them over his eyes. He bopped his head front and back, over and over. I could just imagine him saying, "I'm so cool, my shades are so rad, those kids probably never had a cooler teacher. If I get any cooler the magma in the earth's core would freeze over."

—*Donovan Odo (Grade 8)*

1

The Assignment

The Hawaiian word for passion is konikoni.
kaunu: *to be absorbed*
koni: *to throb, pulsate, tingle, beat; to flutter, as the heart*
hekili: *to thunder*

Needless to say, my students like to engage in hyperbole and, like many young teenagers, enjoy poking fun at others. Especially adults. Especially teachers. Especially teachers who have poked fun at *them*. In any case, I accept their remarks as compliments (backhanded though they may be) because many of them have gained a measure of confidence as writers, while a few have grown fearless enough to express an oblique affection for me.

Now, just as many of my students feel a certain panic when I tell them we will be writing poetry for the first few months of school, I, too, felt a sudden nausea and dread when Jim Gray, former director of the National Writing Project, asked me to speak to five hundred site directors and teacher/consultants at their annual meeting. My God, I was no public speaker. Also, I had recently lost a lower front tooth, whose absence resulted in a slight slur. Besides, I had nothing to say. Nothing, at least, that I could expand upon with any coherence beyond a few minutes, much less anything insightful or frightfully new. And even if I had, who would listen to me? Who was I? Such was the noise that echoed through the canyons in my head.

But I couldn't refuse. For Jim Gray, you understand, was like the academe's godfather. If he asked you to run a workshop, write letters to your congressman, or create a local Writing Project site, you simply did it, inspired by his curmudgeonly charisma and his belief that you had many important ideas worth sharing with others—many more than you thought you had—and his confidence—greater than yours—that you would share them with a certain grace. He was irresistible, making everything sound so simple in his offhand way. *Of course you'll do fine.* Sure. It was easy for him to say (as I imagine my students saying about their teacher). But I didn't want to let Gray down and have him discover the truth, that he was wrong about me.

———————

Back in Hawaii, I worried over the speech for several months before putting sweaty fingers to dusty keyboard. The result is called "The Affective Teacher." It organized for me the disconnected words and feelings, like loose change, that jingled noisily in my brain. It enabled me to grasp more clearly the source and power behind great teaching. It quieted my anxiety.

And though much of what I said was not new, while some of the things I said would seem to run contrary to the current ideas favoring a "student-centered classroom," my audience of teacher-writers was nevertheless sympathetic. (I had a cold, I told them, and my voice was hoarse and gruff from rooting on my son's soccer team in the rain. I imagined myself sounding, at times, like a New York hit man). Here is my speech:

> Let me begin by reading you a piece I wrote at the 1987 English Coalition Conference, where we wrote and argued and rewrote and, as local Hawaiians say, "talked story," as a way of narrowing and grasping the issues that we felt were critical to contemporary education. My story is called "Practice in Search of Theory."

>> It seems that all his life he had been searching for a theory that would explain the mystery of his behavior in the classroom, since, upon reflection, much of what he did did not seem rational. That is, much of his life had been consumed in the search for a language that, in addition to improving his teaching, would clarify what it was that he did right; that explained why his students had found him an effective teacher. For it was said that he was strange, distant, and tyrannical.

>> The pivotal point in his early life was his meeting the Greek poet, Professor Konstantinos Lardas, who, for the first few weeks of class did little more than read Hopkins, Sacco's farewell speech before his execution, whale names at the beginning of *Moby Dick*, Sappho, and Lorca's "Divertisement on the Duende," which speaks of the *duende* as that "mysterious power that all may feel and no philosophy explain."

>> Which is to say, what he learned was Lardas—Lardas' passionate love of language and what he was trying to show through his deep and tremulous reading. That English, rather than architecture, became his major was something that precluded his freedom of choice.

>> Thereafter, he had the fortune of witnessing a similar passion in other teachers he had—an angry passion, a quiet passion, a querulous passion—despite the subjects they taught . . . despite the singular theories according to which they operated. He recognized that, with this passion, they became, in a sense, what they taught, transcending personality, transporting the students to a world that was finer, purer, and nobler than any they had previously known. So he too aspired to the creatiion of such worlds.

To his disappointment, however, fate would have him create worlds not in poetry, but in prose. Then, to his devastation (despite the efforts of his teachers—Leonard Kriegel, Joseph Heller, and Donald Barthelme)—he learned that he would not be creating worlds in prose, either. So, in want of money for a pair of trousers, he became an English teacher. Yet the spirit is forever preserved—for at the end of the seventh year of obsessive work, he suddenly understood, in the middle of a crosswalk, that he, too, could create similarly honest worlds through his teaching; that that, in his own perverse way, was precisely what he had been trying to do all along, precisely what he had been doing successfully. It was for these reasons that he had confidently said to his wife (whom, of course, we cannot forget), "What is ultimately taught is the teacher, he who embodies the idea that his students have the power to create their own worlds." That they did so astonished him throughout his life.

So in this way did his students inspire him. And so in this way was he defined.

But let me end according to the precepts of his will with "Everything and Nothing" from Borges' *Labyrinths*:

> In short, the parable recounts the history of Shakespeare's role-playing: as an actor, director, playwright, businessman—the creator of characters *par excellence*. According to Borges, just before or after Shakespeare's death, Shakespeare, finding himself in the presence of God, asks God, "'I who have been so many men in vain want to be one and myself.' [Whereupon] the voice of the Lord answered from a whirlwind: 'Neither am I anyone; I have dreamt the world, as you dreamt your work, my Shakespeare, and among the forms in my dream are you, who like myself are many and no one.'"

In understanding better how the teacher can be "many and no one," I'd like to talk more about my first poetry teacher, Konstantinos Lardas, of CCNY.

He was a soft-spoken man, soft as the maroon and brown fabrics he wore, or the old, thin, leather-bound books he carried. He seemed doddering, stammering, always groping for words with his hands—which I suppose was a pretense to get us to talk. In any case, he was altogether different when he read to us—for the walls and windows shook, the chairs shook, and we shook, but not through any effect of the volume of his voice. I can hear him now reading the opening of Lorca's "Duende":

> Whoever inhabits that bull's hide stretched between the Jucar, the Guadalete, the Sil, or the Pisuerga—no need to mention those lion-colored waves churned up by the Plata—has heard it said with a certain frequency: "Now that has *duende!*

At such moments, when he read, or spoke in a similar manner, old Lardas would disappear. Where had he gone?

Why is it we can remember so few of our teachers? Better yet: What is it that makes a teacher memorable or great?

Theodore Sizer wrote, in the first issue of *The Teacher's Journal*, 1988, p. 5:

> We win or lose with kids to some considerable measure with our personalities. Good teachers use their personas even at the risk of being characters.

Sizer, for the most part, is right. The good teacher uses her unique personality as an integral part of her teaching, even though, as in a growing number of classrooms today, that personality is manifested through the configuration of the classroom; through the ways her students huddle in groups; through the ways they converse with each other in a forum; and customarily, vitally, through her presence, her posture, her gestures, her countenance; through her voice and language, written and spoken. The good teacher can never be discounted. She is precursor, proviso, and impetus, who makes learning a stimulating and productive experience.

To be sure, original personality and its extension through theoretical models are important. But the *great* teacher—or, as is more often the case, instances of *great* teaching by good teachers—transcends personality and philosophy, which, we now see, are merely vehicles for the illumination of wisdom—or knowledge made beautiful beyond any rhetorical game.

At such instances, the teacher is so immersed in his reading, or in his speaking, or in his characterization, that he sheds all consciousness of self. And the students see embodied before them the very *spirit* of learning: the very *subject* to be learned. So that it can be said that what is ultimately learned is the teacher.

In this way is teaching an art: the teacher, the poem, the students—*all bodies*—vibrating in sympathetic consonance.

I am reminded of this whenever my students write about teachers they carry in their hearts. For example, the following poem was written by a seventh-grade girl. It is called: "And He Teaches at Punahou?"

> Playing "She's so unusual"
> after school.
> Hanging Cyndi Lauper posters
> around the room;
> with her red hair and make-up
> it looks like Picasso was her beautician.
> Asking what happened over the weekend,
> telling us about teaching in Amsterdam,

Bringing vegemite to school for tasting,
dressed as Reptile Man for Halloween,
going sky-diving,
taking pictures of blue starfish in Fiji;
Explaining why he puts Oil of Olay
on his sun-puffed eyes,
thinking of names for our mathematical battle teams,
boys against girls;
Betting us that Philadelphia would beat the Orioles,
writing a poem in chalk
while we did our Friday math quiz.

Sitting behind his front desk
with windmill, calendar of rare words,
answer book, and signed picture of Miss Chinatown;
wearing Magnum-style shirts on his thin body
and a mustache that never quite
matched his curly brown hair.
His voice had a resonance of jello,
it wasn't built for yelling.
We learned more than math or
science.
We learned how to howl at the Moon!

—Keli Sato

Of course, we sometimes retain the memory of a teacher who was simply mean. This poem, called "Kindergarten," was written by a seventh-grade boy.

When you think of kindergarten teachers,
you think of a nice, pretty lady,
but not Mrs. Williams.
She was old. At the time we
thought she was 600 years old,
her long seaweed hair,
with a long pointy nose like a peg
for a coat hanger; round, metal-rimmed
glasses surrounding those green beady eyes;
but her fingers were her meanest feature
long, bony fingers, black painted nails
and wrinkly skin like an old leather glove.
She would take away our crayons,
break them then throw them away,

she would have been a witch
if she had a wart on her nose.
She even had a cat named Spooky
                    —Scott Kaalele

As sometimes happens, poems like the last can encourage us to write our own. I wrote the following poem inspired by a rodent-faced administrator who tyrannized over my teaching. It is called "Curse."

From the void
From emptiness
Arise! Guinea pig face!
I've embers for your eyes.

Feel now
my words, like glass slivers,
enter your Pekingese brain—
your Galapagos ass:

a cypress of ice
a stiletto
a wire nest of fire and
driver ants an army of them
    black as an elevator shaft
Manute Bol;

and the granite sky shatters,
the bat, the monkey, the toucan
screeching,
like Saskatchewan; and more

a chimney, an Oreo, a menthol suppository
the beak of the south wind, cockney, a twelve-point buck
a peacock, Mozambique
—a nebulae of membrane on the counter top, an oil spill
on the toe of a brogan, a barracuda
cut cleanly with a stainless sword,
the fingers and tonsils of your memory;

at each pin prick
a bee sting
a tire iron
an injection of cholera.

Clutching the torso
I pronounce upon the blank face:
Poetry is voodoo.

It seems to me that we need to do more nationally to right the balance between affect and intellect in our teaching, where—to state the condition in the extreme—our talks, our materials, our methods, and even our postures are dominated by a language impoverished of passion.

I am constantly forced to ask myself: How can the mind be reached except through the heart? Especially young minds?

There are several ways, in my experience, that we can gradually right the balance.

First is encouraging ourselves to indulge, without embarrassment, our feelings. This can be easily practiced by reading the works we love to our students—reading not, however, as though they were seated before us, but with the whole of our attention upon images and sounds, as though we were reading to ourselves in a lofty cavern. Second is allowing ourselves to succumb to those moments when the heart is in ascendance. The first time, as you know, occurs as propitious accident, like the accident experienced by the character, in the 1988 novel *Stoner* pp. 112–113. The author, John Williams, says,

> When [Stoner] lectured, he now and then found himself so lost in his subject that he became forgetful of his inadequacy, of himself, and even the students before him. Now and then he became so caught up by his enthusiasm that he stuttered, gesticulated, and ignored the lecture notes that usually guided his talks. At first he was disturbed by his outbursts, as if he presumed too familiarly upon his subject, and he apologized to his students; but when they began coming up to him after class, and when in their papers they began to show hints of imagination and the revelation of a tentative love, he was encouraged to do what he had never been taught to do. The love of literature, of language, of the mystery of the mind and the heart showing themselves in the minute, strange, and unexpected combinations of letters and words, in the blackest and coldest print—the love which he had hidden as if it were illicit and dangerous, he began to display, tentatively at first, and then boldly, and then proudly.

I would assert that, like the best language, the best teaching and learning are unrestrainedly physical.

The third way we can right the balance between heart and mind is by teaching poetry: first of all, the poetry of our contemporaries and our students' peers, poetry that speaks particularly to our age and issues of our times, through the language of our streets and boulevards, through the language of the barrio, farms, and coastal fisheries, through the language used for its noblest function—without fear that Shakespeare, Keats, Dickinson, or Langston Hughes should be neglected or beg our defense.

As a complement, we should also teach our students to write their own poetry, to speak their own hearts—allowing language to prove its own efficacy. As one eighth grader said, "It's a great feeling to know that there is a way to express my emotions without any fear of persecution and to even get praise for it." True—only poetry can accommodate, can celebrate, such speech.

And if we teach our students to write poetry, we ought to write and share our own, in the very same ways we have shared with our students our prose. This is the fourth way we can right the balance and perhaps the most difficult way, since we must reveal, for the scrutiny of our students, our feelings and ideas, our peculiar visions, our biases and flaws. But what better way exists to know a thing—to know the various ways a thing can be made—than to be a maker of things ourselves? What better way to forewarn our students of the difficulties, and guide their prosperity along the way, than by having preceded them, having reconnoitered the terrain ourselves?

Besides, as one eighth-grade veteran put it, "Anyone can write poetry. I know, because I've heard my classmates reading theirs."

He was earnest. There is *no more* fertile soil than poetry for psychological growth. Writing it and reading it aloud.

And you yourselves have heard many poetical utterances here at these conventions. You have heard the quiet wisdom of a Jix Lloyd-Jones. You have heard the disarming vulnerability and humanity of Peter Elbow. Last year many of you heard the terseness, power, and piquancy of Janet Emig's inaugural speech—as many of you heard the music of Maya Angelou.

I guess—for more than any other reason—we come to conferences to be passionately reminded of things fundamental—of things "invisible." Put another way, we come thirsting for the nouns that will transform us into verbs: to seek the wisdom in our own hearts that enable us to light bonfires in our students.

There are many ways to pique our students' interest and arouse their curiosity, no less than the ways of personality, passion, and poetry I mentioned in my speech. And if not through poetry, then through prose or drama, or through all three; through ever-emerging thoughts, ideas, principles, and theories, new and renewed; through the endless, bubbling, variety of talk, question-and-response and counter-question, as the mind cartwheels, doubles back, or leaps between solar systems; and through the tasks we assign: the papers and projects and presentations; through the carefully ordered sequence of "units," often governed by both practicality and an intuition cultivated upon the bedrock of experience, plying, at the moment, our pedagogical and psychological stratagems—of ice cream, plunger, and ax. And if we do not teach kindergarteners or graduate students, then we might teach seventh and eighth graders, as I do, and know in general what interests them, as well as what makes them hesitate or hide; know that Marcus, a local Chinese-Hawaiiian, likes surfing and is good at singing, things we can appeal to, for his benefit and ours.

But none of this is easy. Nor is it easily had.

Teaching, in my mind, is akin to writing. Both require premeditation and spontaneity, revision and refinement, so you may do it better the next time—year after year. It took me twenty-plus years of study and practice to be able speak for twenty minutes. It has taken me at least that long to become a good teacher.

Which is to say, teaching is an intellectually demanding, complex affair, misunderstood by a penurious, lay public quick to condemn and trivialize the profession, generous with its lip service, speaking from both sides of its mouth.

My English-teacher office mate (fluent in Esperanto), deeply ensconced in the lounge chair, says, from behind his newspaper, "Old Korean saying: 'All worked up/lucky he has two nostrils.'"

This book contains working assumptions, writing assignments, exercises, a few adult examples, and many, many student writings that I've collected over the years like dried leaves and flowers and shapely shells. These writings perhaps speak more about the students' talents as individuals than they do about my teaching, but, as I said to a professor who claimed that he was the sole reason one of his students experienced a change of heart and developed into a fine writer, "Well you gotta remember that many of us had a hand in preparing the soil so the seed could take." I did not intend to diminish his truly commendable achievement as a teacher. I just wanted to remind him that teaching is a *joint* affair, that we are all in this thing together.

Which is to say, I must credit not only the students themselves, but also their previous teachers, as well as crediting myself.

The students who attend Punahou School, where I teach, have passed through an admissions process similar to a college's. The school is said to be the most prestigious in the islands. It *is* the biggest. In fact, Punahou, Kamehameha, and Iolani, in that order, are the biggest independent schools west of the Mississippi. Punahou spans grades K through 12, has a student population of about 3,500 and a faculty and staff of over 260, on a campus of forty school buildings over seventy-six acres at the mouth of rainy Manoa Valley in Honolulu. The great majority of the students are of Caucasian and Asian and Pacific Islander background, and many were born of mixed marriages—so many that an ethnographic study based on last names alone would be impossible. Because of the school's endowment, all students are in one way or another on partial scholarship. The tuition is about $10,000 a year, half of Dalton's tuition in Manhattan and much less than many of the other well-known prep schools on the East Coast. And while steps are being taken to continually expand the number of scholarships for local kids from money-strapped families, many parents are working their brains out to keep their kids at Punahou.

Other than tuition, the collegelike facilities, and a weekly chapel program, Punahou on the surface would seem little different than a good public school almost anywhere in the States, the kids especially. I remember going to school with a number of very bright kids at Junior High School 43 on the Upper West Side of Manhattan, in Harlem. My colleagues, hailing from teaching posts at public schools all over the States, claim the kids that they've taught are very bright. And though we teach a proportionately higher number of smart, quick, hard-working students than teachers at most public schools do, we teach, as they do in public schools, many who struggle in one way or another. Otherwise, we do not have thuggery, guns, or blatant use of drugs; we have few students who are labeled as handicapped and few pregnancies, though we have our share of dyslexics, kids from broken homes and reconstructed families, slow readers, many latchkey kids, and kids on Ritalin.

Kids are kids, and kids are kids in a particular society at a particular time. I'm glad I'm not a kid, and I'm doubly glad I'm not an adolescent, especially the kind I used to be. As I said elsewhere, if I had me as a student I would've kicked me out of class.

2
Beginning with Poetry Writing

Mere air, these words, but delicious to taste.
—Sappho

The way of comets is the poet's way
—Marina Tsvetaeva

"There they all are with no place to hide," I say as I walk into class. I write my name on the board and say, "Hopefully, you're in the right room . . . By the way, those of you who've heard rumors about me from my previous students—about my being mean and so forth—well . . . they're all true." They laugh nervously.

Good.

After answering some questions about having the right books and other materials, I tell them that they will be introducing each other to the class.

"One of the things that I want to hear, and want the class to hear, is how every one of us is unique, if not peculiar. We as listeners and readers are interested in the personal and the intimate. So, among the facts that you garner from each other in five minutes, tell your partner one thing that you do that is odd or eccentric, something you think only you do. For example, I am what is known as a nomadic sleeper. I start the night sleeping in my bedroom with my wife, but sometime during the night, while half-awake, I'll go to the living room and sleep on the rug, or I'll go to my son's room and sleep on his bed, since he likes to sleep on the living room couch. I sleep in all three places, sometimes two or three times. Then before dawn I go back to sleep in my own bed." One kid, I learn, has a pet pig that the family keeps in the house and even takes for walks on a leash. Another, when she was younger, liked to read in her mother's closet using a flashlight even when it was daytime. And so forth. It's a quick and fun icebreaker, gets them on their feet in front of the class, and hints at the writing expectations to come.

The next day I tell them, "Take out the marble notebooks I told you to get yesterday—what? Well, just write for now on some folder paper and copy it into your book later. Date it. Date everything. I will be dictating to you a

11

number of ideas throughout the year. So when I tell you the date, you know what's coming. Ready? *8/28/99: The number one goal of English is the development of mind—the caring, critical, creative mind—which subsumes (which means includes) a knowledgeable mind.*" I repeat parts of this quickly several times. I don't write it on the blackboard; I rarely use the board. One of my intentions from the outset is to train the students' ears, so important in the study and practice of language.

"Now I don't know about you, but I don't know anyone *uninterested* in the quality of his or her own mind. Therefore, what you say, write, think, and feel will be at the center of this classroom. Our foremost concern. *Capisce?* That's Italian for *understand.* When I say *Capisce?* and you understand, you say *Capisce.* Everyone, repeat after me: *Capisce.*"

"CAPISCE!"

"Okay, now, write down this next idea. *You will learn more from each other than you will from your teacher.*" They dutifully record this. But some of them look skeptical. "Like the other claims I made about English and about how your thinking will be at the center of this class, this idea too is a *thesis,* a claim or an assertion or a promise that you will find true or not true as the year draws on. *Capisce?*"

"CAPISCE!"

Then, as many of the students anticipate, having heard about me, I say, "For nearly this entire trimester you will be writing poetry." They groan, their heads drop or tilt dramatically toward the heavens, their eyes roll, while friends stare at each other in apprehension. My face remains stone. "On the other hand, there will be no spelling tests, or vocabulary tests, or grammar workbooks. Nor am I fond of pencils; use blue or black ink only. If you make a mistake just cross it out. This isn't a penmanship class. All final drafts will be typed or word processed. *Capisce?*"

"*capisce.*" Still moping about writing poetry—ha! But that will change. It always does.

Now down to business.

"Your first assignment is the Two-Word Poem."

"Huh?!" The befuddlement begins.

"Now, form two lines in front of my desk and pick up your assignment. Both stacks of handouts contain the same things, so take just one—c'mon, c'mon," I say, mimicking Archie Bunker. My classes, after all, are only forty minutes long.

"A two-word poem?"

"Hey, you guys, the end of the line is back there," I say, pointing. "This isn't the cafeteria."

"*Two words?*"

They laugh at some of the examples that I read to them from the handout—pairs of words suggesting identity: "Grandmother/raisin," "Marriage/handcuffs," "Bra/hammock," and so forth.

Newness is everything—especially for kids entering or in the midst of puberty; especially when the high court of opinion is the society of their peers, and their major interest is the intrigue and drama played out among classmates and friends. Newness is everything—especially when their experience of English over the years has been pretty much the same from class to class. What else besides poetry is as emotional and songlike as they are? What else can be as different from the singsong rhymes of their elementary days—that they understand as *all* poetry? What else besides poetry is as idealistic, using language for its noblest ends—expressing the self's soul, heart, and mind on behalf of the universe?

Where to begin? The best place, of course, is with yourself: you who must teach the craft, you who have been trained in the discipline having read a variety of exemplary works. Remember that power and beauty of language that first drew you, like most of us, into the discipline? Think of those poems and stories and speeches that, as the kids say, *blew you out of the tub*, made you say *wow*, took your breath, or brought tears to your eyes; the ones that you honor in your personal library.

Go ahead. Choose from your library, from among your favorite works, your initial models and examples. Maybe even include your own writing. Label the assignment, say, Transformation Poem or Revenge Poem, whatever label your collection would seem to fit.

Now think of the teachers who read those stories and poems aloud to you, and the physical reaction you experienced, and of how that reaction could be recreated in your own students. Think of the writers and teachers and family members and friends who stand tallest in the pantheon of your mind—can you hear those voices? I know I sometimes can, having assimilated their voices into my own through some aural osmosis. I hear my old poetry teacher Lardas, who held nothing back. I hear my friend Tommy Muller-Thym and his street-talking rap and his political harangue. I hear Mark Anthony vowing revenge and blood and chaos over Caesar's corpse and "Let loose the dogs of war." In some of my prose, I like to build up speed through many long sentences, like Melville, or tear off the rear-view mirror and rush headlong through the wilderness, like Faulkner. And though, like most teachers, I'm enamored of a *variety* of different voices and tones and moods—a great variety of works—and try to show that great variety to my students, I'm well aware of my bias, which is of no small advantage to me. For it's that breathless tumbling stuff that I read aloud the best, and I take advantage of that strength as I try to shatter my students' cool complacency.

One of my own poems that I share with my students comes at the end of reading aloud a number of examples for the Bitterness Poem, a fairly simple assignment that asks kids to write about feeling bitter or angry. Their knowing that you sometimes write yourself will earn you some measure of respect, for here is a practitioner, here is someone not afraid to open him- or herself up to public scrutiny, even if the work that is shared isn't that great. By way of preparing the students for my poem, I tell them that the names mentioned in the poem refer to famous writers, whom, for now, they don't need to know. Otherwise I explain nothing.

Mantis
(The Horror Show)
The sound of maple-black, thumb-length roaches
gently rattling in a bag of aluminum cans
not fire or radioactive rain dripping from eaves:
so unnerving I can hear their scratching two rooms away
and think ax, baseball bat, outrage, my brain a mandible
think of the line from *The Fly*: "I am an insect
who dreamed he was a man and believed the dream" before
his bubbling face split open, his body cracking, an aperture
from which a mechanical leg like a saw
was stepping from the threshold of a dark room.

This is the Egypt of every man's past that haunts
like buzzing, the attic of memory:
the heaped and dusty carapace from which we hatched:
the armor, the haircoat, the silkworm gown
the veil like a spider's web—Cocktails at
Dachau? Breakfast in Beirut?
or a thousand rebellious slaves crucified
along the Appian Way
or crushed like a species of beetle
in Tianamen Square, though a kiln were better
for Dresden china, the crock pot of Troy, the fruits fresh
from Nagasaki we spray with spectrocide, the chemistry
of My Lai—reel after reel in the Arabian Night.

As a chronicler of darkness (here, you can see my badge)
I wonder what Mahfouz, Kundera, or Marquez would say
or the suicide, Kawabata, while I know Capote's
been working on the crime for forty years now
finding nothing in the Mongolia of our faces
nothing in the heart of the Congolese dark, no tiger
wasp, or discipline of ants. No *nada*. No metaphors
to give it shape, to grasp. Nothing that frightens.
Nothing to kill. But noise in the pantry!
Out of rage, revulsion, disgust—in bloody vengeance
I tear off their arms like wings and devour people.
Record the chewing.

I see in their faces and hear in their voices "Oh, yuck!"
The hypocrites. For they will turn out poems equally bitter or angry, and
equally dark.

Another way to begin is by referring to books that offer a whole repertoire of poetry writing assignments, including many examples that teachers can use immediately in their classrooms. Most such books include a section on theory that provides teachers a rationale for their choices, establishing both order and a simple teaching/writing routine. Since the book I know best is my own, *Teaching Poetry Writing to Adolescents*, I will elaborate on important parts of it briefly. But first, let me introduce a poetry writing assignment I have used in recent years that's not included in my book. I want to present evidence of what seventh and eighth graders are capable of achieving and illustrate the importance of providing *many* examples.

At this point in the first trimester, the students have written approximately fifteen poems. The sixteenth comes quickly:

"Your next assignment is the Holiness Poem. I want you to write about what you find holy or sacred, or what you hold supremely dear. And, again, forget technique; it's already in your fingers. Just write from your gut. Make us feel what you feel." The following is the updated collection of student examples that I read to my class.

My Savior
You stand before me
like a lighthouse
in which no light shines.
And you dare not make a sound.
But I know you are there
on the shore.

Now, I do not believe,
but when something is wrong,
my faith in you will return.
Like the tide
it comes and goes.

When I kneel
before you.
I will ask for your forgiveness.
As storms of emotions swell inside me.
Begging for you to save me!
Then the lighthouse will be lit,
and a sound will fill the air.
Then I will be saved,
and I will believe.
—Lauren Kawehionalani Chang (Grade 7)

"I like the way that Lauren uses images from the setting to communicate and underscore her meanings: For example, 'Like the tide,' her faith—like the faith of many people—comes and goes; and 'storms of emotion' suggests the degree of fear or even panic we might experience when we are immersed in a difficult situation—when 'something is wrong'—a feeling that may come upon us just because we are alive; when we think what may befall us after we die. But by the end we will be saved from the sea. Rescued. Interesting. Is she saying that in order to believe, she and other people must experience bad or hard times?"

Starvation
Religion is food
and we are starving people.
Those who understand and believe in it feast.
Those who accept it are fed.
Those who have a closed mind starve.
Those who taste a certain kind of food and don't like it find other foods,
other religions.
Like starving people some are too quick to eat, too quick to believe.
The table is set,
but I am not hungry.
—Matthew Moss (Grade 8)

"As you did in your extended metaphor poems on poetry, Matt uses a variation of that form to catalog traditional beliefs about religion, but at the end he undercuts our expectations, for at the moment he, like a number of kids his age, has no need for organized religion."

Believe
The golden spike of reality and magic,
like a secret bride so only the truly worthy may find it.
Across the boundary of mind you will see,
once upon a time,
radiant dragons socializing among the palaces
upon silver lined clouds.
While below,
goblins and witches spook
unicorns peacefully grazing in the meadow,
like scattered daisies in a breezy field,
and yesterday's nightmares lurk from behind each tree.

Nowadays it is only proper to throw away the treasure map,
we deserved so many years ago,
that lead us to the magnificent treasure of imagination.

We refuse to believe in
Santa Claus,
ghosts and ghouls.

You don't own a key to this place,
you don't greet the flowers each morning,
you don't even wave good-bye to the Easter Bunny.

But I do.

      —Beth Liebert (Grade 8)

"How many of you feel you've lost something in growing up?"

Little Brown Box

I praise you every night
for you bring hours of entertainment
into my life
Shedding a holy glow across the room
You rest on hallowed ground
shining, while I stand in awe of your mystical powers
playing music or telling jokes on your own accord
I may change the channel, but you decide what plays
Truly you are a T.V. set among T.V. sets

Although only 16″ wide,
you are, and always have been my own
Lasting 13 years without a glitch or power surge,
you are invulnerable to diseases
most likely because you are American made

As I vegetate in front of you,
I hear a man whom I shall never meet
droning endlessly in a monotone voice
about a new brand of moisturizer
Yet strangely, I consider it entertainment
I sometimes sit blankly and ponder

who truly owns who?

      —Jonathan Chock (Grade 8)

"I like the way that Jon satirizes his and our own reverence for television. I like his voice, his deliberate, measured pace so reminiscent of religious talk and prayer. He creates incongruity through his manner of speaking to a TV set. And, like all effective humor, there is a certain amount of truth in what he says."

In the Clearing
With homework done,
And nobody home,
I glance at my watch.
A special watch my grandfather gave me,
The kind that opens up to reveal the intricacy inside.
Such perfectly fitting parts,
That could be damaged without thought.

It tells me it's late,
But a burning fire in my gut calls to me . . .
It is time.

Out the back door,
With wings underfoot.
I fly past the garden
And through the green yonder,
Over the creek and down a trail,
Through the flowers, so pretty, almost fake.
Jump the nettles and duck the branch.
The path is my spine,
The creek a leg,
The meadow an arm,
The trees the features of my face.
I know it all so well,
The back of my hand.

I arrive at my spot,
Untouched by man,
With the exception of me.
All how I left it,
The rock, the stump, even the spider web.
Everything sleeping beautifully,
Awaiting: the kiss from the prince.

"Hello, friends!" I cry,
Sitting down upon my stone.
I gaze at some ants,
Wondering what drives them on,
Those tiny robots programmed to march.
I am enjoying myself greatly,
As I do whenever I come.
I turn some somersaults in the clearing,
And I bump something hard

—Something . . . Foreign!
It is a sign,
A developer's sign,
"Soon to be Green Acres,
15 wonderful half-acre parcels!"
Suddenly my arm falls off,
And my leg disintegrates.
My spine snaps,
And my features burn.

My body,
Is gone.
   —Ryan Meyer (Grade 8)

"Look again at Ryan's first stanza. See how it sets up and foreshadows the body of the poem? The grandfather's watch is the keepsake or patrimony or legacy passed on by previous generations to the young: the kind of watch, like a poem, 'that opens up to reveal the intricacy inside. / Such perfectly fitting parts [that inter-relatedness], / that could [like nature] be damaged without thought.' The body of the poem tells us that nature and the self or mankind are one, and when we damage nature we damage ourselves; we damage the future of our children, whose representative is the young poet, Ryan."

Ha'ena, Kaua'i

Climbing higher, higher
up the steep, rocky slope of the mountain,
we finally reached the *pa hula*
My back and legs were oh-so sore.
The sun beats down, I let out a sigh.
Hula skirt in hand, I looked up at the mountain,
and down to the sea below;
Breathtaking!
Pele, Hi'iaka, and Lohi'au
I couldn't believe we were really there.
We stumbled over each other getting in line.
Kunihi ka mauna i ka la'i e . . ."
Our voices echoed against the mountain behind us.
The sound excited me,
a chill swept up my spine.
Water trickled down mossy rocks,
la'i swayed to our chanting.
Hala leaves danced in the wind

in rhythm to the pounding of the *ipu*.
Our feet touched lightly on the soft grass,
leaving no prints.
As our dance came to an end,
a mist rolled in, blessing our little group.
Hi'iaka's *pa'u* swirled upward, spreading out to the sea.
Silently we filed by the *'ahu*,
laying our *ho'okupu* on her mossy shrine.
We retraced our steps down the ancient trail,
leaving the sacred home of the hula.
                                        —Sara Saffery (Grade 8)

Pele is the goddess of the volcano; Hi'iaka is her sister. Lohi'au was an *alii*, a person of royal blood. *Kunihi ka . . .* is part of a chant: *toward the mountain ridge, the tranquility. La'i* means ti-leaves. *Ipu* is gourd drum. *'Ahu* means alter. *Ho'okupu* means gifts. *Pa'u* is Hi'iaka's skirt, which is made of mist.

The Locker Room
Others see it as sweaty boys talking in dirty language in a stink place. What it really is is an important part of a boy's life, filled with new experiences.

It's a place where your emotions are released, sometimes resulting in fights. Even with that, it is a place where you are more easy-going and open than you would be at school.

When you begin a sport, most everything changes. Ties between players on a team become stronger.

When you walk in after a day of practice you see tired faces and smell the salty sweat of perseverance.
After a defeat the locker room is as quiet as a calm summer's day. You can see the gloomy expressions and feel the needles poking each player's heart.
When a team is pronounced victorious the locker room is louder than a herd of stampeding bulls, there is laughter in the air and you can taste the sweet apple of victory.

And we go through these experiences and feelings in the way God wanted us to, completely naked.
                                        —Amit Aurora (Grade 8)

After Amit had finished reading his poem at an eighth-grade chapel meeting, he was greeted by unanimous applause, chirping kudos, and joyful laughter. It struck a chord especially among the boys.

Angels Among Us
You see them behind
the doors of every home.
You hear them in
the hearts of those
around you.
They're ordinary people,
no wings, no harps, and no halos.
But for each criminal, liar, and convict
there lives one person
strong enough to free you.

With hardships and suffering,
you wait until the time comes when
darkness masks you,
but in a flash of
white light
you have security again.

Angels in plain clothes
walk among us.
It's doubts in your mind
that disguises
their true meaning.
There's nothing
supernatural about it.
—Kristin Izumi (Grade 8)

"I like the conviction and strength of Kristin's voice, her hard-edged, illuminating perspective."

Memories
My mind wanders, roves, it drifts
and twists.
I can't recall the date of the
Revolutionary War.
But I still see the ocean, its waves
ebbing like graceful fingers edging its
way along the sand
I can't remember Einstein's theory of
relativity.
But I can still smell the scent of freshly
popped buttered popcorn and cotton candy,
and hear the petrified screams on the rides

at the carnival.
I can't remember the names of all the
U.S. Presidents.
But I can still visualize my first puppy,
his sorrowful eyes, and rough tongue
slobbering over my face.
I forget the four elements of matter.
But I still feel the ecstasy of hitting my
first baseball, the sound of the crack of the
bat, and the power I felt running
through my arms.
Memories are like wisps of fresh air
that weave through my mind.
They bring back special times,
places, and feeling.
Time may rob me of my youth.
Years may snatch some of my hair.
Age will consume my flawless physique.
But simple memories, like holy gifts,
will sparkle in my mind.
                    —Lance Mitsunaga (Grade 8)

"And what better way to grasp those memories than through writing? In fact, the more you write, the more you recall, the more you unearth, and the more one memory leads to another . . . and the more you make them permanent. And that's good when you get old like me. For example, how many times, Shane, have I forgotten your name?"

"It's Sean."

"Sean."

"Lots."

After Life
Sweet strawberries, blueberries, raspberries
Any kind of fruit or berry that you can think of,
Overfills this place
As you pick them,
Ripening in your hand

Dressed in white
You are a dove
Gracefully soaring above the earth
Independent and free

As the main character in a cartoon,
You're a clown
Always filled with joy and parading around with your friends
Hakuna Matata, "no worries."

All of your wishes will be granted
All that you have to do is ask
Pleasure is in the air
There is pleasure everywhere it goes

At dusk,
When the sun slowly sinks farther and further into the ground
You think, "Wow! Eternity!"
                                        —Kimberly Polomsky (Grade 8)

"Yeah. I can see it. All the colors of the sunset—just like fruit."

Family
With a familiar screech and droning engine
They pull up in Uncle Larry's muddy gray truck
Relatives pour out of the back seat
Like rain off a corrugated aluminum roof
Uncles, countless cousins, and dignified grandparents
Aunties scolding my young cousins about this and that
"Wipe your feet!
What they gon tink of you!"

With a chorus of pidgin greetings they burst in
Invading my family's home like African snails in Auntie's garden
Each family bearing a dish
A paper plate wrapped in foil or a Tupperware container
Held like a revered idol
Spam musubi, beef stew
Tako poke, bagong

Every room is filled with relatives talking story
Uncles in the living room watching the Rainbows on T.V.
Grandparents laughing at each other's jokes
My brother showing off pictures of *halalu* he caught
Aunties in the kitchen chattering lively about their families
Children everywhere
Climbing everywhere
Climbing the lichee tree, throwing stones at the dog
Screaming and laughing like mynah birds

Mountains of savory, irresistible food pile up
People are drawn to the spot like hungry flies
Paper plates and chopsticks in every hand
Sashimi, ox tail soup, musubi, macaroni salad, lemon chicken
The creaking wood floor disappears
Under a wave of quilted, homemade cushions
Family, young and old, gathered together

The seated children fall silent as they listen quietly
To the adults talking of Uncle J. J.'s last goat hunt
Auntie Colleen's diet, Uncle Tommy's leaking sam-pan
Gossiping about friends no one seems to remember
A guitar appears under someone's arm
An old Pahinui song fills the room
With its sweet, mystical melody
Evoking bittersweet memories of the past
Aunties, uncles, and wise grandparents
Pause in their conversation
Perhaps to remember a past long gone
When they sat entranced as we were
At the gathering of family

—Matthew Ishida (Grade 7)

"Note how, when he creates similes, Matt looks to *local* experiences for his details and images, befitting the content of his poem. For example: 'Like rain off a corrugated aluminumn roof' or 'like African snails in Auntie's garden' or 'Screaming and laughing like mynah birds.' Part of the effectiveness of similes often stems from how well a simile fits with the content and language of the poem, or, put another way, how naturally the simile seems part of the verbal 'family.'

"This is a wonderfully rich list poem in homage to the extended family of second and third cousins, neighbors, and friends—Japanese, Chinese, Filipino, Korean, Spanish, Hawaiian, Irish, Samoan—as mixed and bountiful as the lavish foods. You've experienced such homey celebrations yourselves, when every adult, related to you or not, is called 'auntie' or 'uncle.' Coming from a small family myself, I admire and feel a little envy when local folks get together like this."

If there's time, I share my own poem with the students. "The only thing you need to know is that the two names I mention, Florelle and Christine, refer to my friend's wife and thirteen-year-old daughter, who died in an electrical fire in Canada. My father died when I was eleven. The poem resurrects him for a moment and honors all fathers, like yours, like me, who adore their children."

Big Trees and Lots of Light
(Christmas, Honolulu)
Urged on by your son,
You buy the tree early this year
a modest one a hermit might hew deep in the woods
Pretending the rain were snow
you pull your son's red hood over his head
while he sings "Jingle Bells"
and you remember the ice festival in Quebec
the white plastic canes filled with brandy
Florelle and Christine alive again
and it's twenty below
You stuff the tree into the back seat
your fingers gummy, turn on the air conditioner
and breathe in the resin-sweet perfume of pine needles
as though your son were one again
asleep in the crook of your arm
beneath a tree that would fill, you think, a cathedral.
And you remember the beginning, the winter clothes
you've shed, the mitten with the hole
in the thumb, the scarf like a sail
as you slid down the icy hill, the sound
of long zippers, the frozen hair like menthol
deep in your nostrils. And for a moment
your father stands at the end of the dining room table
an engineer's cap on his head, watching
like a kid, the train go round and round
in its endless circle, whistling
white smoke from its chimney,
through tunnels, over trestles
into the countryside
perhaps to pick up a load of coal
or fir trees for city families
like ours, for fathers who require big trees
and lots of light and loved you
beyond the dimness of your memory.
The star over your Bethlehem.

The reason for providing a host of examples is to immerse students in the sea of poetic language and to show off the variety of tropical fish that swim in its shoals: the many ways of speaking and feeling and seeing and maneuvering. Examples which, I caution the students, they must not imitate if they are to produce something original. However, the examples suggest what else might be done were the writer to assume a slightly different stance or perspective, creating a different species at a different depth. And the sea is vast and inexhaustible, with space enough for variant upon variant, derivative poem upon derivative poem; space where something can always be modified or placed in opposition to something else; space where something can always be born of something else, whether from a student example or something that exists in the writer's mind.

For human beings, nothing can be created from nothing.

For this reason alone, in order to increase the possibility of students creating something new, we ought to expose them to many examples.

Although I do use adult models, my *primary* examples are student examples. This approach is especially effective for young adolescents and, according to colleagues, can be equally effective for high school seniors and elementary kids. There are several reasons for this.

Probably the most important reason is that the writings strike an immediate interest in students. As well they might, for the poems or stories or papers were written by kids their own age whom they know by name and face, if only through glimpses from the end of the hallway; kids who have passed through this class before them, by several years or several hours; kids just like themselves with similar interests, conditions, desires, and hangups; kids with emerging skills, strengths, and sensitivities, sometimes heretofore unknown. The students' first reaction is untainted curiosity for the unfolding words, ideas, images, rhythms, sounds—quickly followed by the perking of their critical ears, equivalent in degree, perhaps, to the tightening muscles that narrow their eyes. "I can do that"—or better! Or an image or memory or an idea is inspired as it hovers in the vicinity of their brow, and they think, "I can do this." It's all unspoken, of course. Not surprisingly, many students start into their work immediately, silently, some like saboteurs, giving the impression that they know what they're doing and where they're going.

By contrast, as I note in *Teaching Poetry Writing to Adolescents* (1988, p.10), "if students know that a work was authored by an adult (because they have been told or because it is evident through sophistication of language or ideas), the work will appear beyond the students' reach . . . Often, what makes the adult work inaccessible is not so much its language or ideas (which we can lead them to understand), as it is the impossibility of their 'duplicating' such work. Skills aside, they have little interest in wanting to," as if adults were a different species ("Well, in a way, you guys *are*").

Funny: In all my years of schooling, from grade school through college and graduate school, never once was I given examples written by my peers; exemplary papers that could have clearly shown me what I had to do; papers I could study, watching the movement of the writer's mind, showing me where, at what points, the writer dwelled, where and how to shift gears; papers that showed me what things were permissible or even admired by my teachers. I wonder how much more quickly and easily I might have learned had I been given such papers. Then again, I doubt I would have bothered to read them as an eighth grader, unless the teacher read the papers to us, as we read along with her, and pointed out their virtues along the way.

Another reason I use student works as my primary examples is that, taken together, they reveal and establish the general range of excellence that students themselves can achieve—or, in fact, exceed. Further, through their efforts at emulating the quality of work produced by their predecessors, students automatically participate in a literary tradition distinctly and proudly their own. Such traditions can be established with any age group, so long as you have at hand the best of the poems and papers your former students wrote. And the body of exemplary work you've collected over time will help simplify the difficulty of grading by grounding your judgment on the proper plateau of achievement as determined by your eighth-grade students.

In those instances when we *do* want students to imitate certain things—such as by writing the Two-Word Poem or learning how to prepare for and comment on quotations or how to marshal evidence—many examples create a helpful redundancy. Imagine, for example, having one or two function-paper examples for each chapter of *To Kill a Mockingbird*.

My day-to-day routine is the one thing that is predictable in class.

On the first day of a new assignment, I give the class a handout, which includes a number of student examples. I read the assignment, reminding the students about originality, trusting that the reader will naturally generalize from the specifics they offer, and keeping their total attention on their subject as they write. Then—focusing my own attention, girding my emotional loins, and adjusting my voice to the voice of the poem—I read the examples, and others I didn't hand out, as well as I can. For I know that how well I read the examples will determine, in great part, how well the examples will be received. The only time I raise my head is when I comment on the poems along the way.

The next day, the students return with their first drafts and enter feedback groups, whose configuration varies from one assignment to the next. They might meet in pairs or in groups of three, four, five, or six, or with the whole class during Circle Revision. I sometimes ask them to choose their own groups, then later ask them to choose the kind of feedback strategy they want to practice, or to direct their group in the kind of feedback they want. But most of the time I organize the groups, sometimes mixing genders and sometimes separating them; sometimes grouping kids at random, by number, or by the proximity of their seating, for one of the things they must learn to do is work with *any*body. They must learn how to navigate gracefully among all kinds of people; they must learn how to be tactful, patient, flexible—and forthright. All of which takes time and frequent practice. That's why we start right away.

And it takes time to learn how to be of practical help to each other, to learn what to look for, what to comment on, what to say. And whom do students learn from in order to be teachers and editors themselves? Who else but the teacher at the front of the room, who, in looking over their "final" drafts, does not stint in his or her criticism and suggestions. For the sake of compression, I use a squiggly underline and write "cut" or ask "need?", or I'll suggest in the margin a word or a phrase or an image as a substitute for a line. For the sake of precise or more vivid diction, I'll list two or three words as alternatives to consider. For the sake of more dramatic movement, I'll rewrite several lines alongside the original and write "compare." I use arrows to suggest reconsidering the order of progression. In all these instances, I give the students alternatives to weigh in order to improve the qualitative effect of the poem. I give them options. Which is precisely what I want the students to offer their classmates, precisely what their classmates need, for revising one's own work can be supremely difficult. All writers, even professional writers, need feedback. The response "good" is useless, while the suggestion "add similes" is inadequate. The question is always the same: "What changes would you make if this work were yours?"

I also use check marks to indicate that a word, a phrase, or a line is very effective. And I write "old," "trite," "cliche," "flat," and "ugh" where the writing is disappointing. I don't stint on the truth either. "How long did you work on this at home? Five minutes?"

"No."

"Six?"

"No."

"Well, what?"

"Ten about."

"TEN MINUTES? IS THAT IT? YOU GOTTA BE KIDDING ME!"

Or another will answer, "Maybe . . . an hour."

"An *hour?*" I ask, skeptically.

"I think around there."

Then making my face dark and grim in a comical kind of way, I bark, "YOU LIE!" Which they find funny and repeat back to me in the hallway. The message is clear. As I tell their parents during Open House (before I read them a few student poems, which they love): "There is no easy way—no shortcuts—to learn how to write except to do it honestly, day after day, expending the necessary emotional and intellectual sweat. It's the only way to grow. And, as you know, individual growth is our primary concern. But, oh my, when they do commit themselves, it's amazing what they can do."

On the third day, before I collect their final drafts, which several will revise again and again, I remove myself to the back of the room and say, "The floor is open." Here, everyone has the opportunity to publicize their work by reading it to the class. I lean over a clipboard with a list of the students' names and place a mark next to the names of those who volunteer to read. They all know that 20 percent of their grade is based on class participation and that one very important goal is to become an effective, all-around language user. But, alas, how poorly some of them read! At times it drives me crazy to hear so many students mangle and suffocate their own words, oftentimes good words, never giving them their proper chance, their rightful due, killing the words in their shells. So, while they are up at the front of the room, I coach them. "EMPHASIZE YOUR LIP MOVE-MENT!" is another pet saying the kids grow fond of, knowing how foolish we all look while saying it—and we repeat it over and over as exercise—especially when mouthing "you*uuur*" and "m*ooo*vement."

Another way I publish students' work is by putting a C next to a check-plus grade, which means make a clean copy and stick it up on the board at the back of the class. By the end of the unit, everyone has had at least one work pinned to the board. I make sure of that, for, believe me, nothing makes them prouder.

Midway through the trimester we hold a public reading for parents and rela-tives who can get away from work for a while. More often than not, several moth-ers end up teary-eyed. The next day I read to the students their parents' very positive responses, which the adults returned to me at the end of the reading.

Finally, at the end of the long unit, the kids put together individual poetry books, with table of contents, introductory essay, copyright and dedication pages, index—the whole works. Then they give them away as Christmas presents.

They never forget.

If you start your year with poetry writing and sustain that focus for a meaningful length of time, say at least six weeks, I promise you that *most* of the students along the way, at different points, will not only grow in literary competence, but will also undergo a subtle change of a different sort. Their attitudes toward language, toward English, and toward themselves as writers will grow more positive. For some, a hidden or repressed or dormant enthusiasm for learning will reemerge. And through their writing, you and their parents will see the invisible, psycholog-ical growth going on beneath the surface.

On the following page is a copy of the eighth-grade syllabus that I give to my stu-dents on the first day of class. I have students write in the blanks in the upper-right corner the names and phone numbers of two of their classmates. If, when at home, they have questions or need information about work they have missed, students should seek help first from the students they have listed on their syl-labus, reserving their teacher as a last resort.

On the back of the syllabus is an explanation of the grading rubrics that ap-pear on the students' report cards. I have both the students and their parents sign and date the bottom as confirmation that they have read and understood the ex-planation.

English 8   Name_____ #_____

Mr. Tsujimoto   Name_____ #_____

GOALS: To make deeper, more complex, more original, and clearer meanings

To become more knowledgeable of language and literature

To increase one's capacity to work with others and appreciate other points of view

To increase one's confidence and competence in, and appreciation for, writing, reading, class discussion, and public presentation

APPROACH: <u>Poetry</u>: writing, reading, reading aloud, and publishing individual poetry book; narrative writing; learning log and journal writing (throughout the year). <u>Texts</u>: numerous adult and student handouts.

<u>Drama, Novel, & Literary Analysis</u>: reading, discussion, speech writing & presentation, argumentative writing, paper presentation, dramatic performance, group presentation on an adult poem. <u>Texts</u>: *Oedipus the King, Julius Caesar, To Kill a Mockingbird*.

CONVENTIONS: Grammar, usage, and mechanics will be individually addressed according to each student's needs.

ASSESSMENT: A letter grade will symbolize the student's cumulative mastery and growth in four broad curriculum areas—PREPARATION, PARTICIPATION, BEHAVIOR, AND ACHIEVEMENT (see back)—and will be reported to parents each trimester.

Note: Late final drafts will be penalized a full grade; preparatory work, a partial grade. If you submit work late 5 times, I will inform your parents.

If you are absent from class, it is YOUR responsibility to find out and make up what you have missed—you'll be given one extra day. If you need help, ask. I am available before and after school. Otherwise, you may call me at home, but <u>never</u> after 9 PM and <u>never</u> on Sunday.

NOTE: <u>Only the **Labels** in **BOLD** print</u> will appear on the trimester report card. <u>Percentages will change for Behavior & Achievement for the second & third trimesters.</u>

	Excellent	Good	Fair	Needs Work

PREPARATION   [20%]   /_____/_____/_____/_____/
Homework is submitted on time
It is complete
It is neat
Written work has been PROOFREAD
Student comes to class with necessary materials (pen, paper, etc.)

PARTICIPATION   [20%]   /_____/_____/_____/_____/
The student shares his/her work with the class in poetry readings and dramatic readings
The student works effectively with others to provide feedback or to create a common product, presentation, or performance
The student engages others in spontaneous, meaningful talk: asks questions, answers questions; offers opinions, feelings, anecdotes; amplifies, modifies, extends, contradicts, paraphrases, and generalizes ideas, etc., during class discussion

BEHAVIOR   [20%/10%]   /_____/_____/_____/_____/
The student comes to class on time
The student does not disrupt instruction or learning
The student is an attentive listener, especially when others speak, read, or perform for the class
The student seeks, when necessary, the help of the teacher and keeps conference appointments

ACHIEVEMENT   [40%/50%]   /_____/_____/_____/_____/
Quality of Work/Mastery of Subject Matter as demonstrated through papers, exams, presentations, etc.

Student signature_____Date_____

Parent signature_____Date_____

3

Reflection

We remember best what we put our own tongue to.
—Wittgenstein

Call me Ishmael. *Some years ago—never mind how long precisely—*flying home over the Pacific from a National Council of Teachers of English (NCTE) conference on the mainland, I found myself sitting next to Hodera, a fellow teacher who just happened to work at the school where I first began teaching in the late 1970s, Seabury Hall on the island of Maui. When he mentioned the school, a host of images washed over me—the cow pastures, the mountain mists, the glass-enclosed breakfast room where we worked on papers between classes; the up-country mansion, Cooper House, the main building on campus, where, in the living room, the boarders would gather with faculty before dinner to hear announcements and prayer; lily pads in the reflection pond; student John Ivey, in senior English class, telling us—and making me conscious of the fact—that my intention was to teach them to think more deeply; breaking my ankle in a softball game, faculty against the girls; the smell of ginger, pikake, and maile leis at graduation, the girls dressed like brides; Roger calling it a holiday when it snowed on the volcano; the senior class weekend at the Seven Sacred Pools, where, lying on the grass next to a low stone wall, I got the title to a poem that I would write a year after quitting; a contemplative, serene campus at the start of summer; moving back to Honolulu for David's birth.

Had we been seated on a couch after dinner with wine glasses in our hands, instead of cinched in narrow chairs in coach, and the talk had drifted back to faculty or locals we both knew, or to Makawao town, I might have read Hodera my poem:

Archeological Site
(Do Not Remove Stones)
I am sitting at the crossroads of Makawao
population 2500
where Baldwin Avenue meets Olinda Road
which sweeps steeply uphill

for the town leans like splintered siding
on the slope of Haleakala   House of the Sun
an extinct volcano
on the stillness of Sunday,   fled
to a vacant beach
despite the shade of musty eaves
and monkeypod trees.

The rock & rollers I teach call Makawao
Hippie Town
of surfers, craftsmen, farmers, entrepreneurs
from Newport, Boston, Canada, Missouri
from elsewhere from long ago
like some of their grandparents
in rusty pickups and four-wheel drives
in shacks and pole houses
breeding orchids on their back porch
or pot in forest pockets
where maile grow
on the shoulders
of ghosts.

It's really a town of Portuguese cowboys of
     mainland steaks
     and Hawaiian fish
       ono
       uku
       mahimahi
of barnyard nights at Longhi's Saloon
where the men are grizzly   dusty
leathery as jerky or a chaw of tobacco
where the women are horses, saltier than the men,
who don't need Colts or bullwhips
to kill each other.   Alex
known as geek
was already bustin' broncs at 17
while Derek
back from U. of Davis
makes Maui wine   and Suzanne
turns English into Spanish
for the Sandinistas.   —Ahkoi?
She simply chucked the whole thing
went back to the peninsula
wraps laulau with her own taro leaves

dances ancient hulas
under purple shower trees
the jacaranda.

I teach up Olinda Rd., through eucalyptus
across Oskie Rice's Rodeo. Take a right
between two rows of cypress trees
across a rattling cattle guard, through the gate
which opens
upon
> a lettuce-green campus
> the chapel
> the West Maui Mountains
> the ocean
> the pasture of drifting cows

It is dusk
and in the vesper light
you can almost hear.

I told Hodera, as he himself knew, how heartbreakingly beautiful the campus was, how it would have been better had my wife and I lived at Seabury and worked somewhere else, or lived somewhere else, like Kula, and worked at Seabury. For it takes someone special, like Hodera, to teach and coach and live at a boarding school twenty-four hours a day. I told him that after three years I no longer had the desire or the energy or the dedication to devote my total life to the school, but that I *could* understand how *he* could, because of his children. What a healthful, peaceful, wonderful place to bring up your kids, as well as to give them a good education.

After sharing anecdotes about our students, I asked Hodera whether he had his students practice reflection writing. I had just left a Conference on English Leadership luncheon where I delivered a not-so-exciting paper on the subject. I had been invited to speak because a couple of years earlier I had given the conference teachers my "Affective Teacher" speech, which they thought was uplifting and fun, a good way to end a conference. I should have picked up on their hint that they wanted something similar.

Hodera wrote me a letter a couple of months later informing me of what had happened in his classes since our separation at Honolulu Airport. Near the end of his letter, he wrote,

> The learning process I've been outlining . . . is not a linear process but spirals back upon itself, turning over as students modify their initial responses based on new information. Of course, this is where reflection is vital. You asked if my students "practice reflection." My answer is, now they do. Re-

flection writing was the missing link in my instruction up till now. I've always had an irksome feeling about "moving on" to a new unit; now I see why. Reflection journals give students a chance to come to some sort of closure, to discuss both of the major outcomes of their learning journey—what they think they've "learned," and what they've learned about their own learning. This semester, I'm having students write reflection journals at least every other week. Of all my students' writings it is the thing I enjoy reading the most.

I was happy for Hodera, for I knew he learned a lot from his students. I told him to be wary of cowpies when cutting across the field, and wished him well the rest of the year.

In tandem with poetry writing and the other activities they engage in throughout the year, I have my students periodically write learning logs in response to questions that compel them to sum up and clarify their understanding. For example, early in the year, after students have written three poems, I ask them to write a learning log in response to two questions, (1) What did you learn about making poems? and (2) What did you learn about yourself as a writer and thinker?

One seventh-grade girl wrote:

> So far I've learned that poems should create surprise and interest, that they should be unpredictable, and I've learned to play around with stanzas and use variation, to make my poems more clear and complex.

This student established demanding standards or goals for her poems—unpredictability, clarity, complexity. These she chose as the characteristics that make a good poem. And she had an idea about how to meet those goals in the future. She had, in effect, set forth for herself a writing agenda. Her response to the second question, about herself as a writer and thinker, began:

> I've learned that I'm not that afraid or nervous about reading my work to other people but I kind of anticipate their response. It happens with everybody. The poem you worked on at home that was good and made sense suddenly becomes stupid as you read it aloud, so you're afraid of what they'll think. I've learned to appreciate other points of view more, and accept and make changes quickly. It's a little difficult for me to make a poem jump around to other places because last year we mainly focused on one given subject. I find that I take a while to write something I'm really satisfied with and especially when I compare my work with those of others.

Apart from feeling ambivalence about reading her work aloud to classmates, appreciating more the suggestions of others, and wanting to write poems that are as good as her peers', the student also said that she had a difficult time making a poem "jump around." This idea, I learned after talking with her, was connected to her ideas of playing around with stanzas and using the variation that she mentioned in her response to the first question. I told her that, though she might admire such "moves," not all successful poems employ them, and that she need not feel that her poems were lacking because hers did not contain them—that there were many ways to write poems and that "the best way to write them is usually discovered along the way, as you write."

"Through reflection," one eighth-grade science teacher said to me, "I've come to know my students more quickly, and have been able to help them earlier, more expeditiously." Not only can we have our students clarify to themselves what it is that they learned, but we can also come to their aid when they feel confused or, as in the above case, they operate according to narrow assumptions that limit their options and their freedom to create.

One of the questions I always ask students to respond to during Week Nine concerns reflection itself: How does writing about what you've learned, in learning logs, help you? In looking over the one hundred logs, their mini-discussions addressing the topic, I extract the students' basic assertions and categorize them under three broad areas. While many students make more than one assertion, many mention the same ones. These apparent redundancies are, I've come to realize, students' very particular ways of seeing and giving value to their findings. Here are some of the assertions they commonly make:

Memory
I can remember what I've learned.
I can remember what I've accomplished.
I can remember what I did wrong or right.
I can remember what I wish I had done.
I can remember how I felt.
It helps me remember what I need to learn.
It helps me remember important things I may have forgotten.
It helps me remember what I want to remember.

Realization
Some things I didn't even know I learned until I put them in words.
It helps you see things you never saw before . . . things you think you
      learned, but really haven't.
I find that I've learned many new writing skills and hadn't really noticed
      them, even though I use them in my writing every day.
Even what I'm writing now is helping me understand what is in my
      mind.
When I reflect on what I've learned, it reminds me to apply it.
The more I have to say, the more I've learned.

Process

It is important to keep a record of what you are learning to see how much
you've learned and how much you've progressed.

It makes me compare early work to current work and see the differences and
improvement.

It becomes clearer to me that I am learning something and exactly what
it is.

It gives me a better understanding of myself . . . of how much my mind has
grown.

It makes me think how proud I am about what I've done.

In addition to having our students make what they have learned clear to
themselves and to us, they also can lead us to improve our teaching, for as often
as not, students learn lesser, greater, more, and different things than we intend.
This shouldn't trouble us—as individuals at different stages of development, students will focus their attention on their own particular *growing points*. One student might mention how he has improved in handing in his work on time, while
another might say she has difficulty with wordiness and is trying to follow the advice that "simplicity can lead you to the profundity you seek." Sometimes, unknown to the teacher, the same concern or growing point is shared by many in
the class.

One year, after five days of sensory exercises—a blind walk focusing on
touch, blind smelling, blind tasting, listening to music, drawing an object from
various angles and perspectives (each class ending with their writing and sharing
several similes)—I asked students to respond to the question What did you learn
from the five sensory exercises you just experienced? I expected that they would
talk about how the senses other than sight, which was annulled in four of the exercises, grew in sensitivity and strength; how these other senses took on a life of
their own and grew in importance, where before they were taken for granted or
ignored; how it was almost impossible to convey to others a sensory experience
except through the use of similes, which liken an experience that's unique to one
that most people have gone through, appealing to the imagination; how similes
make a piece of writing richer and more interesting; and so forth. And many students did talk of some of these things. But, to my quiet surprise, many also talked
about how scared or anxious they felt being blindfolded and led around by their
partner (who was of the opposite sex). They said they were initially afraid of being led into a wall or cracking their shins or tripping; some said they were fearful
of what their partners might have them touch, touch being the focus of the exercise. They said that it took them awhile before they could trust their partners
with their lives. Others said that they understood blind people better.

Though many talked about things that I didn't expect or want, they revealed what was uppermost in their minds, what was important to them: Security. Trust. These are large words for seventh and eighth graders who must

work closely with each other through the rest of the year. And I should have anticipated their fears. Wasn't my responsibility as observer to ensure their safety? Did I not constantly say, "Slow down" and "Hey, you're supposed to make your partner feel comfortable" and "No, too far. I can't see you. Come this way"? And most of all I tell them "Elbow and wrist! Elbow and wrist!" since, paired up as boy and girl, they shy away from human touch—fearful of communicating the wrong message to their partner and anyone possibly watching and giggling at the other end of the hall—their hold on the blind partner is so limp and feeble, so tenuous and void of strength as to say to the one being led, "I might leave you at any moment" or "I'm not really watching where you're going."

The following year I emphasized, before the blind walk, the importance of the care students must use in leading their blindfolded partners through the halls and out into the field; the importance of conveying—through *firm* hands, one at the elbow and the other at the wrist—that everything will be all right. "Think of the person you're leading around as a grandmother or a toddler."

This experience taught me that we can learn from what our students say and teach them better in the future—since, when first trying something new, we cannot anticipate everything.

One thing I take great care in is the wording of my learning log questions, which should be treated as seriously as homework, essay, or exam questions. As you know, when questions are imprecise or otherwise flawed, they can easily be misinterpreted or point students in unintended directions, yielding unfortunate responses. I'd like to give you examples of my own poor questions, but I have erased them from my consciousness, since I already have too many reminders of my fallibility.

There is no formula for *when* learning log questions should be posed, though logic suggests it be done at the end of a study unit or at the end of a mini-unit within the larger unit (the sensory exercises are a mini-unit within the larger poetry writing unit). Depending on what you want students to reflect on or what *you* want to know about their learning or thinking, you might assign learning logs at other logical places in the curriculum, such as before you assign a new poem, or in the school schedule, such as before school events, holidays, or weekends.

I asked students the following learning log questions during the poetry writing unit last year. Some of these issues are addressed elsewhere in this book, so I don't talk here about students' responses to every question.

Week One: What was your reaction to the logs you read?

After quickly introducing the course through the syllabus, I handed out a batch of final learning logs written by kids in previous years. The students read and exchanged as many logs as the period allowed. The logs addressed two questions, What was the most important thing you learned? and How has the shape of your mind changed?

It was a good way for my new students to preview the class and hear other students' testimony about individual change, development, and growth in several areas across the year. Many pointed out in *their* logs the repetition of certain themes previous students had addressed: students learning how to read metaphorically, students gaining the courage and wherewithal to engage in class discussion, students learning to value the classmates who are pivotal to their own growth. Most everyone remarked on the high quality of the writing and, to my surprise, hoped that they themselves would rise by year's end to a similar level of competence!

More important than getting a sense of my new students' abilities as writers (which I would soon discover anyway) was this general expression of hope. I simply did not expect it, my mind focused on lesser intentions. What a happy surprise!

> *Week 2: (1) What does it mean to write a Two-Word Poem? Use examples and explain how meaning is suggested. (2) What does it mean to learn something? Note: Don't allow your reader to ask questions about what you think—give answers before the reader can ask those questions.*

Learning logs are like mini-papers, and at the beginning, especially from my seventh graders, they are *very* mini. I know I should expect as much. But my hope is boundless!

I treat these papers as rigorously as I do students' poems, so that many end up having to rewrite their logs, sometimes two and three times. They rewrite according to my questions and directions scribbled over their papers, which ask them to expand on their thinking, write in greater detail, provide examples, and define what they mean. It is here that I begin identifying students' individual shortcomings: what they do not know about grammar, usage, punctuation, and other conventions.

The students keep these drafts and rewrites in their writing folders along with their poems and use them as references when writing their next logs. Some of them actually *do* look back at the drafts. More important, the folders become the record of students' development as writers, making them conscious that, yes, they have made progress.

Although learning log writing is relatively infrequent, it prepares the way for other kinds of writing, such as narrative writing, exposition, speeches, and literary argument.

> *Week 6: (1) Evaluate yourself on your willingness, honesty, and thoroughness in giving your classmates feedback. Give yourself a letter grade. (2) What things must you work on in your poetry writing? Explain.*

I have students work with each other frequently. Group work is pivotal to my teaching and my students' learning; students spread the critical perceptions pointed out in their own papers among themselves, applying my observations second-, third-, and fourthhand; practice editing; and, most important, cultivate the social skills that enable them to work with others. I need to know early if any of the students are experiencing difficulties with their social skills. Based on their responses to Question 1, I give them a little talk that runs something like this:

> Some of you said in your logs that you have a hard time working with so-and-so because of some minor reason. Oh, the personal and social barriers we erect for ourselves! What, he's too quiet? What, you don't like her perfume? What, he's a *geek*? And *you're* perfect? Give me a break. And some girls, not in this class, are unabashed in expressing their insensitivity. I mean, they can be downright mean. Though I'm a pacifist, I sometimes get the urge to slap them in the face.
>
> Anyway, the very fact that someone might be different from you is a benefit, since there is a greater likelihood of hearing responses different from those who think like you, who offer you what you already know, which is not what you want when seeking feedback, right? Unless all you want is approval.
>
> Which takes me to *honesty*. Many of you eighth graders said that you have a difficult time giving your friends honest feedback—you just say that their work is "good" out of fear of hurting your friends' feelings. How wonderful. Everybody lies to each other and no one's work is improved. How nice, the disservice we perform for each other. And when someone is truly deluded into believing his or her work is indeed good and reads the final draft before the whole class, which realizes, as the writer suddenly does, that the work is doo-doo . . . well, how nice.
>
> Think of it this way: Are you concerned about your friends' welfare and growth? Your own? Beyond that, one of the goals you were challenged with at the beginning of the year was broadening your capacity to work with anybody. Even people of the opposite sex, for I know that some of you are shy.
>
> As for being *thorough* with your feedback, which some of you said you had difficulty doing, just continue to review carefully the kind of feedback others offer *you*. What to look for and what to say, and how to say it as completely as you can, will come to you as your knowledge and understanding grow. Remember, we all start at different places and learn at different rates. Those of you who do try your best, wanting to return the quantity of good feedback that others have given you: Do not stint on your feedback to students who do not give you as much as you give them. I promise you that their feedback will change as they grow.

Those few of you who receive good feedback and don't return in kind, but are able to: You guys are both lazy and cheap. And those very few who don't care or who believe all this feedback stuff is a sham—well, all I can say is that you have the option *not* to participate and may sit in the back and doctor your own work.

According to your drafts and the interesting comments scribbled on them by your peers, and according to your final products, many of you are developing nicely as editors.

In response to the question about what they must work on in their poetry writing, most students mention *diction*—using richer words and phrases or more original language—and *compression*—cutting words and phrases that slow down reading and dilute meaning or effect. Some say they want to write longer poems. Most students repeat back what I emphasize on their individual papers, which informs me that they are aware of what they must work on.

Week 8: (1) What is the importance of including personal experience in your writing? (2) What things must you work on when writing learning logs?

Students' responses to Question 2 vary from proofreading spelling, to grammar concerns (such as fragments and run-on sentences), to providing examples, to being aware of easy generalizations—the usual—and, again, the responses are based on comments I've made on their papers. "And now that you know what you must work on, you can direct others in giving you specific feedback outside of class. Ask your classmates or your friends or your older sister or your parents, or your next-door neighbors if they aren't grumps. From now on, remember, all learning logs must be submitted with drafts. How do you like them apples?" Groan.

Some teachers might argue that log writing—usually called exploratory writing or freewriting—ought not be treated as "formal" writing and should not be graded or submitted with drafts. That's fine if you're just going to walk around the room and see if students have done the writing—and not actually look at their work. But I need to read their work, I need to know what's going on. And I can't stand reading raw, unedited, undisciplined, uncrystallized thoughts that rarely move beyond the toddler or primitive stage; that are rife with easy abstractions and generalizations and disconnected, fragmentary ideas; that are unconcerned with audience, including the writers themselves. I have yet to read any research that suggests that such writing, *if left as is*, amounts to anything except a rough draft, a foundation for the further, deeper, clearer thinking and writing that arises in the next draft. I'll take that kind of thinking and writing every time.

Week 9: (1) What are the most important things you have learned in English so far? End your discussion by talking about the most important. (2) How does writing about what you've learned, in learning logs, help you?

Week 10: (1) List the names of the classmates who have given you effective feedback. Describe the kind of feedback they give. (2) On average I spend ___ minutes writing my first draft. (3) ___ minutes on my final drafts. (4) The letter grade I would give myself for overall achievement ___ .

Twenty percent of students' trimester grade depends on participation. Half that is determined by the number of times they volunteer to read their poems to the class. That half is easy to keep track of, since I do the recording. The other half is determined by how helpful students are to others in feedback groups or in whole-class circle revision, in which they make suggestions on each other's drafts, then sign their names after their general comments. I learn how effective they've been by reading their self-evaluations and their classmates' descriptions.

Some students make a list of names that includes more than half the class, which may be legitimate. Large numbers do not trouble me. Nor does it trouble me that some students are very picky and may only mention two names. What concerns me is when one or two students are not mentioned at all, and another one or two are mentioned only once. It's at this point that I start conferring with these kids to find out what's holding them back. Usually, it's some kind of fear, such as the fear of appearing dumb or ignorant in commenting on a work that they think is far superior to their own. After talking to these kids as a group and extracting their promises that they will at least try, I break off and repeat, in different words to the whole class, the importance of giving each other their opinions:

> Your opinions are invaluable. You, too, are part of the writer's audience, and he or she wants to know if any part of the work makes you hesitate or stumble when you read it or listen to it; wants to know if it is clear or trite or moves you. I sometimes write myself, and I always test my writing on my wife or my friends or my colleagues. In fact, all the writers I know want exactly what most of you try to give each other: feedback, reaction, even saying that this part of the poem is better than that part; suggestions, especially, about how the work may be changed for the better, or even changed to create a different effect, *even a different poem.*
>
> And believe me, once you try and try again, your skill in giving feedback will improve. You will see the change first in the changing way you judge your own work. *Capisce?*
> "*CAPISCE!*"

In the second trimester, I ask students to list the names of their classmates who have helped them the most.

Week 11: (1) Describe how poetry is similar to and different from (a) an autobiography and (b) a fictional short story. (2) Now considering what you've written above, write your definition for poetry. Beware: Are ALL points of your definition ALWAYS true?

Some of the students will incorporate their definitions of poetry in the introductory essays to their poetry books. These essays are like "grand reflections," since many students adopt the before/after writing strategy to talk about the changes they've undergone as poets and writers throughout the unit. I tell them,

Your essays should be as powerful and beautiful as your best poetry. And though you are writing an essay—where you must lead us by the hand through your thinking—use what you have learned in poetry writing: Use personal experience, use similes and metaphors and picture writing, use the voice that defines you best.

I also tell them *not* to talk about me, their teacher; that the essays are about *them*. But, as history shows, saying this is fruitless—nor will your students be able to stop themselves from mentioning you. I then guide students through a sequence of drafts as suggested by the feedback they receive from their peers. The whole process spans about five days. The following essay is one of the examples that I read to the students to give them an idea of what an introduction might sound like. It was written by Jason Morrison, an eighth grader.

Introduction

As I walked into class that first day of the year, I remember Mr. Tsujimoto sitting at his desk and doing nothing more. What he looked like was no surprise to me. I'd seen him before. I was still worried about class, though. All the rumors roared through my head. But I figured English wouldn't be as bad as some of the stories I had heard.

Finally class began and the teacher spoke. The distinct voice spoke of New York. He acted Italian, though he was Japanese. He then talked about his class, then moved into poetry.

That very night we had to write our first poems. I hated poetry, and I was going to have to face a whole trimester of poems. I dreaded the thought, as I struggled to write my first poem.

To my surprise, we had to read our poems to the entire class. I hated reading aloud almost as much as poetry. I hated it because it got me real nervous, and all I could do was worry about reading. It reminded me about my first baseball game under the lights at night. "What if I can't see the ball in a blind spot? What if I can't see because of the glare?" Those were my worries then, similar to my worries in class. It was a fairly new experience for me and I didn't want to screw it up. Yet they were both something I really wanted to do.

"Morrison! EMPHASIZE YOUR LIP MOVEMENT!" That was Mr. Tsujimoto's reaction to my poem. He got on my case and everybody else's that day. I figured I could do better, but this teacher would be hard to please.

The next few poems were just as bad.

"Morrison! Speak up!"

"Morrison! Your poem does not use rich language!"

"Morrison! Your poem lacks interest and dramatic leaps in time!"

I remember those words well. I ended up rewriting most of those first poems.

Almost every night we'd have to write a new poem. With each poem came a handout with examples of poems he liked. These examples were what saved my poetry.

I began to examine the examples closely. If I found a style or an idea, however small, I'd try to express my feelings in that style or format, or something that moved along similarly. I began to write poems that pleased Mr. Tsujimoto, not just what I felt was enough work.

Eventually I would sometimes be able to take a single thought in my mind, and I would spring a gusher of words that would flow over the paper, sometimes so fast I couldn't grab them before they disappeared. With one feeling in mind, poems became easier to write, and they drastically improved. My poetry began to please the teacher, but it also began to please me. I realized that poetry was taking one thought, or one idea, and transforming it into a brief picture that would tell the whole story, and nothing else.

Or, as an unknown seventh grader wrote,

Poetry is like painting, creating a lasting picture, not by pictures or sculpture, but by thoughts, feelings, emotions. Like Homer and Poe, people who saw the world differently, not black and white, but flowing with color, blues, greens, yellows, oranges, pinks. Like music, flowing through the air, piercing the silent reaches of your mind and sweet.

After the narrative writing unit, which follows on the heels of the poetry writing unit, I give students the following handout:

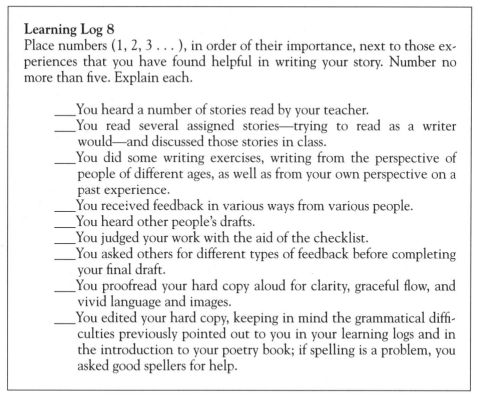

Learning Log 8
Place numbers (1, 2, 3 . . .), in order of their importance, next to those ex-periences that you have found helpful in writing your story. Number no more than five. Explain each.

____You heard a number of stories read by your teacher.

____You read several assigned stories—trying to read as a writer would—and discussed those stories in class.

____You did some writing exercises, writing from the perspective of people of different ages, as well as from your own perspective on a past experience.

____You received feedback in various ways from various people.

____You heard other people's drafts.

____You judged your work with the aid of the checklist.

____You asked others for different types of feedback before completing your final draft.

____You proofread your hard copy aloud for clarity, graceful flow, and vivid language and images.

____You edited your hard copy, keeping in mind the grammatical diffi-culties previously pointed out to you in your learning logs and in the introduction to your poetry book; if spelling is a problem, you asked good spellers for help.

The responses to this handout benefit both the students and me. Students become more conscious of the things that contribute to their writing and may heed those things more closely the next time they write. I learn what activities I ought to retain or modify or drop. Interesting to note is that, year after year, the responses—students' choice of the three most helpful activities—vary, which has led me to retain all the activities I assign in helping them write their stories.

After the winter break, I begin the six-day free-reading cycle by making this an-nouncement to the students:

The next cycle will be devoted to free reading. Tomorrow, you will bring into class your three favorite books from your personal library at home and display them on your desk. Keep a blank sheet of paper next to the books for people wanting to borrow them, so they can sign their names. Prepare to read to the class a passage from one of the books in order to tempt the audience. Limit the length of the passage to a third of a page. Also, list on an index card your top-seven book recommendations and we'll stick them on the board. You may also bring in pillows or cushions and lie on the floor as you read.

As they read, I confer with students about their recent stories.

After the free-reading cycle I ask students to respond to the following in a learning log:

1. What is your reaction to the cycle on free reading?
2. Point out one new writing strategy you learned from your reading.

Many students appreciate being able to read for themselves, something they have not had time to do since moving on from sixth grade because of increased homework responsibilities and greater participation in different classes, clubs, after school sports, music, and dance. They also like the idea of choosing what to read from recommendations made by their classmates, their peers, their friends—people whose taste and judgment they trust—and that leads to quick choices. Many will read two or three books during the six days, and most will ask that another cycle be set aside for free reading in the future (which I can't oblige). Some will talk about the books they read, from Stephen King novels to *Catcher in the Rye* and *Nineteen-Eighty-Four* to young adult classics like *Where the Red Fern Grows* and *Tuck Everlasting*.

After the month-long speech unit, which follows the free-reading unit, I ask students to submit learning logs answering two questions:

1. Evaluate your own speech performance and summarize the evaluations given to you by your classmates. Then give yourself a letter grade for both the substance of your speech and the effectiveness of your performance.
2. What things must you work on?

I consider their responses against my own evaluation of their performance. I operate similarly for their group analysis and presentation of an adult poem near the end of the year.

Most of the learning log questions I ask during the remainder of the year refer to the literature the students read. For example, after my eighth graders have read aloud Anthony Burgess' translation of *Oedipus the King*—when students readily volunteer to read dramatically with others at the front of the room—I ask them to write their response to the play. The following are excerpts from some of their logs:

I personally feel that Oedipus should have saved his sword for the oracle and knocked the living daylights out of it for being the cause of all this.

The anger that Oedipus shows was a result of pride; when he felt his authority was being challenged he used his anger to try and defend himself. Anger and pride were the causes of Oedipus' tragedy.

Something which I found to be very unrealistic was that Oedipus had no knowledge of how King Laius died. I find it hard to believe that in all the years in which Oedipus and Jocasta were married, they never once talked about her ex-husband or how he came to his death. Also, Oedipus is described in the story as quite smart and clever, but it certainly doesn't show before page 52, when he finally begins to realize what he's done. After all, it seems a bit strange that, just after he killed a man of obviously very high stature (Laius was riding in a carriage and had servants with him at the time of his death), Oedipus arrived at a city which that man was coming from and their king had just been murdered. Only an idiot would never have pieced this together.

I felt pity for Oedipus as he realized he was the killer of his own father. I felt sorry for Jocasta when she found out that her husband was her long lost son. I think that all of the characters in the story suffered, not one was untouched. Creon was accused of treason by his own brother-in-law. Tiresias was branded a liar, and the people of Thebes suffered with blights on their cattle, fields, and women.

Some of the words I learned were *scourge* (punishment), *rebuke* (reprimand sharply), and *blazon* (announce publicly). One of the places where I found a hidden meaning was when Oedipus was talking: "I am kin to the seasons—four-legged spring, summer upright in its pride, tottering winter." This sentence reminds me of the answer to the Sphinx's riddle. Man: walking on four legs at the dawn of his life, two legs in the noon of his life, and three legs at the end of his life. Also, Tireseus said of the future, "A stick shall tap his way into exile."

I also feel bad for Jocasta. She did not know that Oedipus was her son. Many years ago she had to suffer the loss of her son so that her husband would presumably live. However, he did die, and she was left to marry the killer of the Sphinx—whoever that may be, no matter how old, ugly, or awful. It seems to me she was even more a puppet of the gods than Oedipus. Women overall in the book seem to be very lowly and not very important. This is shown when the Chorus Leader says, "You need a woman's calm . . ." Is this all the women are around for? Jocasta denied to Oedipus that there was any truth in prophecy. Yet I wonder if she was saying that just to make him—and herself—feel better, fulfilling her role as comfort-giver. In the end Jocasta has absolutely no control over her life—except to end it. Oedipus, it seems, had many more choices: to leave home or not to leave home; to move aside from the carriage or not to move aside; to answer the riddle or not.

I would hate to be in Oedipus' position; he saved a city from the Sphinx. Then he was found guilty of murdering his father and marrying his mother. I'd rather nothing tragic or rewarding happen to me than both be a hero one minute and a villain the next . . . I think it was really interesting to follow the actions of a man not conscious of the grave consequences his actions would lead to. At first I truly believed that, if he knew his destiny and it couldn't be avoided, he should just sit there and wait for it to happen. After finishing the play I realized that I would have to at least try to overcome my fate and push past it. I'd really make an attempt to pave my own path and not have it paved for me.

Many of the students' observations are keen. This was not an easy read for eighth graders, who at first had to read the play on their own. But, as we do with *Julius Caesar*, which is even more challenging than *Oedipus*, we read the play aloud in class—as dramatically as the kids can with my prompting—and the archaic language, the poetry, the drama, the characters, and the ideas become more accessible to the students. In the end, with both plays, the students feel pride that they can read more and more of the writer's language on their own. I know they are impressed with the writer's genius. I know who students might choose to be, despite gender, were they to act as one of the characters in the play. I know these things because I ask, and the students tell me in their learning logs.

To sum up, I have students write learning logs:

1. So they can clarify for themselves what they have learned, telling me at the same time so I can decide whether to intervene or not;
2. So they can evaluate themselves, taking greater control of their own learning in the future;
3. So they can inform me about the curriculum and my teaching; and
4. So they can practice writing explanatory prose.

In the end, we may find, as the Seabury Hall teacher, Hodera, wrote about his students' reflection journals:

Of all my students' writing it is the thing I enjoy reading the most.

4
Working Assumptions

Did our talking together make a difference?
. . . This is why you come to school.
—Mr. T.

As a modestly successful part-time writer, an experienced reader, and a seasoned classroom speaker, I asked myself this question a number of years ago: What ideas guided your development as a writer, reader, and speaker? This led to another question: How many of these ideas are hidden in the way you teach these skills to others; that is, how many are merely implied? Finally, I asked: If these ideas worked for you, wouldn't they work for your students, if you made them explicit for your students?

I decided they would.

As to the first two questions: I often spouted certain general ideas that I wanted my students to adopt to help them learn how to write and read and speak better. But few of those ideas adhered. Further, I wasn't sure that I had told the students all that I wanted to. For these reasons I felt that I had to formalize my spouting by dictating to students, at timely and convenient moments, the assumptions that I myself follow. That forced me to write my assumptions down in some orderly fashion.

The assumptions that follow come primarily from my work as a teacher and a writer, but many come from graduate school; Writing Project Summer Institutes; readings on process writing, collaborative learning, and reader-response theory; other writers and teachers; and even students. As you will see, many of the assumptions sound as humdrum and dry as curriculum guides or mission statements that threaten to unhinge and vanish with the first puff of wind. But students' writings—their final learning logs—ground the abstractions, giving the ideas meat and bone and heart, investing the ideas with concrete meaning.

As I dictate the assumptions, the students take them down in their marble notebooks, which also contain writing exercises, grammar notes, and literature journals. Their taking down my words guarantees nothing. If the ideas are to truly become part of the students, they will have to live and experience the ideas themselves. That takes time—sometimes a semester, sometimes a whole year, sometimes more than that. For that reason, I pose the assumptions as theses, claims to be tested and proved or disproved during students' stay in my classroom.

And—what? Do the assumptions merely sit there in their marble notebooks? For the most part, yes, though I will repeat an assumption orally when the students need a reminder or, more frequently, when the assumption appears valid or true. The telling point comes at the end of the year when I ask two questions for the final learning log:

1. What is the most important thing you learned in English this year?
2. How has the shape of your mind changed?

In addition to looking in their folders, which contain all their writings and logs, students look at the assumptions they have taken down throughout the year to help them answer questions.

One last thing before I present the assumptions. This may sound strange, but students need not remember most of the assumptions once they have learned them. That is, once students have assimilated the assumptions and can demonstrate through their actions that they know them, it is *less* important for them to be able to recall the assumptions in words. Though many might be able to, they ought not be quizzed.

Further, learning and remembering, though similar, are two different creatures. For example, when I look back on my own schooling, I'd be hard-pressed to tell you what I learned in fourth or seventh or tenth grade. I would fare much better with college and graduate school, but not much and not without some effort. What I remember best are some teachers and classmates and instances of failure and success, like the time I cheated on an art exam or the time Mr. Bellay told the class I had allowed Judith Wilkes to catch a pop-up in the vicinity of third base (which, alas, she dropped). I remember atypical things: The same Mr. Bellay would, every Friday before assembly, line us up at the side of the classroom, and, one-by-one, examine our ears and fingernails for dirt—and woe to the boy who forgot his handkerchief! I remember in third grade, Mrs. Thompson saying to someone in class, "You should wash your bowels every night," and Bonnie Brown and another girl in class chortled. The rest of us had no idea what "bowels" meant, though I learned it and a host of other anatomical words, colloquial and otherwise, from the family dictionary that night.

Other things I can recall occurred outside the classroom: accidents, fights, crushes; Perry the cop who roamed the streets outside George Washington High School; my ninth-grade social studies teacher, Mrs. Oppenheimer, run over by a bus on 125th Street; atomic-bomb drills; polio shots; Kennedy's assassination.

Oftentimes, events peripheral to the curriculum have an impact on us that few classroom experiences can equal. Their unique fingerprints become so indelibly impressed upon our consciousness that just the slightest reminder seems to set these events in motion again. Which is to say, the replaying of these events are memories and not things necessarily learned, as they are re-lived for a moment. On the other hand, remembering what we've learned—knowledge—is self-contradictory. We know what we know. There is no need to remember, for what we've learned is simply there or quietly goes about directing us.

I learned how to read and think about literature in certain ways, thus forming my assumptions. I know when my students have adopted some of the assumptions. They do not have to tell me, though they always do in the end.

The following is a partial list of the working assumptions that I dictate to students during the poetry and narrative writing units. They are grouped under three areas of study, writing, reading, and speaking, but the first few under writing apply to *all* areas of study. To help explain some of the ideas, I have included excerpts from the best of my students' final learning logs.

Part I: Writing

The first assumption is this:

The number one goal of school is the development of mind—the caring, critical, creative mind—which subsumes a knowledgeable mind.

I just learned the most important thing from the Art of Writing [a summer school class] this week. It is that grades don't matter, but to see the benefit of the course is to see how much your mind has changed or expanded.

I think this is a big deal because when report cards come, my parents just look for the grade, not noticing my improved skills. Therefore, I try my best in school for the grade, instead of what really matters. After my mom looked over my report card that I received today, she didn't believe that anything had changed. Then, after I read to her all of my writing, she was very surprised and agreed with my dad that my writing had improved tremendously.

—Meredith Tanaka (Grade 8)

This quote says that three parts of mind would be developed over the course of the school year. One of these was the caring mind. Mr. T. wanted us to care about the world around us, to feel what others are feeling and to experience all of life's aspects so we could make our writing alive. Our writing is what we experience in *our* words. We read other works to experience what others feel in *their* words.

Mr. T. wanted us to develop the critical mind so we can constantly criticize our works and others'. By doing this, we are always changing our writing, using richer language, breathing life into our work. By always having a critical eye, we can help others make their work alive . . .

There are so many things to say about the creative mind: always finding original things to write about, organizing jumbled ideas until they take form into a wonderful shape, and understanding the deeper meaning of literature. The creative mind is always changing perspective and looking at things from someone else's point of view. They do things to learn, not just because they have to.

—Sarah Aldinger (Grade 7)

In English, the development of mind is approached through the study and practice of language—through the making of meaning—through writing, reading, speaking, and reflecting.

"When I was in high school, where I didn't last too long"—the students kind of jerk when I say this—"I don't recall any of my teachers telling me the point of taking their classes. And if they did, none of their reasons were pertinent to my life at the time. From college on, I wanted to know the point of studying anything. Nothing was too obvious for me. Nothing would be hidden from me. Just as nothing will be hidden from you."

The development of one language area (like speaking) will positively affect the development of other language areas (like writing or reading).

"So," I tell the students, "it is important that you talk. It's like writing out loud, composing at the tip of your tongue."

You will learn more from each other than you will from your teacher. We are all involved in each other's development as writers, readers, and speakers, and in each other's development as sensitive human beings.

Many of my students acknowledge that learning from their peers is the most important experience of the year, and I will hear it mentioned repeatedly. They learn through continually giving each other feedback on their writing and through listening to their classmates in discussions about literature.

I think the most important thing that I learned is the significance of listening and learning from my peers. This was brought to light through all the poetry, prose, speeches, presentations, and assignments we wrote. In class discussions we collaborated and expressed our unique insights. We independently interpreted and commented on each other's work. A new idea would create an innovative spark or a new zest for the poem. Through the process of feedback stale ideas were revived with the flavors others provided. Everybody's minds are triggered differently by the same poem or piece of writing. We think at different wave lengths because of our different backgrounds, experiences, morals. We are affected and react differently from each other based on our individual characters. What counts, especially in writing, is if you choose to utilize those insights to help others grow as well as yourself!

—Romy Trigg-Smith (Grade 8)

Over the year I have learned countless things, most of which I am not able to put into words. But the most important thing I've learned is that I'm not as good in English as I once thought. By learning and accepting this I have been able to take in others' ideas and not think that I had the only right answer (which usually wasn't the case). I have been ever so humbled by all of my classmates' extraordinary minds and opinions. Of course, for anyone, realizing you're not as smart and perceptive as you thought is a let down. But I am glad I realized this and have not blocked out anyone else's opinions and views. For, if I had, I would now be a lot more stupid and wouldn't even begin to realize what I was missing. But I still need to work on getting my ego out of the way of learning and growing, emotionally and mentally.

—Heather Hodges (Grade 7)

The most important thing that I have learned in English this year is that people can change. I have always thought deeply, always read beyond the page. I have always seen the bigger picture and preferred the story told between the lines. But I have no practice in telling others what I see and read in the untold story. I tried to tell friends about the things I could get from reading, but the kindest responses were strange looks and quiet laughter behind my back (you can imagine the unkindest). Even my mother, who encouraged this way of thinking, and who told me I was a "neat kid," never seemed to appreciate what I said in the way I wanted her to.

So, I have been thinking this way ever since I read *Charlotte's Web*, my first real chapter book. I would read the stories alone and get all I could out of them. But I would never share them. They would stay with me, and I would read in my own little world. Not in the way most kids do, where they space-out the world around them. I would read a book and think I was the only one in the world that knew what was really there, and that made reading a way to disconnect from reality in the way only I could.

When we first began reading in class, I was skeptical. I thought that no one else would understand, and if I showed that I did, I ran the risk of being jeered at, just like when I was young. And even though you said that no one would laugh at anyone else, well, six years of being taught something is hard to undo with one sentence.

But when we moved on into the text, and my classmates began to show that, not only could they read in the way I always had, but that they wanted to, I began to feel less afraid of how I could read, and more proud of it. I could see that for some it was not easy, and that some stretched a bit to find meaning, but I saw my peers, kids who could easily have joked about me six years ago, strive to achieve what I had told them about. As Nick Tatoppolis said in *Godzilla*, "People do change," and that's the most important thing I learned this year.

—Leoni Leduc (Grade 8)

The bottom line in all your writing is ORIGINALITY . . . which provides information through a new way of speaking, seeing, or understanding. This goes beyond being unique. It means being significant in some way.

Aside from pointing out cliches and hackneyed expressions, teaching means disabusing students of unquestioned, commonplace ideas they borrow from everyday conversation and media—ideas that do not originate in the students themselves.

This procedure [writing like her classmates] worked except for the fact that soon I started to hate English. What was the point of writing poems anyway? There was no fun writing them, and it was pure torture after awhile. It was getting harder and harder to squeeze my brain for "their" topics, and more of those strange ideas, my ideas, would seep through the crevices of my brain.

   Then one night, I was completely blank and could not think of absolutely anything to write, so I decided to try to write down one of my ideas as a last-minute resort. As a million words flew from my head to the paper at the speed of light, I realized how fun and easy writing poetry could be. I also discovered that I was able to write with a passion that I never felt before, like I was able to express everything I was into that one poem. From then on, I wrote about what I wanted, even though it wasn't anything like the poetry of my peers. Strangely enough, Mr. T. seemed to like and rate my poetry higher . . . I realized that poetry is like a mirror to your soul. Earlier, that mirror was reflecting my peers, but now it wasn't reflecting anyone else but me . . . I found that being original in your writing helps you to express yourself and be yourself.

—Marife Molina (Grade 8)

You must write from your gut, your heart, your muscles—with 100 percent attention on your subject. That is, you must commit yourself to writing honestly.

When I was younger, I thought it was long words and elaborate sentences that got you good grades. However, now I realize that it's how much you write from the heart and what you feel that counts . . .

I found the poems where I wrote my straight, simple thoughts were the most effective. I thought the poems about my grandfather and my sister were my best, and they were about as honest as they come.

—Kristina Izumi (Grade 8)

To be original in my writings, I also had to express my feelings honestly. To me, a paper or writing that is not expressed honestly is boring.

—Stephanie Lee (Grade 8)

The most effective writing is based on personal experience and knowledge. There isn't anything else.

When we had to write poems and stories for English, I noticed that some of the best stories and poems I had written were those that included my own experiences. I learned that personal experience is important to writing because with it I am able to create powerful similes and metaphors.

. . . With personal experience . . . you can express the fear, happiness, or sadness you felt much better than someone who hasn't had the experience because you have been there and done that. For example, a person who has lost a loved one can explain their mixed emotions of grief, pain, and sorrow better than someone who hasn't lost a loved one before. The person with the experience can explain the shock of terror as they receive the death phone call. He/she can also explain how the reality of never seeing their loved one again doesn't soak in until a day later, and then turns into depression or sadness that overcomes his/her body like a deadly disease. The person who experiences this is able to write his/her feelings better than a writer who is guessing how he/she might have felt in that person's situation. Personal experience is the greatest tool of writing I have learned this year in English.

—Mari Oishi (Grade 7)

Good writing appeals to the five senses.

There are three things that intrigue intelligent readers: new information or insight, other people, and complexity or richness.

The only good writing is rewriting.

From the very first class, Mr. T. made it clear that he expected a draft with every submission. If there was not a draft attached, I would be penalized. At first, I thought he was just being cynical by finding petty details to penalize me for. I felt this way because I was too lazy to put the extra effort into the rewriting process. Little did I know that over the course of the next nine months my attitude toward rewriting would take a full 180 degree turn . . . for the best.

Obviously, reworking a paper definitely helps to improve the paper. Through feedback, I am able to use the suggestions to make my paper more appealing and grammatically correct. For each rewrite I do, I am continuing to improve my paper. To understand what I mean, it might be easier to think of what I would be missing if I did not rewrite my paper. If I turn in a paper that has not been read by anyone else, I could be turning in a paper with many flaws. Mr. T. would see this and my grade would suffer. I am biased when it comes to judging the quality of my own work. Because I wrote it, I tend to think that it is perfect the way it is. However, when others who are not blinded by bias read it, they find the errors and flaws that I've overlooked. That's why it is important to have others read your work when rewriting.

Another reason why rewriting is so important to me is because it helps me to not procrastinate. Although that may seem farfetched, it actually isn't. I procrastinate because I have an anxiety of failure. For some psychological reason, I feel I am delaying failure by delaying the start of a paper. However, now that I rewrite my papers before submitting them, I know that I will not fail. Because I no longer fear failure, I no longer procrastinate or delay writing my paper.

—Natalie Watanabe (Grade 8)

The most powerful revisionary influence is other people. Other people free your mind: they show you other ways to think and see, giving you options, choices—thereby freeing you from the tyranny of your first draft.

"Nor, by the way, does it matter that a single suggestion offered to you is superior to what you already have. All you ask is that the suggestion be different from what you already have so that you have a basis for comparison. What you want is lots of suggestions from lots of different people. *Capisce?*"
"*CAPISCE!*"

After writing as much as you can, focus on compression.

"Consider this: The more you compress a thing the denser it gets, and the denser it gets, the more intense it becomes, so that, if you were to touch it, it will explode. So cut the fat and find the words that will do their job with ruthless speed."

The idea of perfection in writing is an illusion. Any work can be reshaped or transformed, infinitely.

One of the most difficult things for kids to do is give their classmates honest feedback. At first, kids fear offending others (especially their friends). Kids fear appearing dumb or wrong. They do not give suggestions—what the writer needs most, what they themselves want most from their readers.

"Instead, kids—like some of you—merely write 'good' on your classmates' papers, not spending the time and effort to express their real opinions and give others advice and examples. For some of you, giving others honest feedback will remain a challenge for some time. For you others—Don't be cheap! Reciprocate!"

Your Attitude As a Reader: This is what I would do if this writing were mine. No one is an expert here. Obviously, the writer has the choice of whether or not to heed a reader's advice or accept any suggestion.

One of the most difficult things for kids to do is to be open minded—receptive—to the criticism and suggestions their peers offer in response to their writing.

At the time, I thought of feedback as something people gave you to compliment you on your work. If by chance someone criticized me or told me to fix something in my writing, I thought of it as a threat to my work and to my ideas. I wouldn't even consider or listen to what the person was talking about. I would merely think that they had no idea as to what they were saying, and that I was right and they were wrong.

I now know that the best kind of feedback that you can get is the feedback that tells you exactly what doesn't make sense or what the person doesn't like in your writing. Now, I actually think of the "nice" comments as a waste of time. I barely even glance at them. It's the constructive criticism that I love to get. It is through feedback that you see things that must be fixed in order for your work to be clearer, more thorough, and for you to become a great writer.

—Lauren Chang (Grade 8)

I have learned to step outside of myself and become a third person. As a third person, I can see the same thing as the person commenting. After I have looked at my own idea or piece of work from this perspective, I can either agree or disagree with the person commenting.

What I have learned also includes the courage to keep on trying. I have learned to voice my opinions even after having my other ideas rejected repeatedly. When I have been criticized, I don't sulk and think to myself that everybody is trying to be rude. I make an effort to see what the person is criticizing. I learn and try again.

—James Schulmeister (Grade 7)

Generally, for young writers, being clear means being thorough.

"Let's face it," I tell my students, "it's easy to make generalizations. Your second-grade sister can make them. It's another story to supply the details and thinking behind your beliefs and opinions.

"In my lunchtime banter with other eighth-grade teachers and from talking with science and social studies teachers and many high school teachers, I've heard their number one complaint or criticism of student writers: that they fail to elaborate on their thinking, and do not adequately discuss the ideas they assert. To put this another way, the only way you can achieve complexity and depth— *clarity*—is to write at detailed length. If you develop the capacity to do this one thing during the school year, everything else you will have learned will seem small by comparison, for your power of mind will have taken a leap."

The seeds of what to develop in your writing—what to write next or at greater length or depth—exist in what you have already written. Therefore, constantly look back and question what you have written.

When I sit down to write a paper I try to write an introduction and what little I can think of to write about, to answer the question presented to me. Usually I start off with very little on my paper, but then I start to look back at what I've already written and I start to get ideas on how to make it better and longer. When looking at what I have, I do one of two things. I either think of ways to elaborate on present subjects, or I make connections to new ideas through what I already have on my paper. Sometimes I find that I thought that I had written down ideas when I didn't, or I have only written parts of them.

—Keith Beers (Grade 8)

As you move toward the completion of any draft, consider the needs and expectations of your audience.

As James Moffett says best, "People at first assume that minds match, that other people see the world as they do, think about it the same way, mean the same thing when they use the same words, and fill in the gaps of language as they do . . . The assumptions, furthermore, are hidden. People don't know what they don't know." He calls such thinking *egocentric*, the type of thinking that results in what Nancy Martin calls *writer-based prose*, writing that fails to communicate because it ignores the differences between the writer and his or her audience. Identifying the students' audience will be of some help. However, the telling point is when students know they must do something more with their writing when their classmates look confused or less than satisfied.

I tell the students, "Put yourself in your readers' position. Put yourself, say, in your grade level supervisor's, Mr. Woody's, chair. You know, the bald-headed guy who doesn't smile. Then ask yourself what more your writing might need in order for Mr. Woody to completely understand what you're saying. And knowing that he's a picky thinker and loves graceful language, ask yourself what more you could do to make him smile."

The most important thing that I learned in English is the fact that clarity takes precedence over what you are trying to say, and that if you are not clear, the material that you are trying to convey is irrelevant.

For me, it is significantly easier to get from "point A to point B" than most people. However, in order to do that, I need to show how to get from point A to point B. In doing so, I must cut out some of my argument if it cannot be proven.

When I write, I have learned that there are levels of understanding, which may necessitate either making the writing simpler or more complex. All opinions must be stated clearly, but they cannot be simplistic, for then they do not introduce anything new. Metaphors and similes must be made complex enough so that they are original, yet simple enough that they can be understood.

My prose writing needs to be more understandable, a process I am still working on. It must use only facts that can be proven, not opinions, to support what you are writing about.

My mind has expanded to be more susceptible to other ideas. Some poetry is simpler than I interpret, and other writings are more complicated than I think they are. I have grown in my ability to communicate with other people, a process that will need to grow more as my years at school progress.

—Kenji Matsumoto (Grade 8)

Always seek feedback before going public with your work.

I would say that the most important thing I've learned this year in English is that clarity is the ultimate goal of a writer. By that I mean a writer needs, as a courtesy to his/her audience, to be clear and direct about getting his/her views across. All too often I ignored the readers' needs and assumed they knew what I talked about.

This occurred in multiple instances, such as the Damon Speech, my learning logs, and in my short stories. For the first draft of my speech on cloning, nearly everything needed amendment because I had forgotten that people didn't know quite as much as I did when it came to cloning (after all, I was the only one in the class that researched it). A more in depth explanation was needed . . . No, I couldn't touch on all of the aspects of cloning, but what I *did* touch on was understood by everybody. The all-important feedback factor was what straightened me out. Feedback was how I came to realize that the class didn't know what I was talking about.

. . . From beginning to near end, clarity has been something I have neglected in the attempt to look a little fancy.

—David Campana (Grade 8)

Continually proofread your work aloud. Let the ear reinforce your eyes. As well as hearing the sound and rhythm of your own unique voice, you will catch omissions and cringe at the awkward words, expressions, and constructions that you'd never speak to another human being.

"I cannot tell you how invaluable the practice of reading your own work aloud can be. It is the most dependable way you can judge your work against your highest personal standards, leading you to refine and polish your language. But many of you won't heed this advice until I interrogate you publicly, sometimes more than once—am I right, Scooter?—using as evidence your so-called final drafts. And despite your weak claims to the contrary, I will say—now all together, class—YOU LIE!"

At the end, proofread the hardcopy with a partner for acceptable spelling, clear punctuation and mechanics, and other conventions appropriate to the genre you are writing in.

I think that the most important thing that I learned across the year, that will help me in later years, is proofreading. In the beginning of the school year, Mr. T. told us that the only good writing is rewriting. Before I absorbed this statement I would have little or no drafts at all. Either that or when I rewrote my work, there would still be a lot of errors because of my poor proofreading skills. I wouldn't check for grammar errors, instead only spelling errors. Throughout the course of the year Mr. T. showed us new techniques for better proofreading. An example is run-on sentences. He taught us many ways to fix them: the colon, semi-colon, comma, etc. Run-on sentences are no longer as big of a problem for me as they were before. Since I spend more time on my work I now can catch many of the small errors too!

One last thing that I found out: the more people that I get to give me feedback, the better my paper will usually be. I now always get feedback from not only myself, but from family, friends, etc.

—Kahai Macdonald (Grade 8)

Part II: Reading

According to many of my students' final learning logs, more powerful than the impact of poetry writing was their learning how to *read*, which began in the narrative writing unit. Perhaps this was true because their learning how to read was gradual, spanning a good portion of the school year, and required a lot of intellectual sweat, which at first resulted in little except frustration. "How come I couldn't think of that? How come I can't see what Malia sees?"

During the poetry writing unit, students experienced at least a modicum of success from poem to poem, rarely earning less than a B. And they knew they were making progress in their skills. At the beginning, while learning to read in this "new" way, the students did not feel successful, nor was it evident that they were improving in their new skills.

Also new were the kinds of stories they were asked to read—stories from different genres (which I hoped would broaden their range and appreciation); stories with increasingly sophisticated vocabulary; stories whose protagonists are frequently adults; stories where character, motivation, revelation, changing relationships, and other issues of the heart become the plot, where much of the action is "internal"; and stories that employ almost invisible strategies to convey their meanings, hiding their art. And my questions, whose answers are not explicitly written in the story, were new to them, too.

Through patience, practice, listening to their peers, and venturing forth with their own tentative ideas, the students found that the kindling caught and the night and the forest grew lighter and lighter.

In the middle of the year, Mr. T. said to us, "You must become better readers." I never knew there was such a thing as a good reader. When I read books, it was all about the text, where, as long as I knew what the words meant, I was fine. In English, I had to overcome hills and mountains to get to the reading level I am today.

At the beginning of the year, I was doing really bad because everything was literal to me. Never could I see behind the words where the true meanings were. This year, during our class discussions, I have used metaphorical meanings to deepen my knowledge of the questions we discussed. My mind has grown better at interpreting lines. The depth of my understanding has grown so much that I laugh at what I considered "reading" in the year(s) before.

The different angles of approach through which you can understand a piece of writing have helped me to think deeper. This was shown in *Julius Caesar*, where Cassius said that Caesar should be "stripped of his wings." I raised my hand to talk and, luckily, Mr. T. called on me. I thought it meant that the conspirators thought that Caesar's power should be taken away so he would descend into mediocrity. In the adult poetry unit, my mind was put to the test. A good example of this was in the poem "258" by Emily Dickinson. One of the questions asked was, "What does 'sent us of air' mean?" Many of my classmates said it meant that the "imperial affliction" was sent through the air, which is all around us, can't be avoided. Then Josh brought up that the word "air" could also mean music. This means that air could represent sad or happy music, which is a metaphor for our feelings, whether we are full of despair or feel joy. The imagination is a phenomenal thing, especially when you can picture the metaphor.

—Andrew Lee (Grade 8)

We are interested in what the text does not tell us directly and plainly.

Rather than testing students' recall of what they've read as a means of teaching them to be more attentive, more sensitive readers, I ask them for their interpretations, for the meanings I ultimately want them to construct with increasing sophistication. Paying attention to what is important will lead students back to the text itself, giving value to the words and passages that inspired their interpretations in the first place, and thereby giving practical value to accurate and precise reading. Similarly, in writing, I ask not for sentences and paragraphs, but for whole works, because students' *care* for the whole work reveals and underscores the importance of mastering grammar and mechanical conventions. With the higher goal always in mind, like making interpretations or writing whole works, the students and I give due weight to lesser goals, defining their importance in the total meaning-making scheme.

And what is reading? What are writing, speaking, reflecting, language, and literature? As seen from the highest perspective, they are machines, tools, for the development of mind. That is their primary function.

Reading is an interpretive act. We half-create what we read.

"I sometimes think," said the South American writer Jorge Luis Borges, "that good readers are poets as singular, and as awesome, as great authors themselves." Which is to say, reading is a creative act, requiring as much imagination as writing does. For it is the reader who fills in the blanks, puts meat and flesh on the bones, draws the detailed pictures in the planetarium of our minds, creating a cosmos from the coldest, blackest print. Good readers can do that.

A piece of writing is like a page of hieroglyphics, which need to be read and reread to uncover its true meanings. Behind these simple carvings lies a story. Depending on what knowledge you have of archeology and reading hieroglyphics, these inscriptions may translate into different things for each person. This is why reading—like archeology—is something that requires practice in order to master it. Sure, almost anyone can read the sentence "See Spot run," but it takes an experienced reader to be able to take that sentence and do something with it. They are the ones who are able to unmask these simple black and white words, show us the color that is hidden by them, and can tell us what they mean.

—Robyn Nakamoto (Grade 8)

Everything in a work of literature is significant or can be made significant through skillful interpretation.

"If you recall revising your own writing, especially your poems, one of the things you did was eliminate anything that did not serve a purpose and that slowed down the reading, diluting the effect you wanted to create. This is also true for prose writers and storytellers. In theory, nothing is present in the story that does not have a function. Now write this down: *This assumption encourages us to question the purpose of anything or everything found in a text.*"

Now, thanks to reading three books and discussing them at length during class, I read much differently. I pick out the subtle meanings, examine the metaphors. I find the insights in the writing; I get to know the characters much better, their purposes, goals, and achievements. I understand the problems they face at a deeper level and question what it means to my life. I understand what kind of people the characters are and changes they go through.

These past few weeks we have been reading *The Contender*. I read this book a few years ago when my older brother was in 7th grade and read the same book. Back then I interpreted the book and its meaning as follows: Alfred is a boxer with a friend who uses drugs. Alfred is undefeated in his first three fights but retires after the fourth because he loses. He saves his friend at the end.

Reading the book for the second time was much more enjoyable, even though I knew the ending. Knowing the ending used to be important, but now the important part is the hidden meanings and life lessons you can discover along the way as you read.

—Kyle Morgan (Grade 7)

There are no single right answers to meaningful questions about literature. Multiple answers lead to richness and complexity. But this is not to say that there are no wrong answers or that all answers are of equal value.

I anticipate that my students will come up with a few outlandish interpretations. When they do, I understand that it is not that they are wrong in their observations but that they are limited in what they are able to see at this point in their development as readers. More often than not, their peers will persuade them that more "elegant" interpretations are likely.

The most important thing I have learned in English is that nothing can be viewed from only one perspective to be fully understood, and that in order for something to be seen clearly your own perspective must change. Everything can be seen from a different point of view, in a different light. If you were to look at a two-dimensional side of a three-dimensional object, you would probably not guess that the rectangle you see is part of a cube, unless you obtained a different view of a different side and put them together. This might change your perspective for the side that you view and give you a clearer understanding of the whole object that you are looking at, or the whole meaning which you have missed. One perspective is not enough to recognize the rectangle as part of a cube. The changing of your perspective, because of the input from the other person, would now allow you to see two sides of the cube, which would allow you to guess at the whole object. But even if that other person gave you input, but your perspective did not change, then you have wasted their view, because you can still only see one side. You need input from other people, thereby increasing your understanding.

—Kevin Takasaki (Grade 7)

One quote I've always known (but now understand more thoroughly) is the following: "We don't see things as they are, we see things as we are." This has finally made sense for me . . . I used to wonder why we have arguments in English. Why we all have different views. Now I know too.

—Sharaya Llanes (Grade 7)

Understanding other people's explanation is like opening a door to something new. You are allowed to see things you were blind about before . . .

I connected this idea to the "walking in his shoes" saying. You can't judge someone until you've walked in their shoes, until you've seen what they've seen, been where they've been.

When you've been where they've been, you are able to understand what they say and how they think.

—Koa Nuuhiva (Grade 8)

I will teach you, as you will teach yourselves and each other, how to read metaphorically.

The most important thing I learned this year is how to read literature metaphorically. I learned how to do this when we started reading *Heroes, Gods, and Monsters of Greek Myth* and had to write triple-entry journals. Finding the significance of a quote forced me to find connections with some other part of the text or find metaphors. After awhile, it became fun. I found it interesting that literature could have so many meanings. It also amazed me that the author could be so brilliant to write these little connections consciously or sub-consciously. Now when I read something, I sort of automatically find a metaphorical meaning in my mind. For conceited reasons, this makes me feel smart—like I've done something no one else has. I enjoy finding metaphors because it makes me think on a deeper level. I actually have to think harder to grasp a concept I know is in my head. The extra thinking I have to go through to reach a satisfactory or better paper makes me feel prouder of what I have done.

—Megan Lau (Grade 7)

Always read with a pen in your hand; mark up your text (if it is yours). Experienced readers often hold a conversation with the text or the author, never allowing themselves to be totally consumed by the words.

The only good reading is rereading.

Part III: Speaking

I dictate this assumption to the students early in the year:

> *Another hard thing for kids to do is to read their own work aloud to the class, to give speeches and other kinds of public presentations. Weighed down by the psychological baggage they shoulder to the front of the room, students unintentionally place emphasis on themselves rather than on their work, where the emphasis ought to be.*

The body begins to sway, while different appendages assume a life of their own—a wayward ankle and foot, a bouncy knee, a hand tugging the front of the shirt or blouse—drawing attention away from the words. Students speak, or read their own words, too softly, too swiftly, often in a monotone, slurring their words; their voice dying at the ends of lines, sentences, paragraphs, at the end of the whole work; running, while still speaking, from the front of the room. Like any other valuable skill, speaking effectively in front of an audience takes practice and experience.

> Disgust was the first distinct pose struck across my face the moment I found out how important presentations and participation was going to be in the following year. It was like standing on the shore watching a rushing tsunami, no escape . . . no hope of survival. From that moment, the words, "EMphasize your lip movement" (Mr. T's favorite saying) were engraved into my brain. I had practically never worked on speaking in any other class before. Speaking in front of others is still one of my biggest fears and hates. It is also the most important thing I have learned this year.
>
> Obviously, important knowledge does not come without great challenge and hard work. It took me awhile to figure this out. As I sat there, understanding the questions, knowing the answer, I yet said nothing. I slowly worked my way up, reading my poems to the class or occasionally giving my input. When it was time for final presentation, I was ready. Being up there didn't faze me at all. I was perfectly comfortable up in front of the class, despite the cold chills prickling my arms. I was fine. Afterwards I was really shocked. It was the first time I had done so well in front of a crowd.

I'm not saying that I have completely mastered the skill of presentation. In fact, I'm far from it. But it's the baby steps that count.

— Kimiko Thornton (Grade 8)

Mr. T. has taught me how to get brave enough to read aloud to the class . . . The worst thing that can happen is Mr. T. yelling at you, which isn't so bad because he practically yells at everyone by the time summer school is over.

—Michael China (Grade 8)

My students have a predilection for hyperbole. My voice is generally loud and may sound arch or angry, which most certainly isn't what I intend. One day after class, Michael, together with another student, caught me at the threshold and asked, "Mr. T., how come you don't smile in class?" I hesitated for a moment, then answered, "Would you smile if you were missing teeth?" I showed him my teeth through a wide, sardonic grin. He and his friend shrank back a little and laughed, now well armed with an anecdote that he could share with his folks, probably at the dinner table over stir-fried noodles. "So you're Mr. Tsujimoto. It's true, you always wear your sunglasses on top of your head. Even at night."

Beware. Everything you wear, do, or say comes home.

Both prepared speech and impromptu talk need the voice and body to communicate the scripted words or the words, ideas, feelings, and images swimming about in the speaker's head. The difference between the two is plain: Just as free or spontaneous writing originates at the tip of a pen, impromptu talk originates at the tip of the tongue. However natural such talk may seem, it amazes me that we are able to do it. It's a wonderful mystery. It amazes me what people can sometimes say off the top of their heads, especially in casual talk among friends, colleagues, and family, when the larynx is most free and relaxed. At these moments, people can be witty, ingenious, insightful, and even profound. In smaller measure, and to a lesser degree, similar characteristics can be found in a classroom of eighth graders discussing a piece of writing.

The problem is that, for too many of *my* eighth-grade students, the larynx is not free and relaxed. And I know that part of the problem is me, their very demanding teacher. My voice is loud; it is also deep and resonant; and because I can get carried away sometimes with my histrionics, my voice sometimes resounds, passing through the walls into the adjoining rooms. Further, I can be impatient and abrupt and give short shrift, while my humor, sometimes directed at individual students, can bite too deeply. My "big," often formal, language can be intimidating, though I often translate along the way. I refuse to talk down to my students, treating them instead as the intelligent human beings that they are, some of whom retain greater native talents than I do. The other shortcoming— the one I *can't* improve upon—is my being the authority in the classroom, the person who must judge the students and give them a grade. They are already wary of grades—though for some, especially the smart ones, their fears transcend grades. As I said, I am only part of the problem.

That my students do not speak as much as they could, or sooner, is problematic for me because so much of my teaching is dependent upon student interaction and the interchange of ideas. More important—where their writing is concerned—is that students hear and heed their own public voice and language, which are more indicative of who they are than the voice and language that sometimes appear in their writing. How often must I write in the margin, "Write more closely to the way you speak"? To hear themselves, to hear their voice, manner of speaking, natural rhythms, can only aid students in their search for a writing voice, especially for those who see writing as a creature distinctly different from the way they speak.

> *For many of you, volunteering to speak in class discussion will be your biggest challenge. On the other hand, those who meet this challenge will experience great pride and satisfaction over their achievement.*

A variation of the flaws that are apparent in prepared presentations emerges during class discussion, with this difference: Students—through lack of interest or through fear, mostly—can choose *not* to talk. And many of them, through much of the year, choose not to. It seems to me that publicly proffering ideas and opinions is a greater risk to their public image and self-esteem than, say, reading their poems to the class is (that's something that *all* my students volunteer to do at least three or four times in the unit). Much, much more than their initial fears in feedback groups, which they overcome over time, is the magnified fear of raising one's hand and talking to the *entire* class.

Students' first fear is the fear of being wrong, which is generally dissolved when the class begins to embrace the assumption *There are no single right answers to meaningful questions about literature.* Their second fear is of appearing ignorant and of being ridiculed. This is gradually overcome by constantly working with each other and coming to understand that each of us arrives in class with a different configuration of global knowledge and that all of us are experts and novices in different fields by continual turns: from our knowledge of skate boarding to yours of rap music to hers of hula to his of computers or to my wife's of our peach-face love bird.

Students' third fear, which poses the greatest threat, is of appearing stupid or dumb before their peers, the society from which they desire respect and esteem. In general, students confuse stupidity with ignorance or being wrong. I try to make them aware of this mistake; and, pointing out that we have all been, at one time or another, a victim of that confusion, I appeal to their generosity of feeling.

Wanting to learn and having a possible answer to a question, but fearing imagined consequences, gives the student a poignant dilemma. Several *want* to raise their hands and talk. You can sometimes see it in their postures—as though they are physically preparing themselves to act—often too late. You can see it in the changing glow or shadows or shades of color in their faces. You can see it in their eyes, which they think are secret, as they attend upon a wavering resolve. You might see it in the hesitant movement of their hands, whose palms might be moist, whose fingers might tremble beneath the desk. I can sometimes recognize some of these signs and call on a student, making the decision for him or her, which is sometimes a necessary first step. But sometimes I don't see very well and the moment passes by, the focus of talk is suddenly elsewhere, the opportunity lost; perhaps this is a step that must repeat itself. I suppose for many of us a certain price, some little pain or anxiety, must be paid for learning.

To ask me to pinpoint the one, the best, the most important thing is like asking me to pick the best card from six aces. If I were to sum up my entire English experience I would begin with the most important: *courage*. Without courage there is only regret. Regret for not reading a poem to the class, regret for not sharing opinions, and regret for not being all that I could be.

Courage is the ability to stand up to danger with confidence. Danger in English class, in my eyes, involves a somewhat social image that is damaged by having my comments seemingly rejected by the class. Learning to ignore and overcome that danger and understand that there is no wrong answer is what English has taught me this year. Bringing that confidence and self-esteem to other classes has been a plus in my academic potential and achievement, not to mention the way I feel about myself.

Some are born with courage, and those like me must learn it. English has been a learning experience, a first step in the continual gathering of courage into myself.

—Rory Hennessy (Grade 9)

Not only do we learn a great deal from others by listening to the kinds of questions they ask and noting the various reactions to those questions, we spur, extend, modify, expand, and complete each other's thinking. As a result, we experience the power of our joint effort in the making of meaning—meaning that no single one of us could construct alone.

The most important thing I've learned in English this year is that participation is the key to a successful class period. When I say successful class period, I'm talking about a class session in which everyone learns something. When I leave class, I expect to have somewhat broadened my knowledge. If, in a discussion, someone limits their speech, you will never know if good ideas had been floating in their mind. The whole class will suffer if one person with even a fraction of a good idea does not share their thoughts because the class can expand on it. I say this in regards to my own personal experience. In the third trimester, ideas kept popping up in my head, but together they meant nothing. The whole class period I tried to arrange them in a way that made sense. I realized that I should've spoken up because my classmates could've helped to clarify the idea. And together, it would clarify the poem a little more.

Previously, I always felt there was no need for me to participate in discussions because someone would eventually say what was needed to be stated. I felt that anything I might add would be nonsense. Since we had so many discussions this year, I learned how much you can get out of participation. Not only does it force you to stay awake and focused; it helps you understand the topic of discussion. If you present a question or idea, the class can help you. The only way that the class can help is if everyone's ideas are voiced. Since I am a part of this class, I realized how essential it is for me to participate.

—Nicole Saito (Grade 8)

We can create an atmosphere, then, where students can render each other support and courage; a place where they can see each other as genuine sources of information, where they can grow and witness the dramatic growth of others, as Rory and Nicole did.

Let me sum this chapter up this way: A teacher can ask him- or herself: What are the general principles and assumptions that guide my own approach to writing, reading, and speaking? Or, put another way, What are the general principles and working assumptions that I want my students to adopt as a guide for writing, reading, and speaking? My belief is that, by offering students governing ideas that they can apply to the general process of reading literature, writing, or speaking, we give them ways to modify their present practices. And if they try out an idea and it helps them see and understand more deeply, they will assimilate the idea into their personal approach to reading literature or writing or speaking.

Practicing reflection (as through learning logs) helps students immensely, so long as they have something to reflect on. "What was the most important thing you learned in English this year?" Always, they gravitate toward a "metalinguistic tool," a governing idea—a principle or working assumption that has proved itself a boon to their development as language users.

5

Narrative Writing

Tell me a story of deep delight.
—*Robert Penn Warren*

After allowing my students a week to put together their poetry books, I spend the next three weeks preparing them to write either a fictional short story or a nonfiction story about an experience they've had. I focus on two things: training students to read as writers (learning some of the tools of the craft) and helping them generate story options (for, as students claim, the number one difficulty in writing is finding a topic).

During much of this preparation, I operate, to use the current jargon, a "teacher-centered classroom" and do so without apology. My classes are only forty-minutes long, so I must pick judiciously those instances where I can "facilitate" students' learning for themselves. Really, these terms drive me crazy. Which is why, for the most part, I follow poetry. Listen to Basho:

> Four temple gates
> Four ways
> Beneath a single moon.

Put otherwise, there are many ways to the top of the mountain.

Day 1: Learning to Read

At the very beginning of the narrative writing unit, I announce to the students, "I will teach you how to read."

Eyes squint—"Huh?"—or roll up into their heads, accompanied by deep exhalations. Guffaws.

"You're kidding, right?"

I love it.

"First, all that you will be doing in the next three weeks will work, in some way, toward your writing a fictional story or a story about an experience you had."

70

"How long should it be?"

"Did I answer that question when people asked how long their poem should be or how long their introduction to their poetry book should be?"

"No."

"Just ask yourself how *good* it should be."

"I asked and nobody answered," says one wit.

"He asked and no one was home," volunteers another.

"Just ask yourself then how good you *want* it to be. Nathan, do you *want* to write something good?" He nods, sideways.

"Now about stories. How did your learn to tell stories? You heard them from people around you, just as you learned how to speak English, just as you learned new vocabulary. You heard and listened and imitated and added your own touch to the basic pattern. Think of all the fairy tales and children's stories your parents read to you. My mother used to read me Uncle Remus stories and Golden Books and children's Bible stories. One story that comes to mind is *Ping*, the duck; another is about that little train that would never give up—I forget the title—"

"The Little Engine That Could."

"That's the one. And how did you learn how to write stories? That is, how did you learn to *improve* at writing them?"

"Reading."

"That's right, through reading. And as some of you have sensed through poetry writing, *there are more moves in writing than Michael Jordan has on a basketball court*. Some of those moves you already know, having practiced them. But there are so many more you will discover as you read. So many more yet to be invented. So many styles and compelling voices and stories to tell. So many that catch you by the throat. You have read some yourselves, getting so immersed in them that the outside world must slap you on the back of your head to wake your attention and retrieve you from the dream, so persuasive was the tale, so real—even a story about a spider told through the eyes of a pink pig named Wilbur. So real because that world, that reality, we half-create ourselves. Other stories, despite the fact that we know they are fiction, can, with our unconscious consent, deceive us, for unlike poetry, the art of narration is often hidden, subtle, overlooked.

"So, like writers, who are oftentimes great readers, we must withhold part of ourselves from totally succumbing to the story. We must keep a little part of our mind at a distance so that we may see the crafty stage direction going on just to the left of the curtain. And why must we do this? So that like writers—most of you will be writers of some sort the rest of your lives—we can learn, borrow, and steal from other writers in order to help us tell our own tales better; in order to improve our own craft.

"As fledgling writers, you must read as writers, adopting the attitude of hunters. And strangely, along the way, rather than breaking the story's magic, you'll find it richer and deeper and more satisfying, having, by way of the hunt, become better readers.

"Now before we go on, I want to read you something I wrote about the ideal listener or the ideal reader:

> Our model here is the child or the young learner who takes joy in hearing stories—stories of any kind—so long as they are original and are accessible to her age. These are her only expectations. Because of her openness, subject matter is irrelevant to her; and because she is free of preconceptions, as older students are not, she is capable of viewing spontaneously and freshly each story or poem as a new situation to be contemplated for itself.

According to the short story writer Guy de Maupassant:

> The public as a whole is composed of various groups, whose cry to us writers is:
>
> > "Comfort me."
> > "Amuse me."
> > "Touch me."
> > "Make me dream."
> > "Make me laugh."
> > "Make me shudder."
> > "Make me weep."
> > "Make me think."
>
> And only a few chosen spirits say to the artist:
>
> > "Give me something fine in any form which may
> > suit you best, according to your own temperament."

Children, it seems, are 'chosen spirits,' free of the psychological baggage with which older people burden themselves.

"I want you to remember this idea of openness when you read some of the stories I assign. Like the story about Lencho that I assigned to you on—Friday, was it?"

"Yeah."

"One last thing. Take this down. Today is?"

"December first."

"Okay: 12-1-99":

Everything in a work of literature is significant or can be made significant through skillful interpretation.

"This assumption encourages us to question the purpose of anything and everything in a text. So as I read through this story about Lencho, I'll ask you a few questions. I think you'll begin to agree that the assumption has some validity to it."

———————

Lencho—in Lopez y Fuentes' "A Letter to God"—is hoping for rain to water his kidney bean crops and ensure that his large family will eat. However, instead of rain, hail falls, ruining his crops. After deep meditation, Lencho writes a letter asking God for a hundred pesos, then takes the letter to town and mails it at the post office. The postmaster, through the postman, intercepts the letter and reads it. Wanting to preserve Lencho's impressive faith, he takes up a collection among the post office employees, then places the money in an envelope addressed to Lencho from God. When Lencho returns to the post office, he asks if there is a letter for him. Upon receiving it, he opens it and, without surprise, counts the bills, but becomes angry since he has received only seventy of the hundred pesos he had asked for. God, he thinks, does not make mistakes, nor would he deny Lencho's request. He immediately writes another letter to God (which again is intercepted by the postmaster), advising God to send the rest of his request by some other means since "the post-office employees are a bunch of crooks."

In addition to assigning students the reading, I ask them to make slash marks whenever the author makes a leap in time, which forces them to see how a writer collapses or truncates time in order to focus on important events.

"As we begin, consider all the things the writer does not tell us or does not tell us directly."

Then I ask, "Who is telling this story? Or from whose point of view is the story seen?"

No answer.

"Let me put it this way: Is the storyteller someone in the story or someone outside the story?"

"Outside."

"Can anyone tell me the term teachers use to identify this narrator?"

"Third person?"

"Okay, and what's that mean?"

"The storyteller uses *he* or *she* or a name when talking about the characters."

"Like in a fairy story?"

"Yeah."

"So what's a *first*-person narrator?"

"Someone inside the story. A character is telling the story."

"That's right, and the pronoun she or he uses is 'I.' And when you use 'I' you admit to being a human being who has faults and flaws, meaning sometimes you have to weigh what a first-person narrator might say, for he or she might not be altogether accurate in his or her judgment."

"Is there a second-person narrator?"

"No, nor, for the curious, is there a fourth. Now, what magical power does the third-person narrator have that is impossible in the first-person narrator?"

"He can tell us what's going on in people's heads."

"And hearts."

After they identify places where the narrator exercises this power, I ask, "Why must this story be written in the third person? Or what wouldn't we know if Lencho told this story?"

"We wouldn't know where the money came from."

"And we wouldn't laugh at the end."

I read the first sentence: "'The house—the only one in the entire valley—sat on the crest of a low hill.' Why does the author choose to have Lencho's house the only one in the valley?"

"So that he's alone. To make it hail only on him and his farm."

"So that he can't ask neighbors for help."

"To make him unique."

"He's already unique."

"In what way?"

"Well, I know that kids might write a letter to Santa Claus or maybe even to God. But an adult?"

"Not only that," I say. "Lencho uses the national post office system to send it to God, as though the postal system had some kind of connection to the Almighty. Extraordinary!

"By the way—some of you might want to take this down in your marble notebook, or anything else you find important; it's up to you: All stories present some kind of problem or conflict or raise a question, or a character needs to make a decision. But not all problems may be resolved, or the questions answered. Or a decision might be made and the story doesn't explicitly tell us why. The general question to keep in mind is *What's at stake?*—which is easily apparent in the case of Lencho and his family.

"Now, after Lencho and his wife talk about the need for rain—by the way, why isn't she named? Lencho just calls her *woman*."

"It might be a cultural thing."

"What about Lencho's children?"

"They're not important, really."

"Huh?"

"I mean in the story. They're just there."

"Is anybody given a name?"

"Lencho."

"That's right—anybody else?"

"The postmaster, but that isn't really a name."

"And the postman," I say. "In this way, while denying the other characters in the story a name and favoring only Lencho *with* one, the author emphasizes Lencho's importance. The author, to use a technical term, *foregrounds* Lencho's character. As you continue to read, you will note various other ways writers do this.

"How many—what's the *least* number of children that Lencho has?"

"Two."

"No, four."

"How do you know?"

"It says."

"Where?"

"Right here, a third of the way down."

"Please read it."

"'The oldest boys were working in the field, while the smaller ones were playing near the house.' So the minimum is four."

"Is this information important to know?"

"Yeah, he's Catholic."

"Most likely, and it does connect to the importance that religion plays in Lencho's life. Any other reason?"

"It's a big family."

"And . . . ?"

"Lencho has a lot of people to feed."

"He's responsible for a lot of people, not just himself. Like any parent."

"He must be worried."

"Is it significant that Lencho's children should all be boys?"

"Yeah, boys eat more."

"All the time?" I ask.

The boys look around the room and perhaps recall some female siblings who'd out-eaten them. The girls in the class look at each other knowingly but for the most part, do not enter this exchange. "Maybe not all the time."

"Most of the time."

"At least, tradition would have it so."

"Right after the mother calls everyone to dinner, the narrator says, 'It was during the meal that, just as Lencho had predicted, big drops of rain began to fall.' Now, this is not by accident. Unlike life—though many fictions appear like life and we read them, at least temporarily, *as* life—many events in fiction occur at purposeful times. *When* things occur can be as premeditated as anything else in fiction. One difference between poetry and prose fiction is that, in the latter, the writer often tries to hide his craft; hide her art; hide the order, meaningfulness, and form that exists in and throughout the author's created reality. Which is not historical reality or the reality we live day to day, which often has no apparent order or meaning—and according to which the fictional reality masquerades. Anyway, why does the author have it rain precisely at mealtime?"

"Because it's important."

"How?"

"Because [it takes awhile for these city kids] . . . because rain means food."

"When the rain falls, Lencho says (it's in the middle of the page), 'Those aren't raindrops falling from the sky, they're new coins. The big drops are ten-centavo pieces and the little ones are fives.' Then when the rain is replaced by hailstones, the narrator says, 'These truly did resemble new silver coins'—which soon utterly destroy Lencho's crops. The narrator, through a playful, almost mocking voice at Lencho's expense, underscores the *ironic* turn of events. The reversal of expectations. For example, you hope at the end of the school day, when Mr. T. descends the stairs, he will slip on the steps and fall on his butt. But, at the end of the day, as *you* descend the stairs, *you* slip and fall on your butt. The narrator here is being facetious, which is a subtle form of sarcasm. I am being sarcastic when, as you enter the room and trip over the doorjamb, I say, 'How's it going, *graceful.*' Facetiousness and sarcasm are kind of rough-and-ready forms of *verbal* irony. You've witnessed subtler forms, I'm sure, like when one of your friends makes a critical remark about another friend's character flaw in that person's absence—say, about that person's tendency to create and spread rumors—when you recognize the irony: Your friend's criticism of your other friend, you realize, is really a self-description. Henry Fielding uses this technique often in his hilarious novel *Tom Jones.*

"Where else does irony occur in 'A Letter to God'?"

"At the end."

"Well . . . ?"

"When Lencho blames the post office people for stealing his money, when the post office people were the ones who gave it to him."

"And you found that funny?"

"Yeah."

"At the bottom of the page, the narrator says, 'That night was a sorrowful one:

"'All our work, for nothing!'

"'There's no one who can help us!'

"'We'll all go hungry this year . . .' First, notice the time leap—how many of you guys put a slash mark in front of 'That night was a sorrowful one'?" Many students raise their hands. "Most stories do that; they don't tell you everything that happens from one moment to the next. Some leap years. Next, you see those three dots? They're called an *ellipsis*, meaning usually that words have been omitted and the audience or readers understand why. Here, the ellipsis suggests to me that similar comments are repeated and what is given represents all the complaints and worries. Why is it, I'd like to know, that we aren't told who is saying what? There are no 'said' tags to any of the quotations."

"Because we don't need to know."

"But why?"

"I know. Because they all are thinking the same things."

"They all feel the same way."

"A few lines down, someone says, 'Don't be so upset, even though this seems like a total loss. Remember, no one dies of hunger!' Then someone else says, 'That's what they say: no one dies of hunger . . .' What word or words do you think were omitted here, replaced by the ellipsis?"

Silence.

"What would be *your* first word? Considering what you know of the world?"

"Yet."

"But."

"Yes, sadly, people *do* die of hunger. You've read about such things happening in the newspaper or seen it talked about on TV. So you can imagine how this second person speaks in feeble support of the first person, his voice falling at the end of his sentence, raising great doubt over the family's future.

"The narrator then tells us, 'All through the night, Lencho thought only of his one hope: the help of God, whose eyes, as he had been instructed, see everything.' Then we are told, in the next paragraph, 'The following Sunday, at daybreak, after having convinced himself that there is a protective spirit, he began to write a letter.'"

After talking about whether or not Lencho believed in God prior to the calamitous hailstorm, I ask the class, "Why does the author have Lencho write his letter to God on Sunday?"

"It's a holy day, people go to church on that day?"

"What people?"

"Mostly Catholics."

"And Protestants, too."

"Christians."

"Religions, we might call, of the West?"

"Jewish people go to church on Saturday."

"Go to *temple*. Yes, their sabbath is Saturday. How many of you, by the way are Buddhists?" A half-dozen hands are raised. "When do you go to church—to the temple?"

"Sundays."

"Writers often use special days of the week and the year for their own purposes, while taking advantage of the built-in meanings those days traditionally uphold. They also take advantage of the seasons and the meanings that adhere to each.

"They also take advantage of the time of day. Not only does the author have Lencho write his letter to God on a Sunday, but he also has Lencho write it *at daybreak*. Why daybreak?"

"It's a new day."

"So?"

"It's new. He has hope now, I guess"

"That's right. That guy Lencho finally convinces himself through the night. His faith in God is strong now."

"He's a changed person?"

"It's like the whole world has changed."

"Morning. It's the beginning."

"Like I said, it's a new day."

"Now, after Lencho deposits the letter at the post office, the narrator says,

'One of the employees, who was a postman and also helped at the post office, went to his boss laughing heartily and showed him the letter to God.' Why does the writer need a postman when he could just as easily have the postmaster find the letter?"

"Because the postmaster's too fat to get up from his desk." Ha-ha.

"Because the postman does not believe in God."

"Where did you get that idea?"

"From what the next sentence says about him."

"Please read it."

"'Never in his career as a postman had he known such an address.'"

"Can you tell us how you get from those words that the postman does not believe in God?"

"I don't know, it's just a feeling. Not knowing God's address is like not knowing where God is."

"Or not knowing he can be reached."

"Those are mighty good possibilities. So the postman exists in this story—for what? Because he is *un*like Lencho?"

"Yeah, to emphasize Lencho even more."

"Such a character is a contrast figure, sometimes called a *foil*. You'll see many such figures in Shakespeare's plays, like in *Hamlet*, my favorite and therefore the greatest play ever written." Ha-ha. "You'll see . . ."

"Why does the author make the postmaster (the person most impressed by Lencho's faith, who takes charge of the collection), 'a fat, amiable fellow'?"

"Because he's Santa Claus!"

"Yeah."

"That's good metaphor and I can buy it. Why else might he be fat?"

"He doesn't do much, just sits down and does paperwork."

"True, his work might be like some teachers' work. Very sedentary."

"He eats a lot."

"Like the farmers?"

"No. More."

"Why more?"

"He can afford it."

"And the farmer can't?"

"The farmer has to depend on the weather and such."

"Yeah, and the postmaster'll get paid rain or shine."

"I like him, he feels for Lencho."

"Probably feels guilty, too."

"Yeah, like a lot of fat guys?"

"Pardon me?"

The class talk will sometimes end by questioning the proposition that God *did* have a hand in Lencho's receiving money.

Such discussions pass fairly quickly, so I also give the students questions about the grammar and style peculiar to each of the stories that I assign as overnight reading, to ponder as they write their responses in their marble notebooks, preserving them there to share with the class the next day.

I end the class with a rhetorical question: "Did our talking together make a difference?"

Day 2: More Class Talk, and I Read an Odd Story

For Saki's "Open Window," their second assigned reading, I ask a fourth of the class to account for the author's choice of point of view. I ask another fourth to explain the importance of giving Mr. Nuttel, who Vera will dupe, a nervous condition. I ask another fourth to explain how the story would change if the last sentence of the story, "Romance at short notice was her speciality," was omitted. I ask the final fourth—reminding them that what we're interested in is what the text does not tell us explicitly and directly—to describe fifteen-year-old Vera, what kind of person she seems to be. Much of class talk will center on Vera's talents and, later, on how Saki manages our thinking and feeling as he unfolds his very witty tale.

In brief, Framton Nuttel, recovering from an unnamed nervous condition, has taken to the English countryside to recoup his health. His sister has given him letters of introduction to acquaintances she has made in her travels, and has persuaded Nuttel that associating with other people will hasten his recovery. Upon visiting the home of Mrs. Sappleton, who is detained upstairs, Nuttel is greeted by her niece Vera, who says, "In the meantime you must try and put up with me." (Having read the story, we want to shout, "Look out, Nuttel!")

After asking Nuttel two questions and learning that he knows no one in the area and knows next to nothing about Mrs. Sappleton, Vera makes Nuttel aware of Mrs. Sappleton's "tragedy," which, coincidentally, occurred "three years ago to a day." Because of what happened, Vera says, Mrs. Sappleton is not altogether right in her mind—she expects that, any day, her drowned husband and two younger brothers will arise from the bog, walk across the lawn, and reenter the house through the large French windows. "That is why the window is kept open every evening till it is quite dusk." Vera then explains how her aunt last described the men as they usually went out to hunt. But of course, unbeknownst to Nuttel, they are not dead and indeed are out hunting.

He is horrified upon meeting Mrs. Sappleton, who rambles cheerfully on about shooting and game, all the while distracted, "her eyes straying past him to the open window and lawn beyond." Finally, with Nuttel's back toward the window, Mrs. Sappleton announces, "Here they are at last!" and, "Just in time for tea, and don't they look as if they were muddy up to their eyes!"—at which point, for Nuttel's benefit, Vera stares out the window "with dazed horror in her eyes"; we can also imagine the drama of her body and her face frozen in fright.

When Nuttel turns to the window he sees the three "ghosts" in the twilight and makes a mad dash out of the house and down the road, forcing an oncoming cyclist to crash into a hedge.

To explain Nuttel's strange behavior to the Sappletons, Vera concocts another outlandish story, which—given their last name and Vera's singular gift for storytelling—they will likely believe.

"Some writers like to play with names for their characters, as Dickens did. Nuttel, you know."

"He's a coconut!"

"Does anybody know what a *sap*, the first part of *Sappleton*, is?"

"A sucker."

"Which is?"

"Someone easy to trick. Like my grandmother."

"Or my dumb brother."

"Someone gullible."

"Names are sometimes revealing of character. But what about Vera?"

Silence.

"Vera, I suppose, comes from the word *veracity*, meaning *truth*. How ironic. Vera *never* tells the truth."

Most of the talk about the young teenager Vera speculates on her skill as a very smart, very quick, and very dramatic storyteller. Most of the students like her because she's smarter than the adults around her and has fun fooling them. They wonder why she is there with the Sappletons in the first place. As we talk, the general feeling is that Vera is cloistered in the countryside, perhaps against her will; it's probably in the summer; she is living with her aunt and uncle and her aunt's two brothers, men who seem to occupy themselves hunting all the time. Mrs. Sappleton, given the little we know about her wit, seems poor company for Vera, who no doubt craves society closer to her own age. But no one else is mentioned, much less teenagers. So how might Vera occupy herself? The story is set in a time when there is no radio or TV or video games. So she must read—lots—whence comes her skill as a fabricator. And upon whom might she practice? And who becomes her greatest test? Of course, the contest is fixed; all the writer's powers are set against him; poor Mr. Nuttel has no chance.

The other thing we talk about, very quickly, is the use of *flashback*, which is familiar to the students through film; it is defined as *a scene from the past presented as though it were occurring in the present*. Sometimes the bulk of a tale is in the flashback, which the present frames like a painting, as occurs in Conrad's *Heart of Darkness* or James' *Turn of the Screw*. More important is the idea that, though a story's events occur in time, they need not follow each other in that same sequence in the story. Many writers play with events and time. What's important is how the events accrue in the reader's mind.

Sometimes when teaching Saki's story, I get up out of my chair to reenact the scene where the men return from hunting. But first I ask, "How many of you believe that upon their return home they actually entered the sitting room by climbing through the open window?" Here I mimic climbing through a window, my leg reaching over an imaginary sill. The students laugh heartily, struck by the absurdity of such an idea, as well as by observing their stout teacher in such a ridiculous pose, my pant leg riding up a pale, hairy calf. Of course, they assume that a French window is no different from their window at home. I take on the roll of Vera as she faces the window in mock horror, screwing up my face as best I can. Then I am Nuttel—I turn and, upon seeing the approach of the muddy dead men from their swampy grave, I panic and flee in terror.

"Why does Saki give Nuttel a nervous condition?"

"To make him a little nutty."

"Why?"

"So that he'll believe Vera's story."

"Does Saki have Mrs. Sappleton help at all?"

"Yeah. I mean, if you didn't know her, she *would* seem a little nutty herself."

"How?"

"Well, she keeps talking about hunting and stares over Nuttel's shoulder to see out the window while Nuttel is trying to make conversation."

"Is Vera nuts then? How many of you had thought so at first?" A number raise their hands.

"Or, how many of you believed that the men were ghosts?" More hands are raised.

"Why? Because many of you assumed that Saki's meaning for *romance* in the last sentence of the story—'Romance at short notice was her specialty'—was the same as yours. If it was, how would the sentence connect with the story? Those of you who were assigned to question the last sentence know, because you looked in the dictionary for a meaning beyond the hearts and flowers and kissy-face stuff, beyond your common understanding, since that meaning didn't seem to fit. With that understanding, Michelle, what do we know about Vera?"

"That she's a liar."

"Didi?"

"That she's a terrific storyteller."

Others concur.

"Well, she still could be sick," says Michelle.

"Would that I had such a sickness," I say.

"I still wish there were ghosts," says Scooter.

"Now, since we have some time, I'll read you a story called 'The Historic Fart.'" Several students chuckle. Most are startled, squinting, their heads a-tilt, not sure that they heard me right. "The princess Scheherazade, in the *Arabian Nights*, must entertain the sultan with a story each night if she wishes to keep her head the following morning. She is successful for a *Thousand and One Nights*, which the book of her stories is also called. Remember, keep a pen in your hand and your marble book open, just in case a story idea, a memory, a scene, or even a story title pops up in your mind." I then repeat the title, "The Historic Fart," and read:

> It is related that in the town of Kaukuban, Yemen, there once was a Bedouin of the Fadhli tribe called Abu Hasan, who, having given up the life of the desert and settled down as a townsman, became, after much diligence and enterprise, a merchant of considerable wealth. His wife had died while they were both young, and his friends were always pressing him to marry again. Weary of a widower's life, he at length gave in to their persuasions and engaged the services of an experienced marriage-broker, who found him a bride as beautiful as the moon when it shines on the sea.

I read the description of the wedding guests, the exotic foods served at the feast, and the bride as beautiful as the moon. Then—

> At last came the moment when Abu Hasan was summoned to the bridal chamber. Slowly and solemnly he rose from his divan; but horror of horrors, being bloated with meat and drink, he let go a long and resounding fart. The embarrassed guests, whose attention had been fixed on the bridegroom, turned to one another speaking with raised voices and pretending to have heard nothing at all. Abu Hasan was so mortified with shame that he wished the ground would open up and swallow him. He mumbled a feeble excuse, and, instead of going to the bridal chamber, went straight to the courtyard, saddled his horse, and rode off into the night, weeping bitterly.

As I read, the students learn that Abu Hasan arrives in Lahej, where he boards a ship to India. After ten years, he rises to the captainship of the king's bodyguards. One day the longing for his home seizes him with great heartache, and he leaves India. After much travail and risk he reaches the hill overlooking his native town. He decides first to wander about the town listening to the people's gossip. He prays to Allah that after all these years no one will recognize him and remember what he did. Along the outskirts of the town, he rests in the shadow of a hut and overhears a young girl within saying:

> "Please, mother, what day was I born on? One of my friends wants to tell my fortune."
>
> "My daughter," replied the woman solemnly, "you were born on the very night of Abu Hasan's fart."
>
> When he heard those words, he got up and fled. "Abu Hasan," he said to himself, "the day of your fart has become a date which will surely be remembered till the end of time."
>
> He traveled on until he was back in India, where he remained in exile until his death. May Allah have mercy upon him.

"I read this story to my son when he was about seven and he said, 'That's a sad story, Dad.' And I agreed." I ask the students why the date of Abu Hasan's fart will 'be remembered till the end of time.' They answer variously:

"Because he ran away."

"He had no faith that his friends would ever forgive him."

"What do you mean *forgive?* It was just a fart."

"I know that if I had farted like that, my friends wouldn't let me live it down. They'd tease the heck out of me."

"Some *friends.*"

"So that it wouldn't matter if he stayed or ran away."

"But his running away made the fart bigger than it was."

"Yeah, it was da bomb." Ha-ha-ha.

"Nuts."

"It *is* sad."

"The point I want to make is this: A story can emerge from the most mundane experiences; there is no subject that cannot be made compelling. One boy a few years ago wrote a story about not having enough electrical outlets in his room and ending up with octopus plugs and extension cords everywhere. Whatever you choose to write about will emerge from your experience or be tied to it in some way. You know that from your most successful poems. Even a small gesture, an offhand remark, a change of routine can result in something that might alter your protagonist's life or attitude toward the world. Just as sci fi writers project into the future a technological or social problem, taking the problem to its extreme, you too can take to an extreme a character's sensitivity to, say, human touch or cockroaches or water."

I caution them against imitating certain trite patterns, like ending "it was all just a dream," which is usually a cop-out to avoid resolving a plot. I caution them also against trite variations—ending, "it was all a dream" but leaving evidence that it wasn't a dream; or ending by resolving the problem, but then suggesting that the problem is not totally resolved (the eggs of the monster they killed, say, are overlooked) and will recur, only worse. I also caution them about writing in two genres—fantasy and sci fi—that have proven difficult for young writers to manage. For the most part (and too often at excessive length and with a host of multisyllabic names), student writers fail to persuade us of the reality of their fictional worlds.

Day 3: They Hear Five Stories, and More Class Talk

The third day, English is a double period. During the first half I read five short stories, limiting my comments. This trains students' ears further, as reading poems did, sensitizing them to the various sounds and shapes that stories can take. "The first story was written by a local writer named Wayne Kaneshiro in 1982. —Keep your marble notebooks handy.— The title is 'Sand Castles.'"

The thing I liked best about the beach was the shave ice that we got afterwards. The thing that Caryn liked best about the beach was the sand. Not the soft white sand that tourists hopped on or bikinied girls browned on, but the cool dark sand by the waterline. It was with this sand that my sister built her sand castles.

Caryn's castles were fit for the most delicate of fairy princesses. The walls were tall and thin, smoothed flat with a piece of cardboard. There were a multitude of towers formed from a paper tube brought from home, or if that was forgotten, then with a soda can found half-buried in the sand. Tiny seashells lined the bulwarks. Banners made of toothpicks and matchbook covers flew above the towers, heralding the Prince of Columbia Inn or the Duke of Sheraton Hotels. Bits of cloth, glass, and other discarded things found new service in my sister's castles.

My contribution to my sister's castles were the moats. I dug them deep and wide so they could suck up the waves. Water would not reach the fragile walls. Digging was my specialty. I learned to dig by burying people, my mother mostly. I would dig a great hole for my mother to lie in, then I would cover her entire body with sand, leaving only the head that would slumber in the sun. I couldn't bury my sister, she wouldn't let me. She feared that I would gladly bury her head. I wouldn't have, but it was important for her to think I would. I also didn't bury my father. He didn't like the beach; he never came with us. My mother took us to the beach herself, on the bus; or if we were lucky Aunt Reiko would take us in her station wagon. Then I would bury Aunt Reiko.

I don't remember exactly when we stopped going to the beach together. I only know that we did. As Caryn and I grew older, the beach transformed itself from a place for families to a place just for friends. By the time I was twelve, the beach was only for surfing with other brown-skinned boys with sunbleached hair. Caryn, by then, was fourteen and had no further use for the sand. Graphite, charcoal, paint, and the movies *Moulin Rouge* and *Lust for Life* had replaced it.

When Caryn was fifteen, our family moved into our new home in Kalihi Valley. It was a large white house with a green roof. There were two plumeria trees in the front yard and a large mango tree in the back. My sister and I had rooms in the left side of this house. We didn't bring our friends over to see our rooms. My father didn't like strangers in the house. It was his private domain. *No Trespassing.* Once, in the old place, he had chased some of Caryn's friends out of the house, yelling, swearing, and throwing a half-empty can of beer at them. We did not make the same mistake here.

Our family separated. I grew up outside of the house. Watered by the surf and suckled by the warm city lights. Caryn lived behind her bedroom door, scratching lines on newsprint and splashing paint on prestretched canvasses. Our parents occupied the living and dining rooms. They ate in silence and spent the night watching "Big Time Wrestling."

My father did not want Caryn to go to the University to study art. He would not pay for that. My father was a warehouse man whose job it was to move crates and drink beer; he would not waste his money on art. Caryn fought my father on this. The fight was long, hard, and painful. It ended with my father storming into Caryn's room and tearing up her drawings. Caryn watched the destruction in silence, her throat too raw to scream. My mother, as usual, was powerless. My father would not listen to her pleas. All I could do was hold Caryn while she cried.

Caryn did get to study art, with the help of some of my mother's own money and a part-time job at Sears. She graduated with a Bachelor of Fine Arts degree and a husband. In her senior year, she met and married a fellow art student. They moved into a small apartment in Manoa. There they would spend their time making paintings and love. A few months later, Caryn left the apartment and came back home with a bruise on her arm and a cut above her right eye.

My sister then took her paints and charcoals to California. I drove her to the airport in my Volkswagen and said goodbye to her with an orchid lei. Caryn left me two drawings. One of them was of me.

Over the years I received more drawings from Caryn. A Sacramento café, a San Francisco fisherman, a Colorado landscape. Later there came a sketch of a Mexican funeral procession and then a New York street scene. Somewhere in between there was another marriage that failed. The last thing that I received from her was a painting. An abstract done mostly in blues, greys, and reds titled *Thunder in My Dreams*. That was about four years ago.

Two years ago my father died. I burned incense for him at the funeral. I saw him lying in his coffin, his face white and his lips too red; he looked like a clay doll. I was surprised that I found myself crying.

Since my father's death, my mother sold the house in Kalihi Valley and moved in with Aunt Reiko. I got married and my wife is now expecting a child. I hope it will be a girl.

Every now and then, people bring bits and pieces of news about Caryn. She's teaching in Vancouver or working as a waitress in Ann Arbor. An uncle said he saw her in Paris, sketching something in the Louvre. Lynn Sakata, her best friend from high school, said that Caryn was dead; she burned all her paintings and took some pills.

I don't know.

I have the drawings that Caryn sent me hanging on the walls. But the thing I liked best were her sand castles. Sometimes, at night, behind closed eyes, I see one of them. A castle lined with shells and flags. So beautiful and vulnerable, yet standing bravely on the shore, protected only by a moat that could not hold back the waves.

"You know, every time I read the end of this story I get choked up. All that nostalgia. It echoes my own childhood of long summer days and play. When nobody had yet died . . ."

"Mr. Tsujimoto?"

"Yes?"

"That story is like a circle poem—"

"Yes! Yes, that's very perceptive! Many stories take the form of a circle and return, in a way, to where they began. Very good, Mei Ling," who was born and raised in China and generally does not speak.

"Anyway, this next story was written by a college student in the early 1970s. It's called 'Telescope.' Reading this will be easier."

I wondered how long ago it might have happened, for somewhere between the Big Dipper and the measureless backdrop of space, two anonymous stars collided. The distant explosion registered in the Fourth of July night as a mere spark, a faint glow, almost as though the metallic lip of that famous ladle had caught the light of a larger sun.

From the rooftop of 401, on the heights of Morningside Drive, as I lay on the abrasive surface of roofing paper that sparkled like formica, the distant glow reminded me of the tingling glint of a switchblade.

As I rose, brushed myself off, hitched up my pants, and leaned my fifteen-year-old frame over the edge of the brick roof, I found the Harlem sky prettily bejeweled in fireworks. The big round moon hung in the noose of a skyrocket, while tracers of Roman candles laced the night like shooting stars. The dark patches of Harlem's trapezoidal rooftops seemed to sprawl endlessly eastward, guided by brightly lit avenues that hinted of meeting somewhere beyond.

The headlines of the day said there was a war going on on the other side of the globe. But no one knew much about it. And few seemed to care. Locally, earlier in the evening, the neighborhood tenants gathered together in the lobby of 419 with police representatives, social workers, and superintendents to discuss the problems of intimidations, threats, insults, and other crimes and misdemeanors perpetrated by us, the Imperial Knights. They hadn't known yet of the Sinners. And as I looked down from the rooftop I could see them coming up the Drive.

"They're coming!" Leo roared as he rushed through the rooftop door shaking a pipe in his hand.

"How many they got?" I said, pulling a zip-gun from my belt beneath my sweatshirt.

"Pops says five. But they might have more," he said, testing the pipe in the palm of his hand.

"Sammy and the rest downstairs?" I asked.

"Yeah, man. They're laying in the basement."

"Let's go then. Let's pop 'em," I said, as we made for the door. But when we reached the street the fight was already on.

One Sinner was on the sidewalk leaning against a fire pump with his stomach in his arms. While another ran down the middle of the street with a scarf of fire trailing from his jacket. Ping! Ping! Ping! And pellets flew mindlessly, ripping through cottoned flesh, crashing through windows and windshields, ricocheting off pavement and lamp posts.

Dazzled with the sight, Leo and I rushed into the street where Pops, Smitty, Sammy, and his brothers were fighting with Sinners. I jumped on the back of a leather-jacketed boy who was stomping the face for Skinny Murphy's head. I slipped and fell, and shot a pellet into a Chevrolet tire as the boy ran off. As Leo got hit by a ringing bicycle chain, someone yelled "Bulls! Bulls! Bulls!" And everyone froze. An instant later everyone scattered to the music of sirens.

Leo got off the asphalt holding his neck and disappeared into the basement of 414. Quickly, I threw my gun under a car; and while running into the foyer of 401, I tripped on the loose marble door jamb of the front door and hit my head against the silver radiator just inside the lobby and I guess I saw stars. When I woke, the rumble seemed distant and remote. The stench of the stale urine and the dirt of the old lobby floor filled my nose, and I felt delirious and nauseous. The flaky, waxy, yellow-enameled ceiling and the filthy green walls started to whirl round and round, until the sound of footsteps on the stairs brought the lobby to a halt.

Shaking my head and holding onto the radiator I got to my feet. I turned and peered through the spider-webbed glass door and found the street empty—empty, that is, except for Mrs. Vera, who seemed to be walking towards me on the tops of the cars, in a floral patterned house dress with an angular bundle in her arms.

As I turned, she walked towards me in slippers as though in a trance, her hair still in rollers. She shuffled slowly, ominously down the green corridor, growing larger and larger until she stopped. Glaring right through me. Burning. Boring a hole right between my eyes. The angular bundle, I saw, was her daughter. She had a pellet hole right above her left eye. I shrank in horror but I could not open the front door. Mrs. Vera's eyes, void of everything save hate, fused my feet to the floor. Deliberately, she lifted the limp body high above her head, then wildly—she flung it at me!—"Take it! Take it! It's the last I have!"

The room is silent. "The collision between the young narrator and the dead child is, in a way inevitable, if not probable. It is set up by a pattern of conflicts and violence through most of the story—first the collision between two stars in distant space, then Fourth of July fireworks in the immediate sky, then war on the other side of the globe, then neighborhood talk of harassment by teenage hoods, then the street fight between the two gangs. Then we 'telescope' into the hallway scene and the confrontation between the narrator and the distraught mother. The pattern is a kind of repetition we might call parallelism. Which is to say, though the end is a shocking surprise and seems like a slick maneuver, it *was* prepared for. It wasn't a trick and it didn't come from nowhere."

My own writing teacher, Joseph Heller, wrote, "I wonder if a mother would throw her child." I answered him in my mind, "You're right. She wouldn't." At the time, I was more concerned with pattern than with plausibility.

"The next three stories were written by former students who passed through this class. The first story, 'The Playroom,' was written by Didi Oi, an eighth grader. It is written from the perspective of a child. I will interrupt now and then to comment on things I find effective."

I still don't know what the fuss was all about. This morning when it was all dark, I went to the playroom to get Mr. Bear off his shelf and saw the window doors open and a funny looking man lying on the floor. He must've had an owie 'cause there was blood all over the place. I shouted at him that it was time to get up, but he wouldn't listen, so me and Mr. Bear climbed the furry carpet stairs to tell Mommy and Daddy. Mommy started making a fuss, saying, "Oh, my God!" while Daddy called the police on the chunky black telephone. [*"Chunky black telephone": what a precise description; I wonder if they are around anymore.*]

After that, Daddy tiptoed down the stairs with Billy's heavy yellow wooden baseball bat and into the room. I reached up to the doorknob and opened the door for Daddy, with both hands. [*This is a terrific way to show us how big she is, rather than saying she's three-foot-two; numbers don't work; we need comparisons to other physical things.*] I looked around the door while Daddy went inside. The funny man was still there. Then Mommy came down. "John, what's wrong?" she said, in a real quiet voice.

"You two, get the others and wait outside for the police," he said to us, so Mommy carried me outside.

Soon, lots of black and white cars with red lights on top came. They made a lot of noise that sounded like a kazillion yelling ducks. Daddy came out and talked to the man with the black suit on.

"You the one who reported an intruder?" the man asked.

Then my Daddy started to tell him about the funny looking man that was sleeping on the floor.

Some more people came and put the man on this really thin bed and covered him with a blanket (so he wouldn't catch cold). They even covered his head. Maybe he covered his head himself because he was afraid of monsters.

A little later, Uncle Willy came. He's a policeman detective. He went into the house and into the playroom. He was staring at the white outline of the funny man on the grassy blue carpet.

"Hi, Unca Willy," I said.

"Hi, Jenny," he said, smiling and ruffling my head. But when I started to go in the room, he said, "Jenny, please don't come in this room until I tell you, because there might be something in here to tell us why that man was here."

"Okay, Unca Willy," I promised. So I didn't go in. That night he slept over to keep us company.

We had a fun dinner, and after, me, Billy, Jack, Sue, and Joey stayed in the kitchen, while Mommy and Daddy went into the living room to talk to Uncle Willy.

I was sitting by the door with my ABC blocks and Mr. Bear. I could hear all the grownups talking. [*Eavesdropping, intentional or otherwise, is one good way to give readers information.*]

". . . but that still doesn't answer the question of why he was here," I heard Mommy say.

"Well," Uncle Willy started, "he was caught robbing a jewelry store. The owner shot him, but he got away with a huge ruby. My boys just called and told me about it. We think he hid it somewhere along his escape route or climbed in the window to escape the police to hide himself and the ruby somewhere in this house.

"Oh, John," Mommy wailed in a whisper.

"Don't worry, you'll be safe," said Uncle Willy.

"We trust you," said Daddy, confidently.

Then they started talking about some other stuff. I couldn't really hear 'cause I was getting tired.

I must've fallen asleep 'cause, when I woke up, I was in my bed. When I went downstairs for breakfast, everybody was already eating. I climbed up in my chair to start eating. Then Uncle Willy went to the playroom to look for that big red rock that looked like jello. I went to the garden right outside the playroom to watch Uncle Willy and to play with Mr. Bear. He was looking over the room and opening drawers and stuff. After awhile, he got tired and sat down.

"Uncle Willy," I shouted, "can I help?!"

He thought a moment and shouted back, "Sure!"

As I was running to the door, I dropped Mr. Bear. I tripped over him and fell down on the crunchy gravel. [*I like that, "crunchy gravel."*]

"Jenny," he said, running to me, "are you okay?"

"Uh huh," I nodded.

All of a sudden he gasped, looking at Mr. Bear. The fall had broken Mr. Bear's tummy stitches open. Inside was all the stuffing and something red.

"Oh no, he's bleeding," I cried.

There, sitting in his stomach, was a big cold hard blot of blood, big as my two hands.

"Well, Jenny," he said, and then he pulled out the red rock he was looking for!

"Mr. Bear will be okay," he said.

Then we both went inside. He told Mommy and Daddy what had happened.

"My goodness!" Mommy said, raising her eyebrows. Then she hugged me and asked if I was okay.

"I'm okay, but look at Mr. Bear," I cried.

"I'll give him a bath and fix him up so he'll be good as new," Mommy promised.

So now, Mr. Bear is in one whole piece again, and Uncle Willy visits us oftener, AND, I never forget to close the windows!

"For the most part, the writer persuades me that a child is telling me this story. She succeeds through the consistency of her voice and vision, speaking as a child and seeing the world as a child. In a way, she has given herself over to being the child.

"The next story, 'My Baby,' by Beth Derby, an eighth grader, is written from the perspective of an adult."

The guilt which I feel sitting up here spying on my only daughter Jean.

She is sitting next to the window with a look of both frustration and disappointment on her face. I don't think this Paul-guy is worth it. Already he is twenty minutes late, and though I don't want to admit it, I don't think he is going to show up.

Look at my baby. She looks like a young lady. She is wearing that new pink shirt we got her the other day. She's also wearing those awful faded blue jeans I told her to throw away months ago. The pink bow in her hair adds a special childlike feature I miss so much in my baby. She is also wearing my high heels. She didn't even tell me she was going to borrow them. When she was young her hair was blondish, but now that I look at it I realize that with time her hair has gotten darker to a chestnut brown. It goes so well with her baby blue eyes. Her face was set. She still had a lot of freckles which of course she hated and I loved. Before I got another look at Jean, she ran up the stairs, probably to check herself in the mirror. *[The verb-tense switch here, for some reason, does not jar me, as such switches usually do.]*

Moments later, as she was walking down the stairs, I noticed that she was wearing makeup. This surprised me, although I've seen her wear it before. I suppose I felt this way because her outfit and her makeup made her look older than I wanted her to be.

As she sat down once again, I was beginning to feel tired for both myself and Jean, and I was hoping she'd soon realize that Paul wasn't worth waiting for, at least not at this hour. I wasn't sure whether I should have gone over to her to comfort her, to sit with her, or to tell her she should just go to sleep. Now, I couldn't figure out how she felt. The look of frustration didn't appear on her face any longer, but a look almost of horror when our eyes met. She saw me! As I began to get up I heard her say in a small voice, which she used when she was a child to manipulate me when she wanted something, "Did you hear my question, Mom?" she said. [*And we didn't hear it either. A subtle touch.*]

"No. I'm sorry, dear, will you say that again?"

"How long have you been up there?"

"Long enough."

Then there was silence. I expected her to yell at me, but instead she asked, "What were you thinking about when you were waiting up there?"

I found myself telling her everything I had felt in those past thirty minutes and even about how I loved her freckles.

She wasn't mad, or didn't appear to be. She wasn't sad, yet there were tears in her eyes.

As I looked again at my baby girl, I realized there was only one way I wanted to love her and only one way she wanted to be loved.

"Now, this writer, too, persuades me. I believe I am listening to a mother talk about her child. No doubt through hearing her own mother talk about *her* and hearing how other mothers talk about *their* daughters, and imagining how sensitive mothers can identify with their children, this writer was able to imagine herself as a mother and convince us through her invented voice and her observations. As one eighth grader said in his poem, 'Imagination is perception here.'

"By the way, a number of years ago, this story and the one that follows won first-place awards at the Language Arts Showcase, an annual student conference sponsored by the Hawaii Council of Teachers of English.

"The final story, 'A Family Christmas,' by Laura Murray, a seventh grader, is written from a fun perspective and is cleverly told." Students admire the writer's sense of humor, feeling deeply satisfied by some of the observations, perhaps echoing some of their own judgments on adult behavior, which is sometimes childish or goofy, if not absurd.

It was Christmas day, and as usual, I was napping on my favorite rug. Just as I started to drift off, the doorbell rang loudly, announcing the arrival of our first guest for the holiday meal.

Christmas was never my favorite time of year. Everyone would hit me and say, "Nice kitty . . ." Didn't they know I had dignity too. I was no ordinary house cat—I was a full-bred Angora. I didn't enjoy their company, but I couldn't deny that watching those humans called "relatives" was amusing.

First, my owner's youngest son, Peter, arrived with his bride and their screaming baby (I wondered where they got the kid). Next, the Halls' only daughter, Priscilla, came with her boyfriend Jacob. That Christmas she hoped Jacob would propose to her. After all, they had been going steady for six long years. Later, senile Great Grandmother Hall arrived with Great Aunt Matilda (why did they look so shriveled up?). As with most families, we also had a neighbor that joined us on holidays. Her name was Mrs. Monsoon, and she was in the living room laughing hysterically and pointing at Uncle Buzz. Uncle had a cigarette in his nose. He was saying, "Where'd my smoke go?" Uncle usually drank too much and that year was no exception.

Last in the door came the oldest son, Bruce, and his unwelcome bride Rene. The family was not happy to see her. Yes, that was the Hall family's get together, all done under the guise of holiday happiness.

Dinner was served. Priscilla said, "Isn't it wonderful how we're all such a happy family. You know, it's marriage that starts a family," as she looked longingly at Jacob.

"Yes, Priscilla, people are brought together through the will of the Lord. In fact, I have an important announcement to make, and with the Lord's blessing, it might as well be now," answered Jacob.

"And what is that, darling," asked Priscilla excitedly.

"I'm going to enter the seminary," said Jacob. Priscilla burst into tears and raced upstairs. That was the beginning of a "wonderful" holiday.

The unwelcome Rene said, "Well, this is a good time to say what I have to say." We all waited, thinking she was going to smooth things over.

"Rene, honey, are you pregnant?" asked Bruce.

"No, Bruce, I want a divorce." Bruce burst into tears and raced upstairs. A long, long uncomfortable period of silence followed. The family's dislike for Rene reached a crescendo. Younger son Peter broke the silence by saying, "We never wanted you to marry Bruce anyway. You're not our kind and never were. We knew that when we found out that your mother's in prison and your brother pushes dope."

"Quit hasslin' me," said Rene. It was then that Great Aunt Matilda uncharacteristically sounded off: "You don't know what family means. You have shameful morals and disgraceful family!"

Jacob stood up and raised his hands shouting, "Do not behave so in the eyes of the Lord!" Everyone said simultaneously, "Shut up!"

Uncle Buzz broke out of his stupor when he heard the word "Lord" and said, "Am I dead? 'cause if this is Heaven, it's hell!" Now everyone was shouting at each other. All I was able to hear over the commotion was Mrs.

Monsoon agreeing with senile Great Grandmother Hall that the gravy gave them gas.

I thought, "I'm a cat and I've never had problems like this. I'm supposed to have a much lower intelligence than humans . . . If only they knew."

Amidst the fracas, all the lights in the house went out. "It's a sign from above," shouted Jacob. It was obvious that the guests thought this a good time to withdraw from the madness. A procession of agitated people marched out of the room, tripping over Uncle Buzz who had fallen unconscious to the floor. Someone opened the front door and gasped, "We're snowed in!"

Sure enough, a heavy blanket of snow surrounded the house. The idea of these people spending several more hours or another day together was truly abysmal.

I, like the guests, wished to get away from the hysteria. I drifted back to sleep to dream of sugar plums and sweets. As I closed my eyes, I realized that I had learned something as a witness to this "cel-abrasion." I finally discovered why family reunions are so rare. Reunions (and Christmases) are simply times when people gather together to fight and say how much they hate each other.

That Christmas also answered one of my life-long questions. It finally became clear to me what "Deck the halls" meant; of course, it occurred to me that using a fist rather than a "bough of holly" would be more appropriate for decking these Halls.

"Your assignment for tomorrow is to write three half-page pieces—hold on, Melissa. I'm coming to that. Josh! What're you doing? Testing your eyelids for leaks?"

"I was just thinking."

"Well, could you take out your notebook and think on paper? I want you to play with point of view, as in the last three stories you heard.

- In the first piece, you will write from the perspective of a child, describing its grandparent or anything else you wish.
- In the second piece, you will write from the perspective of an adult (you can use one of your parents as a model), who is speaking to him- or herself while primping in front of a full-length mirror prior to going to a funeral or party or wedding, etc., that he or she does not want to attend.
- In the third piece, you will write from the perspective of an animal who is observing kids your age, friends, etc., at a party or a canteen or a dance or a sleepover.

"Who knows? You might find a story worth pursuing at length."

During the second half of the double period, the class talks about the short story "The Grandmother," written by local writer Susan Nunez, who, I note on the handout for the students' benefit, is half-Portuguese and half-Japanese.

The story is about a woman looking back on her childhood on the Big Island, where she makes best friends with her neighbor Francis, who was the narrator's "first and *only* Japanese friend" [my emphasis]. What the narrator remembers most is Francis' grandmother, who alters the narrator's life forever. Most of this very short story describes the grandmother's physical appearance, the cooking shed where the grandmother works, and Francis' backyard, where her family raises orchids. It is in the backyard, among the orchids, that the pivotal scene takes place.

> [The grandmother] spoke something in Japanese I couldn't understand. I kept thinking that the cinder hurt my feet.
>
> After a few moments Francis said, "That's the oldest. All the others come from this plant." She stepped around me to join her grandmother. "My father says this one's older than he is." She took the plant from the old woman, placed it back on the shelf, and pulled on some bits of moss.
>
> Again the old woman said something, most of which I didn't understand. But I didn't miss the last word.
>
> "Purebred."
>
> And Francis said again, "It's very, very old." I hardly heard her, though, because I was staring at her grandmother's face, at her toothless mouth, at the purple flesh. Something in the meeting of the word and the experience alienated me. I was alone. Not like them.

In the next paragraph, the narrator says that it was weeks later that she "decided to destroy the plant,"

> to deliberately crush each flower, to snap the stems and grind them into the cinder, to pull from the pot the moss that held the plant and sustained it, to rub from the pot all traces of the white roots.

The young girl's hateful action shocks and puzzles my students:
"Why did she do that?"
"Yeah, how come she killed the plant?"
"Anybody have an idea?"
"Maybe it's because of what the grandmother said."
"What did she say?"
"She said—it's right here—'Purebred.' It was pure."
"Which means? . . . Alana?"
"That the plant wasn't mixed with other plants. You know, like certain dogs. Like a Doberman. Dobermans are born only from other Dobermans, right?"
"So why'd she get all mad about that?"

"I know. Because she's not pure herself. Mr. T. said the author was both Japanese and Portuguese."

"So the grandmother was really talking about the girl and not the plant?" I ask. "Yeah."

"And the girl was standing right there, man. I mean, that's pretty brutal."

"Wait, now. Did the grandmother know that the girl understood some Japanese?" I say.

"I don't know, but I bet the grandmother knew after the girl started staring at her face. She must have known how bad the girl felt."

"How bad?" I ask.

"It says right here that she felt 'alienated. I felt alone. Not like them.' Like she was something less than them, inferior to them. Like there was something wrong with her."

"How many of you have ever been hurt by prejudicial remarks that refer to your race or ethnicity?" A number of students raise their hands.

"Yes?" I point to Patrick, a Caucasian, who was born here.

"Sometimes I don't like it when some of the local kids call me a dumb *haole*."

"Kelly?"

"On the mainland, a lot of the people ask me what country I'm from or what language I speak. I mean, people can be really ignorant." We hear several other stories, many of them having to do with local people and stereotypes, like the *portagee* seen as the local counterpart to the mainland's *dumb polack*.

"How many of you have heard disparaging remarks made by your parents or grandparents or other relatives about other ethnic groups?"

Several students raise their hands.

"It's like a disease, isn't it, that can be passed on from one generation to the next—thinking our own group superior in some way to everyone else's? How many of you, by the way, felt negatively about the grandmother before our talk? Paul?"

"Well, I thought she was kind of ugly."

"I had a funny feeling about her."

"I know what you mean. Let me tell you *why*. Or at least *why* I think why. Let's look at the story. First of all the title, 'The Grandmother,' and the story's tame first paragraph led you to believe that this would be a story about a kind, sweet, frail, and maybe wise old lady. This is probably true because *most* of you— because of your *own* feelings for *your* grandmother—attached similar characteristics to the grandmother of the story. So strong were these feelings that they overrode what the author seems to be saying through her details. She takes advantage of some of your preconceptions or beliefs about grandmothers in general, then socks it to you. Oftentimes, writers like to explode these easy, common beliefs. If you recall, some of you did something similar in your poems.

"Of course, you were also thrown off by the narrator, who says, in the first sentence of the second paragraph, 'Nostalgia tends to select.' The author has the narrator use the word *nostalgia* to deceive you. The word means a kind of wistful, even sweet, yearning to return to the past. Well, heck, the past that the narrator returns to is hardly sweet—call it instead a nightmare. For at the end, she never again makes friends with a Japanese girl, and she finds the part of herself that is Japanese to be something alien or foreign or strange, something that she might even deny.

"Let's look at some of the narrator's descriptions of the grandmother. Jessica, please read the first sentence of the second paragraph."

"First I saw her feet, withered and veined, the color of dried shrimp, with chalk-white nails so long they grew into the flesh."

"How sweet," I say. "In the fifth paragraph, the second on page two, the narrator runs off after hearing a low laugh, but the impression of the grandmother never leaves her. Now picture this. Neil, please read the last sentence."

She comes to me sometimes, even now, just as she was that first day, a shriveled-up shell of a woman standing sideways looking at me, her head sunk low into her narrow shoulders, her veined hands, bent as if they clutched at something, her dress falling loosely from the hump on her back, hanging as if there were nothing underneath. And the low laugh.

"She looks like a witch!"

"Yeah, a witch!"

"Note some of the things in the cooking shed, in the previous paragraph: "empty bottles and odd-shaped flasks, a pit, and a blackened water kettle." And repeated several times through the rest of the story is the phrase 'and charcoal burning.' And so is the word *ashes*. And so is the word *cinder*, which is a hot, orangy coal the color of marigolds. Though the cinders she refers to are those rock chips that they use to make paths, or lazy people put in their front yards so they don't have to mow the lawn. So, what do you make of all this charcoal and ashes and cinder?"

"It's like Hell."

"So one might think. Repetition can be a very effective device for communicating larger ideas and intentions, better than merely stating facts about the setting or the atmosphere. Think of it this way: Repetition is one way the author can communicate to the reader while a character tells the story.

"Okay, let's close this down. Neil, please read the third paragraph on the third page, that ends right before the space break. As Neil reads, think about the logic of your own assumptions about *all* grandmothers."

"C'mon, Neil."

"Hold your horses . . .

Who can remember when wonderment gives way to something else? Mrs. Furisato was old—I could see that. She was also a grandmother. I knew that because Francis said so. But to me, grandmothers were different creatures.

"Stop! 'Grandmothers were different creatures' from *whom?*"
"Francis' grandmother."
"Mrs. Furisato."
"Go on, Neil. Read the last sentence again."
"Again? . . .

But to me, grandmothers were different creatures. When they smiled their gums didn't show. They were tolerant people, closer to you than your own parents, easy to talk to, easy to love. Mrs. Furisato *was* Francis' grandmother, and because everyone loved their grandmothers, I reasoned that Francis had to love hers. I had not pondered upon this logic. It was just so. Still, I saw that her face was more skull than flesh, and there was always about her the aura of old wood and charcoal burning.

"Thanks, Neil. All of you have heard the story 'Little Red Riding Hood,' right? Well, that author was very smart to have the wolf dress up as Little Red Riding Hood's grandmother. Imagine how bad it would be to see how your grandmother can be a wolf. Not all grandmothers are sweet and loving. As a matter of fact, not all mothers are loving. When I was teaching at Seabury Hall on Maui, I remember being part of a parent conference with other teachers, when this mother (her second husband was there, too) told us she disliked her daughter and that was the reason she had put her in boarding school. We tried to argue with her, but she waved our words away; she said she couldn't stand her daughter. That blew me away, destroying the one assumption that I thought was universal: that all mothers love their children. Some of you, by the way, might want to write a story about one of your relatives who might be peculiar in a way or is uniquely colorful. As a matter of fact, I'm thinking about writing about one of my two sisters. I mean, talk about being eccentric or odd. I couldn't go wrong picking either one.
  "Now, tomorrow you'll be sharing your half-page freewrites in small groups. You know, your perspective writings? Oh, and because I might forget to give you Monday's reading, I'll give you the handout now. Read the story and come to class with three questions that you want the class to answer. Tomorrow, if any of the groups end early, you can do the reading in class and be free of English homework for the weekend."

Day 4: Description and Dialogue

After students meet in small groups and receive feedback on their three writings—helping each other determine which of the three seems to promise the best story—I prepare the students for two short writing exercises to be completed over the weekend. Like the perspective writings, these exercises give students the opportunity to try out certain techniques as they continue their search for a topic. One such exercise centers on description. I read the following example, taken from a translation of J. K. Huysmans' *Against the Grain:*

> He won a great reputation as an eccentric—a reputation he crowned by adopting a costume of black velvet worn with a gold-fringed waistcoat and sticking by way of cravat *[a tie]* a bunch of Parma violets in the opening of a very low-necked shirt. Then he would invite parties of literary friends to dinners that set all the world talking. In one instance in particular, modeling the entertainment on a banquet of the eighteenth century, he had organized a funeral feast in celebration of the most unmentionable of minor personal calamities. The dining-room was black and looked over on a strangely metamorphosed garden, the walks being strewn with charcoal, the little basin in the middle of the lawn bordered with a rim of black basalt and filled with ink; and the ordinary shrubs superseded with cypresses and pines. The dinner itself was served on a black cloth, decorated with baskets of violets and scabiosae and illuminated by candelabra in which tall tapers flared.
>
> While a concealed orchestra played funeral marches, the guests were waited on by naked negresses wearing shoes and stockings besprinkled with tears.
>
> The viands were served on black-bordered plates—turtle soup, Russian black bread, ripe olives from Turkey, caviar, mule steaks, Frankfurt smoked sausages, game dished up in sauces coloured to resemble licorice water and boot-blacking, truffles in jelly, chocolate-tinted creams, puddings, nectarines, fruit preserves, mulberries and cherries. The wines were drunk from dark-tinted glasses—wines of Limagne and Rousillon vintages, wines of Tenedos, the Val de Penas and Oporto. After the coffee and walnuts came other unusual beverages, kvas, porter and stout.

"Just for your information, the occasion for the dinner is to mourn the host's temporarily lost virility; which is to say, any reason is as good as another to throw a party, however carefully orchestrated this one may be. Beyond that, notice that in straight description no time passes, there is no immediate action; the embroidery of words, compelling though they may be, remains static—which is consistent with the life led by this French decadent, whose one enemy is *ennui,* or boredom. But like many readers, I am intrigued by the finely formed list rich with things unfamiliar to me, all consistent with the color black and the theme of mourning."

"It's like a poem."

"Yes. Like some of yours. Like your fruit poem or animal poem. Description and action are usually bound together, as James Joyce demonstrates in *A Portrait of the Artist As a Young Man* (1964, p. 171). Listen to this:

A girl stood before him in midstream, alone and still, gazing out to sea. She seemed like one whom magic had changed into the likeness of a strange and beautiful seabird. Her long bare legs were as delicate as a crane's and pure save where an emerald trail of seaweed had fashioned itself as a sign upon the flesh. Her thighs, fuller and softhued as ivory, were bared almost to her hips where the white fringes of her drawers were like featherings of soft white down. Her slate blue skirts were kilted about her waist and dovetailed behind her. Her bosom was as a bird's, soft and slight, slight and soft as the breast of some darkplumaged dove. But her long fair hair was girlish: and girlish, and touched with the wonder of mortal beauty, her face.

She was alone and still, gazing out to sea; and when she felt his presence and the worship of his eyes her eyes turned to him in quiet sufferance of his gaze, without shame or wantonness. Long, long she suffered his gaze and then quietly withdrew her eyes from his and bent them towards the stream, gently stirring the water with her foot hither and thither. The first faint noise of gently moving water broke the silence; hither and thither, hither and thither: and a faint flame trembled upon her cheek.

"Joyce's first paragraph is predominantly description, as seen by his young protagonist Stephen, who likens the young girl to some magical seabird. The explicit action is limited to the opening sentence alone. The first sentence of the second paragraph virtually repeats the action expressed in the first sentence of the first paragraph, as if no time has passed, and the following action of the second paragraph—the young girl's sufferance and reaction to Stephen's worshipful presence—seems to occur at the same time as Stephen's *continuing* gaze.

"I want you to write two descriptions, one dominated by a list, where no time passes, and a second where description is joined to action."

Another writing exercise that I assign students is dialogue writing—attuning their ears and familiarizing them with traditional dialogue conventions such as making a paragraph with each change of speaker, using commas for direct address and connecting quotations to the "said," using capitalization, and so forth. I read them the beginning of a short story by Tia Teves, a seventh grader, as they follow along in the handout.

"Tommy, come here please!"

"Uh, uh, Mommy?"

"Did you pull Jennifer McGrievy's hair in preschool today?"

"No, Mommy."

"Then why did your teacher just call, sweetie?"

"I dunno," Tommy said, looking down at his feet.

"Tommy, look at Mommy. You tell Jennifer that you're sorry tomorrow, okay? Now go wash your hands before dinner."

> I watched my toddler run up the stairs as I sighed. Half hour of fun, nine months of hell, four hours in screaming pain, and this is where I am now, in an apron instead of a business suit like I used to be. How I liked to be.

I point out, in addition to the writer's using dialogue conventions, her use of *interior monologue.* "Look at the second sentence of the last paragraph. Who is she speaking to here?"

"Herself."

"And what verb tense does she use?"

"The present."

"We get some vital information about the mother, don't you think, almost as if we were spying on her mind. This next example I'll just read to you. It's a fictionalized account of my meeting my wife. I want you to pay attention to how action is joined to the dialogue."

> She was seated at one of the middle tables as I approached with a menu, a glass of water, and some table setting. I lit the candle in the blue bowl.
>
> "Hi, I'm Kenj. Can I get you something to drink?"
>
> "Hi, I'm Christine," she said, pretending to study the menu by the blue light.
>
> "A Coke? Beer? Glass of wine? I can make a good grasshopper," I said.
>
> "A 7-Up . . . Oh, and a hamburger," she said, removing her overcoat. She wore this black sweater thing under a wool vest. She was both modest and shapely.
>
> "Look, why don't you sit up at the counter and watch me cook. You know, I don't have much experience with this stuff. Just leave your coat." I rounded the counter to get her drink, glad I had something to do. My face grizzly, I hadn't been home all night—*look like a bum.* As she slid into her stool, I said, "Teacher's College? From Hawaii, right?"

"Many good readers claim that nothing is more involving than dialogue. And I suppose it's true: Overhearing people talk is fun, inviting the voyeur in us, listening to how they speak and what they say, watching as they directly and indirectly describe themselves, revealing who they are, their likes and dislikes, their temper, their moods and attitudes, how smart they are, how they feel about others as well as themselves, and so forth.

"Your assignment for tonight, in addition to the two short descriptions, is to record, outside of class, actual dialogue that you've overheard or participated in yourselves."

Then, if there's time, we play a game. "The situation is this: A very old lady and a ten-year-old boy are riding in an elevator when the power goes off and the elevator stops between floors. The emergency lights come on. Either the boy or the old lady speaks first. Everyone, write down now what is said. Remember, you have the option to include description and narrative action with your dialogue. When you are done, just pass the story to your left, even if the person to your left hasn't finished. When you receive a new story, check, each time, for the correct use of dialogue convention before continuing. When you make a correction, show what you've done to the person who handed you the story."

This helps to some extent reinforce the convention. And you'll probably hear a few outrageous dialogues, but that's part of the game.

Day 5: More Class Talk

John Updike's "A & P," a story as much anthologized as "The Open Window," typifies the speech and thinking of most adolescent males. It might also typify the behavior of some adolescent girls. At least it does in my experience as both a junior high and high school teacher.

Some female teachers, however, who are conscious of all the deplorable sexism prevalent in our world, especially rampant in media and commercialism, think "A & P" should be trashed. I was made aware of this through a story told by Sheridan Blau, whom I worked with for several years on the advisory board of the National Writing Project. One summer, Blau was directing a Literature Institute in California. The women teachers were appalled that Blau would even *consider* including the story in the syllabus. They were furious with him. They would not let him speak, saying, "You need to be quiet and hear what we have to say." My students, both male and female, think that what the narrator, Sammy, says is funny. And it is—for all sorts of readers—because it *is* typical. Which is precisely the women's point. My students—especially the female students—must be made more deeply aware of what Sammy is saying; that is, more aware of how males tend to dehumanize women, turning them into objects.

I also teach the story in order to show students that we must be wary of the observations and assertions told to us by a first-person narrator. Sometimes the narrator unintentionally gives us the wrong information, motivation, reason, or conclusion. And usually, through artful or less obvious means, the author tells us what is really true or more accurate, or presents us with a quandary or dilemma, leaving it up to us to decide the truth.

Except for the very end, the entire story takes place in an A & P supermarket north of Boston, about five miles from the beach. It opens when Sammy, the nineteen-year-old narrator, says, "In walked these three girls with nothing but bathing suits." He describes them minutely, especially their anatomy, and tracks their progress through the aisles of the A & P. All the while he comments on the various customers; Stoksie, the other cashier; city workers beyond the window digging up the street to repair a broken sewer; McMahon, the meat man; and later Lengel, the manager of the store. Near the end, when Lengel rebukes the girls about their improper dress, Sammy, who sees himself as "their unsuspected hero," announces to Lengel that he quits.

When the students come to class on Monday with their three questions, the one that tops their list is, Why does Sammy quit? "How many of you include that question among your three?" Nearly all the students raise their hands. "How many of you feel that this question is the most important among your three?" Again, nearly all raise their hands. "But why?" I ask. "Doesn't Sammy tell us why he quits?"

"Yeah, but—"

"What does he say?"

"He wanted to be their hero. He tried to impress the girls by saying he was quitting," says Adam.

"He tried to stick up for them," says Natalie.

"Would you have been impressed?" I ask.

"No. Why would I? Besides, I would never go into the A & P dressed like that."

"Why not? Is it against the law?"

"No. I mean, it's just not decent," says Natalie.

"You mean they were doing something dirty?" asks Jordan, baiting Natalie. "Like they were wearing a G-string or something?"

"She means," says Nicole, "that it wasn't appropriate."

"Yeah, that's what I meant," says Natalie, giving Jordan a sassy look.

"What's so *inappropriate* about wearing a bathing suit into a supermarket?" asks Jordan. "I've done it."

"Bull," says Ben.

"Where?" says Sandra.

"Manoa Safeway."

"When?" she asks.

"When I was seven." Several chuckle.

"How many of you," I ask the class, "would have done what the three girls did?" A few raise their hands, boys and girls.

"Oh, c'mon," says Nicole.

"What's the big deal?" says Steve.

"With your hollow chest?" says Ben.

"Ben makes a good point," I say. "There's a good reason for having clothes. Let's face it. There're a lot of ugly people out there.—Just kidding." A few laugh.

"For one thing, it's not healthy," says Nicole.

"What do you mean? What are you going to do? roll around with the grape-fruits?" Ha-ha.

"No, smarty. The supermarket is cold."

"How many of you would walk around in Liberty House like that? . . . I guess none of you," I say. "Just as with Manoa Safeway, which is in a valley several miles from Waikiki; we—you and I as a society—we all agree that there are certain ways to dress when going to certain places. We conform to a certain decorum. We learn this when relatively young—except for Jordan." They laugh. "Now, most of you find Sammy's reason for quitting his job at the A & P puzzling, as Adam does. We'll return to this question in a moment. First, let's hear your other questions. Remember, when you refer to a passage in the story, tell us what page, which column, and whereabouts in which paragraph the passage can be found."

"I got one," Steve says with some joy. "Top of the last page, first column. It says—"

"*Sammy* says."

"Sammy says, 'I uncrease the bill, tenderly as you may imagine, it just having come from between the two smoothest scoops of vanilla I had ever known there were'—[*the class laughs*]—I don't get it," Steve says, playing innocent. "Wouldn't the bill be wet?" More laughter.

"What do *you* think?" I counter. "Matter of fact, what do you all think about the way Sammy talks about the girls? Are none of you girls a slight bit offended? Marci?"

"Yeah, kind of. I mean, he talks about the girl's boobs like they were things."

"I like ice cream," says Steve. Ha-ha.

"Steve, let her talk. Marci?"

"He talks about the girl's bottom as a *can* and names the tall girl *Goony-Goony*. Especially when he says—"

"You just called them *boobs*," says Ben.

"'Especially when he says' what?" I ask.

"When Sammy says—let me see."

"Page one," says Adam.

"Yeah, page one, second column, toward the end of the paragraph, he says, 'You never know for sure how girls' minds work (do you really think it's mind in there or just a little buzz like a bee in a glass jar?).' That's a put-down."

"Natalie?"

"It seems to me that Sammy is just talking to the boys."

"Where?"

"Through the whole thing."

"Wow! I never thought of that," I say.

"The way he describes the girls. He wouldn't talk like that if his audience was girls."

"But girls are part of the audience, aren't they?" Ben puts in. But Natalie ignores him.

"Going back to the quote that Steve read, Sammy says, 'I uncrease the bill, tenderly as you may imagine—' Well, *I* don't imagine."

"You know, Natalie, that's a pretty insightful observation. Original," I add. "What do the rest of you think of that idea? That Sammy is talking primarily to the boys in his audience?" Most of the kids agree with Natalie. "Okay, look at page two, second column, at the paragraph before the space break. How many of you had questions about that paragraph?" Several kids raise their hands. "Darren, could you read it for us, please?"

"The whole thing? . . .

"The girls had reached the meat counter and were asking McMahon something. He pointed, they pointed, and they shuffled out of sight behind a pyramid of Diet Delight peaches. All that was left for us to see was old McMahon patting his mouth and looking after them, sizing up their joints. Poor kids, I began to feel sorry for them, they couldn't help it."

"Marilyn?"

"He's checking them out."

"Yeah," says Darren. "'Sizing up their joints.' Like a butcher. They're in the meat section."

"*Things*, again," says Natalie.

"And they pass from view behind what?" I ask.

"I like peaches," says Steve.

"What do you mean?" I ask.

"Nothing. I like peaches."

"I see," says Kyle. "*They're* like peaches. Diet Delight peaches, sweet things. That's pretty neat."

"Yeah, that's pretty neat," says Steve. "Like dessert. As old McMahon checks them out. Did the author really think of this?"

"What do you think? Reiko?"

"Why does Sammy say, 'Poor kids, I began to feel sorry for them, they couldn't help it.' Couldn't help what? And why should Sammy feel sorry for them?"

"Because McMahon's horny," says Kyle.

"So?"

"And Sammy says he's old. And, well, the girls are young and sweet."

"I don't get it."

"He feels sorry for them," says Marilyn, "because these old guys shouldn't be looking at the girls as he does. He thinks that McMahon sees them only as meat."

"Stoksie is checking them out, too, isn't he? And he's married," says Reiko.

"I suppose it doesn't matter," I say, "if you're married or old or crippled. Tia, do girls check out boys?"

"Yeah," she says, smiling. "But not like the guys. We have more class."

"Yeah, right," says Ben. "You should hear them screaming in the hallways."

"Not at *you*," says Tia, her nose in the air.

"Talk about aggressive. Now you don't want me to talk about you and—"

"Other questions? Yes, Brian?"

"Are Sammy and Stoksie gay? I mean, they talk like it."

"I was wondering that, too," says Steve.

"Me, too," says Nicole.

"Where?"

"Same page, at the top, when Sammy says:

"Oh Daddy," Stoksie said beside me. "I feel faint."

"Darling," I said. "Hold me tight."

"Ahhhh, they're just playin' around," says Scooter from the back row of the semicircle. "Acting like girls."

"You ought to know," says Buster, his baseball partner.

"How do you know?" asks Natalie.

"Well, he's always making fun of somebody."

"You mean the three girls?"

"No. The customers."

"He's right," says Adam.

"Look at the description in the previous paragraph," I say. "Sammy says, 'You could see them, when Queenie's white shoulders dawned on them, kind of jerk, or hop, or hiccup, but their eyes snapped back to their own baskets' . . . and further on, 'A few housewives in pin curlers even looked around after pushing their carts past to make sure what they had seen was correct.' And in the next, Stoksie says to Sammy, 'Is it done?' meaning, has the damage been done?"

"In that paragraph, I don't get the rest," says Scooter.

"Like what?"

"He says, 'I forgot to say he—'"

"*He* who?"

"Stoksie."

"Sorry. Please start again."

"'I forgot to say he thinks he's going to be manager some sunny day, maybe in 1990 when it's called the Great Alexandrov and Petrooshki Tea Company or something.' What the heck does that mean?"

"That's one of my questions, too," says Nicole.

"Me, too," says Buster.

"You lie!" says Scooter.

"Well?" There is no answer. "What kinds of names are Alexandrov and Petrooshki?"

"Russian?" says Reiko.

"Okay. So Sammy thinks Stoksie is going to be manager in 1990—remember, this is the early '60s—when the supermarket chain is renamed Alexandrov and Petrooshki. So what's Sammy think?"

"He'll be manager when the U.S. is conquered by the Russians," says Scooter.

"No, you Dufus," says Buster. "He doesn't think that Stoksie will ever be manager."

"He doesn't think Stoksie has much of a future," says Adam. "Is that why Sammy quit?"

"Maybe part of the reason. Marci?"

"And he didn't like the real manager, that guy Lengel. Sammy says he was a dreary, Sunday-school-teacher kind of guy."

"Yeah, someone who's always preaching," says Steve. "Always following the rules. My dad hates his boss and always says he should quit."

"What else might make you feel like quitting?"

"If the work is boring," says Buster.

"Didn't Sammy make up a song on the cash register when he had nothing to do?" I ask. "How does that song go?"

"It's here," says Adam. "Top of the last page: 'Hello (bing) there, you (gung) hap-py pee-pul (splat)!'"

"He's always making fun of people," says Scooter.

"What's he call them?"

"Sheep, which are kind of dumb animals," says Ben. "And he called that old woman a *witch* when she caught Sammy ringing up something twice."

"And he called that old man buying pineapple juice a *bum*," says Nicole. "He even called the men fixing the sewer a bunch of *freeloaders*."

"I got one," says Kyle. "Says here on the bottom of the last page, 'A couple of customers that had been heading for my slot begin to knock against each other, like scared pigs in a chute.'"

"He doesn't like the customers," says Adam. "He doesn't like working in the A & P. That business about being the girls' hero was just an excuse to quit. That's all."

Most of the students agree with Adam's point of view, which answers their number one question.

"Maybe so. But the girls were a big reason," said Marilyn.

"Yeah," says Tia. "They were like an example for him."

"You know, there are all kinds of possible stories that come to mind when I think of Sammy and the work he dislikes. There were some jobs that I just dreaded coming to. Believe me, there's nothing in the world like what I'm doing now."

For homework, I have students exchange the writing exercises they completed over the weekend and write a reaction to their two descriptions and their dialogue.

Day 6: Nonfiction Stories

"Before we begin, please return to your partner the description and dialogue and your reaction to both. Yes, now. C'mon, chop-chop. Today I'm going to read several personal experience stories. The first was written by David Estermann, an eighth grader. The story's forward motion, though organized by events in time, is dominated by the writer's ideas and feelings about an actual experience. There are no real scenes with detailed descriptions of setting or actions or other characters. As in a personal essay, he tries to make logical meaning of his experience, rather than trying to show how the experience occurred at the time. The drama of the story is the movement of his mind. The story is called 'Cut.'"

> As the sweat ran down my face, the coach read off the names of the last three people cut from the basketball team. "Brent, Andrew, and . . . Estermann."
>
> As the coach started his "I-know-you-tried-your-best" speech, I thought about what I had gone through trying to make the team.
>
> I thought about last year, when I was a pathetic basketball player. No shot, no moves, no chance at making the team. I had thought about trying out last year, but I knew I didn't have a prayer. It was at that point that I promised myself I would make the team the next year.
>
> All last year I practiced hard, playing almost every day during the summer, spending hours by myself at the courts near my house. Working on ball handling skills and developing a shot. I joined Summer leagues, got into pickup games, anything to help me get better. Now all that practice seems like wasted time.
>
> I came into tryouts with high hopes and a good deal of confidence. All of that changed quickly. I was put into the "average" player group. Most of those players usually get cut.
>
> I watched a lot of guys leave in the next few weeks, many of whom I considered better than myself. This was a tough time for me because I had mixed feelings after a cut. I was excited that I was still on the team but at the same time I also felt sorry for the people who had been cut. It's hard to console someone when you're happy about what they are upset over.
>
> Cut after cut passed until finally we were down to eighteen players (the coaches keep fifteen players). I was so confident I had made it, having gone through so many cuts already.
>
> I wasn't asking for much, just a spot on the bench. It wouldn't have mattered to me if I didn't play a minute all year. Just making the team would have been enough.
>
> It was supposed to turn out to be one of those stories you tell your kids— about how you practiced hard and finally achieved your goal.
>
> I wonder now whether the coach kept me until the last cut because I deserved it or because we were friends. He probably thought he was doing me a favor by keeping me. I think it hurt more being cut last than it would have if I was cut earlier.
>
> Everyone says life isn't fair. This story proves it. Some people who made the team had never practiced basketball a day in their life. They were, however, all very tall. I guess all that stuff the coaches said about effort and

heart being the most important factor in making the team was B.S. It's strange sometimes how some people get things so effortlessly, and the people that work for it weren't always rewarded.

I'm at the point now where I don't know whether to give up on basketball or start practicing for next year. I had better decide soon before only one option is left.

"This is a sad story, one that perhaps explodes the myth that, if you work hard and try your best, you'll be rewarded. Which is not always true. And it's perhaps most true in sports.

"The next story was written by Chris Chow, a seventh grader. And though it seems like a fiction, the story is factual."

Hero in Disguise

It was about eight o'clock and not a single soul outside. My mother had urged me to go outside and fetch the football. I opened the door carefully . . . then took a step, and stopped. I noticed a hole in the stone wall with two lines of smoke coming out of it like a giant volcano. At this time the moon was practically covered by a cloud, so I strained my neck forward to get a glance at it, and what I saw horrified me.

It had a short gray muzzle with dull crimson eyes. Horrid claws and jaws like man traps from a pack of cur dogs. It had wings as large as a truck, with two lines of smoke from two flaming nostrils. "Dragon," I whispered to myself. With pure instinct, I shot my arm behind me, not daring to take my eyes off it . . . I was frantic. I grabbed pots, pans, shovels, wire and nails until I found what I was looking for, which turned out to be an old, long, rusty knife that my dad kept in the tool shed.

I took my stand facing its hideous face. First I paused, and then charged in fury. It swung its terrible claws at me, a shrewd blow, so I took it on my knife, but fell from the shock. I struggled to my feet and backed off. But before I could summon another attack, it whipped its tail and swept me off my feet. Once again I battled my way up and backed off. But this time it was too slow. I grabbed its cranium, trying to squeeze the life out of it. But knowing this would not work, I gave it a mean cut to the throat, and with continuous blows I hacked off its head.

Victorious, I dragged its body down to the edge of the storm shelter. After pausing to catch my breath, I hurled it down like a sack of potatoes. "Lie there, foul creature of the underworld, and let your soul bother no one anymore," I shouted.

I walked back to the house in a haze and disposed of my knife and tattered attire. I quickly hosed myself down (for I had blood all over me), and dressed into a spare shirt and pants. I walked inside and, greatly to my relief, I saw my mother slouched over the kitchen sink with a coffee cup in her hand.

And to this day, she is unaware of my whereabouts of that frightful night.

"Nor is he aware of his *mother's* whereabouts, while she slouches 'over the kitchen sink with a coffee cup in her hand.' Where, in what place of mind, might she have been during the boy's imaginative fight with the dragon? What different worlds each of us occupies—what thoughts, daydreams, worries; what wishes; what memories that are ours and ours alone are inaccessible to others. Which is why we might grow curious about the mother's world, too, knowing, at least, how vastly different it must be from the boy's.

"The following story, by Shana Rose, an eighth grader, is another example of how a story can be written about the simplest things and result in a successful little drama. It is a depiction of an actual experience, until the end, where she introduces a fictional character."

A Christmas Exchange

I clutched the large gray shopping bag with both hands as I crossed the street towards the little mall. I had put off going as long as possible, because if anyone saw me here, I would die. There was a much better mall on the other side of town, where I always hang out after school and do my shopping. But thanks to Aunty Kitty and those dumb pants she gave me for Christmas, I had to come here to exchange them. Fortunately, she had told me about the neat little shop she had bought them at. I doubted there were any neat little shops in this entire mall. I walked up the few cracked cement stairs leading to the main part of the mall. The four main features of the mall were the Weiner Master, Music-o-rama, Donald's Drug Discounts, and Thrifty Things. The last was where my Aunty Kitty had bought the pants. Now if the name Thrifty Things makes you think that perhaps this is not just another Macy's, the store's merchandise would confirm it. I walked into the store and glanced around. There were maybe seven small racks of "clothing," none of it decent enough to spit on. I walked up to the counter, where an obese blob of a saleslady sat, filing her short, stubby nails. Her huge nest of piled up blond hair perched on top of her broad forehead and, every so often, threatened to collapse. Absentmindedly, she pushed it back up with her right hand and patted it down with her left. By this time, nail filings began to pile up on the counter, and she still hadn't noticed me standing there. I shifted my weight from one foot to another and cleared my throat. She looked up with a start and embarrassedly wiped the nail filings off the counter.

"Can I help you, sweetheart?" she asked, smiling. I noticed that her name tag said "Bonnie."

"Yeah, um . . . I need to exchange these," I said, pulling the plaid brown and orange pants out of the the paper bag.

"Oooooooooooh, how lovely!" she shrieked. "Whatsa matter, too small for you?"

"No, I'd like to find something else," I replied. I was getting uncomfortable.

I always get this really weird feeling when I think someone is watching me. And that was the feeling I was getting.

Slowly, I turned around. At first I didn't see anyone. But when I moved my eyes along the window, I saw a familiar face. It was Heather McArdle, the coolest girl in my whole school, practically. She was staring right at me.

My shoulders fell. By tomorrow, the rumor would be out that Thrifty Things, the store that gets their merchandise from garbage dumps, was my favorite place to shop. Heather held up a hand to say hello, and, as always, waggled a few fingers as if she were drying her fingernails. She was wearing this cute bright red mini skirt outfit and bright red high heels with matching bracelets and big red cherry earrings. I halfheartedly waved and turned back around. Bonnie was still holding up those dumb pants. I wanted to rip them to shreds. Instead, I said quickly, "Thanks a lot for your help, but I think I changed my mind. I'd like to keep the pants."

She looked pleased so I stuffed them in the paper bag and almost ran to the door. I did not want to talk to Heather at all, but she was running towards me, her long, dark brown hair flying out behind her. I thought about making a dash for it, but that would just give her more to gossip about, so I came to a halt and watched her running over. All the guys in our school are totally in love with her, but I think she looks like a monkey, and not just because I'm jealous of her. She really is weird looking.

"Hey, let's see those pants you bought in there!" she said when she had finally reached me. She was all out of breath and her red face was sweating.

"Oh, I was just trying to exchange them because I got them for Christmas from my Aunt and they are really ugly . . ." I said, embarrassed. She grabbed the package and pulled out the pants. I waited for her to start howling with laughter. She didn't.

"These are so cool!" she exclaimed, holding them up to her legs. I looked at her like she was crazy. Why did everyone like them except me?

"Honest! I love them! These are like the style in Paris, yeah?"

"Yeah," I said, like I knew ALL about it.

"Maybe I could borrow them sometime?" She asked hopefully.

"You can have them!" I said a little too eagerly. "I mean, I don't like them anyway . . ." I didn't want her to think I was dumb.

"Thanks!" she said, stuffing them into her purse.

"The details of this simple story are very persusive, joined to the narrator's superior, name-brand attitude. We know kids like this, don't we? Let's face it. Some of you would be crucified if you wore the wrong clothes.

"The next story was written by Joseph Yamamoto, a tenth grader I taught in the early 1980s. His story, too, is based on an actual experience, but he does something more than embellish the end. He creates a kind of frame for his story that parodies the stereotypical horror film. Given your taste, I think you'll find it amusing."

Bus 751: A Horror Story

As soon as I stepped on the bus, I knew something terrible was going to happen. The bus number, which added up to thirteen, was an omen in itself. My friend and I sat down in seats in the last row which we had first inspected in case there was something undesirable to sit on. The bus was just like any bus we had ridden in; graffiti on the wall; dirty windows, and an air conditioner that never seemed to be working. The bus had made its usual stops, and when it had made one of its jerking stops near the capitol building these two sinister looking guys came aboard. We didn't pay much attention to them, but we didn't want them to sit near us. The first guy was wearing worn out fatigues and a t-shirt; he was loud and obnoxious looking. The fellow following him was stolid, silent, and looked like he was in a trance. The first guy was talking very loud and the second wasn't paying much attention to him. To our horror they sat on the seats across the aisle from us. One of them, the quiet sleepy looking one, lay down on one of the seats, his dirty hands rubbing his eyes. The one in the fatigues asked his friend, "You okay o'wot? You look wasted, brah." He was wasted; he looked only semi-conscious.

"I going crash. Wake me up layta," the zoned out guy said. He fell asleep immediately. The other guy drummed his knees and started singing a song that he probably made up walking down the aisle. After he got bored with his song he had several intimate moments alone to himself. We could hear him talking, swearing, and arguing with himself. All at once he jumped up looking out the window and proceeded to shake his buddy out of his deep sleep. His friend groaned and slowly sat up. The guy with the fatigues was already waiting by the exit door in the middle of the bus.

"Try wait," the stoned guy said. He bent over the seat, and then this awful sound came to our ears. It was the sound of a thousand BBs being dropped on a sheet of aluminum, it was the sound of tin foil being crinkled. In reality it was the horrifying sound of vomit hitting the metal floor of bus 751. Seconds later the smell you never forget filled the bus. Soon, it got to the point where we couldn't stand it any longer; the combination of the smell, the hot bus, and the sight of the milky vomit forced us to move to the front of the bus. Even after that the smell of the vomit followed us to the front. We had fears of putting our feet and possessions on the ground as if the whole floor was covered with the stinking vomit. Soon the bus was nearly empty and these two kids came on the bus, went to the rear of the bus, and yelled to the bus driver, "Somebody barfed in your bus!!" My friend and I glanced to the back of the bus where the terror had been spawned. There was the kid stirring the sinister goop with a stick, as if it were his dinner. I couldn't take it anymore; I had to take my things off that cursed bus. At the next stop we got off and watched bus 751 roll away, losing itself in the forest of buildings. Today, I still wonder about what had happened to bus 751, the kid, the driver, and the few innocent people that were still on the bus when my friend and I escaped from the evil vomit.

"Your assignment for tonight [*groan*] is to write a half-page on each of the following. Ready?

1. Your experience with beauty or fear.
2. Your experience with desire or depression.
3. Your experience with meaness or joy.

"In the event that none of these appeals to you, you also have the option of writing on events that had some impact on your life. Any questions? You know what? Make those writings due on Friday. I want you instead to do this reading for tomorrow. It's called 'The Old Kimono.' Take this down: Come in with two statements about the main character that the text does not tell us directly—"

"Could you slow down, Mr. T?"

"Sure." I repeat the assignment a couple of times. "Now, come up and get the handout. Marci?"

"The writings are due on Friday, right?"

"Right. Aloha!"

Day 7: Class Talk

Marie Hara's "Old Kimono" is about a young, local, Japanese woman who purchases a black kimono at a Buddhist bazaar, at a temple located near downtown Honolulu. She is highly fashion-conscious, enamored of the latest styles and designer-label merchandise. The two old Japanese women who sell her the kimono are stunned into silence when the young woman says, "I might change [the kimono] and maybe cut it all up, too. I don't wanna wear dis kine old-fashion stuff." When the old women do not thank the young woman for the purchase, the young woman thinks, "Hypocrites. They think they know how to do things . . . but it's always their way or no way. Typical."

In the entryway at home, holding the kimono against her body in front of a full-length mirror, the narrator says, "The mirror gave proof that her choice, the sophisticated back and exquisite design, were exactly right for her. She would look bold and new: Asian, not oriental. Sexy, not cute." After examining and admiring the kimono's superb workmanship, she glimpses her mother's arrangement of what the mother calls "boy flowahs, anthuriums," which the young woman finds "crude. Not only were they ordinary and not placed in any particular order, they were also in no way fragile or aesthetic. They were so . . . local."

Once she puts the kimono on, the young woman undergoes a gradual transformation into what she believes—based on stereotypical images of Japan and

Japanese movies—to be a traditional Japanese woman. She then fantasizes her role: "Her loyalty would never waver; she would serve her lord courageously." Then, before the mirror, she begins to dance: "Music in her head, ringing with the rollicking cadences of koto and samisen . . . until she collapsed on the bed, giggling at the spectacle," whereupon:

> She caught her breath when she looked backwards at the mirror. The woman in the black kimono was still dancing as if the music had increased its frantic rhythm. Back and forth, back and forth: her motions were hypnotic.
>
> Lifting her face, the dancer, caught in the instance of clapping her hands, froze at the sight of the woman staring at her from the bed.
>
> Both gasped, the young woman and the reflection in the mirror, when the bedroom door opened.

When the mother enters the room, she says, "I thought I heard music." She then corrects the daughter, showing the young woman how to properly wear the kimono: "Fo' real! Anybody who know anyt'ing—all da people who see dat—dey gonna laugh at you." Moments later the story ends with the used kimono left in a heap on the bed.

"Who's first? Jason?"

"I think she's a big snob. She thinks she's better than everybody else. She thinks she knows how to do everything and she doesn't."

"Yeah," says Kenji. "*She's* the hypocrite. She said to the two old ladies that she knew how to wear the kimono, but she doesn't. Her mom had to show her the right way. Then she gets all pissed—"

"*Angry.* Or *grumpy—habuteru* is the Japanese, right?" I say.

"She gets all *habut*," Jennifer says.

"Yeah, she gets the boot," says Mike. "Right in the butt." Laughter.

"She gets this attitude and dumps the dress," Kenji says.

"What do you mean *dumps?* Is she going to throw it away?"

"I don't know. Maybe."

"She's just a spoiled brat," says Nicole. "If she can't have it her way, she won't do it. She *is* a hypocrite."

"You sound like you know," I say, and Nicole gives me a sassy look. "Any of you ever act this way when one of your parents tries to show you how to do something? Jason?"

"One time my father kept getting on my case about the proper way to grip the club when hitting a golf ball. That's why I play tennis."

"You mean, you gave up golf? Just threw the clubs down and—"

"No. If I ever threw down the clubs, my father would strangle me. They belonged to Grandpa."

"They hold a lot of meaning for your father."

"Mr. T? The kimono used to belong to someone who died," says Jamie. "One of the old ladies said at the beginning—here it is: 'The family wen' donate all her clothes after the one-year service.'"

"So what?" says Mike.

"And Jessica and I thought the kimono was haunted—"

"Not *haunted*. Had a spell on it," says Jessica.

"Huh?"

"What spell?" says Jason.

"When she put the kimono on. She started acting like she was Japanese," says Jamie.

"She *is* Japanese," says Mike.

"No, not that kind," says Jennifer. "I know what you mean. Like a Japanese from Japan."

"By the way, Mike, what's your nationality?"

"I'm Irish-Scottish-French-Vietnamese."

"No, you're American," I say. "Nationality stems from nation, what country you belong to. Like others here, you confuse your ethnic background with nationality. They are two different things. I'm sorry, Jamie, please continue."

"Me and Jessica felt that once she put it on she started wanting to be Japanese, when before she said she wanted to be Asian and not Oriental. And she thinks about how a Japanese woman should act, turning her right toe in—"

"And she starts thinking," adds Jessica, "of the Japan she knows from the movies, with rock gardens and lanterns and samurais and ladies in waiting—"

"And she even pretends to act like one of them, serving some lord back in history. Maybe the kimono was from back then and was passed on to the girl who died, and the spirit of the kimono entered her body, because she starts to do a Japanese dance in front of the mirror."

"Maybe it was a curse," says Mike. "'Cause she begins to hear Japanese music."

"That doesn't mean it's a curse," says Estee.

"What about when she stops dancing?" I ask.

"That, too," says Mike. "The dancer in the mirror keeps dancing. Like a ghost."

"That's her, too," says Estee. "It's like part of yourself watching yourself do something. Sometimes it happens to me when I write. Sometimes when I am writing I can see myself doing it at the same time."

"But," says Scooter, "what about when it says here, at the bottom, 'Lifting her face, the dancer, caught in the instance of clapping her hands, froze at the sight of the woman staring at her from the bed. Both gasped—'?"

"They're both surprised or shocked," says Jason.

"Why?"

"Not both," says Estee. "They're the same."

"Okay. The same. What, then, is the dancer in the mirror surprised about in seeing the girl on the bed?" I ask.

"I know," says Jennifer. "She's surprised to see that she—"

"Who?"

"The girl on the bed. The dancer is surprised to see that the girl on the bed is an American girl."

"Why would she be so surprised about that?" says Jamie. "She *is* American."

"But not when she's dancing. She's so into dancing and her fantasy world that she forgets about being American. Until she sees herself on the bed."

"And the girl on the bed is surprised to see herself as a Japanese dancer. As Japanese," adds Estee.

"C'mon," says Mike, "she knows she's Japanese."

"What she means," says Jennifer, "is a Japanese from Japan."

"A traditional Japanese woman," says Nicole.

"But she's not," says Mike.

"But she could be," says Nicole.

"This ain't the movies," says Scooter.

"Maybe she wants to be . . ." says Nicole.

"I don't know about the kimono being magical or having a spell," says Natalie, "but it does connect her to her roots."

"Ahh-soo," says Scooter. Laughter.

"What about the music, then?" asks Jamie.

"That's part of the fantasy," says Jennifer.

"It could be part of her roots, too," says Natalie.

"Who else hears the music?" I ask.

"The mother!" says Buster. "When she comes into the bedroom, she says, 'I thought I heard music.' So it's gotta be real."

"Or it's something they both have," Jason says. "They both come from the same roots."

"The mother wants to be Japanese too?" asks Buster.

"God, she *is* Japanese," says Mike.

"She's just local. They're both local," says Scooter.

"What's wrong with *that?*" asks Nicole.

"Whaooo!"

"The girl doesn't think much of things local," says Mike. "Like her mother's anthuriums. Also, maybe she doesn't like the way her mother talks pidgin."

"She talks pidgin, too," says Buster.

"Maybe that's the reason, too, that she dumped the kimono on the bed."

"It reminded her," says Estee, "of who she really is. A local."

"Too bad," says Scooter smiling.

"You know what, Scooter?" says Nicole.

"What?"

"You're so . . . so *purebred.*"

"Huh?"

"All those fashion magazines must've screwed up her head," says Nicole.

"What's so wrong with being local?" asks Mike. "I'm local."

"Except for you, Mike," Estee says. "Nothing. Absolutely nothing."

"Let me just say that I think you folks did very well in trying to tackle a very mysterious scene. The writer, I think, uses the protagonist's imagination to show the duality that she is as a Japanese-American or 'local,' and to show the subconscious conflict she feels in being both. You might think of employing yourself an instance of apparent unreality in order to communicate what someone is experiencing."

The bell rings. As usual, I say, "Aloha."

Day 8 (Double Period): Beginnings and Voice

"Now before you share your half-page writings in small groups, I want you to work out an interesting beginning to one of them. But before that, I want to read you some story openings authored by well-known adults. The openings focus on the music of language, the sounds and rhythms, the accents and attitudes expressed by various human voices—that make the human voice so compelling.

"Remember, what's at stake at the beginning—beyond the reader being temporarily drawn in by cleverness, sensationalism, or even information, if you really want to get down to the bones of the matter—is whether or not the reader wants to hang out with this writer for the length, say, of three hundred pages. In the quiet living room, study, or library, under that magic pool of lamplight [I draw a circle over my head with a finger], the reader will open the cover of the book and read the opening pages, judging whether or not to read on. And you know yourselves, it doesn't take much for the reader to put the book down and pick up something else.

"This first opening is from E. M. Forster's *A Passage to India*, which, to me, emphasizes the narrator's bitter but beautiful description of the Ganges River and the city of Chandrapore. It hints perhaps at the racial tensions between Indians and their British colonizers. That is, you can communicate a lot through setting, as you saw in 'The Grandmother.'"

Except for the Marabar Caves—and they are twenty miles off—the city of Chandrapore presents nothing extraordinary. Edged rather than washed by the Ganges, it trails for a couple of miles along the bank, scarcely distinguishable from the rubbish it deposits so freely. There are no bathing-steps on the river front, as the Ganges happens not to be holy here; indeed there is no river front, and the bazaars shut out the wide and shifting panorama of the stream. The streets are mean, the temples ineffective, and though a few fine houses exist they are hidden away in gardens or down alleys whose filth deters all but the invited guest. Chandrapore was never large or beautiful, but two hundred years ago it lay on the road between Upper India, then imperial, and the sea, and the fine houses date from that period. The zest for decoration stopped in the eighteenth century, nor was it ever democratic. There is no painting and scarcely any carving in the bazaars. The very wood seems made of mud, the inhabitants of mud moving. So abased, so monotonous is everything that meets the eye, that when the Ganges comes down it might be expected to wash the excrescence back into the soil. Houses do fall, people are drowned and left rotting, but the general outline of the town persists, swelling here, shrinking there, like some low but indestructible form of life.

"Though the writing is powerful, the picture the writer paints is not very pretty; his tone or attitude is one of bitterness, even disgust in places—for the river, the town, the inhabitants who seem as primitive as the mud. So why would I want to read about Chandrapore—except for that voice? When you begin your own story, think of the mood or attitude of your own narrator and how his emotions might color all that he relates.

"The next opening is from Ernest Hemingway's *A Farewell to Arms*, which takes place during World War I. The writer's style almost mesmerizes with its incantatory repetitions of 'leaves' and 'trees' and 'dust,' and through the rhythm of its sentences, which emphasize nouns, the names of things. Simple verbs and the subtle 'and' bind the words together into something almost like an elegy, as if the war had already happened. The end of the second paragraph makes the whole passage sound ominous."

In the late summer of that year we lived in a house in a village that looked across the river and the plain to the mountains. In the bed of the river there were pebbles and boulders, dry and white in the sun, and the water was clear and swiftly moving and blue in the channels. Troops went by the house and down the road and the dust they raised powdered the leaves of the trees. The trunks of the trees too were dusty and the leaves fell early that year and we saw the troops marching along the road and the dust rising and leaves, stirred by the breeze, falling and the soldiers marching and afterward the road bare and white except for the leaves.

The plain was rich with crops; there were many orchards of fruit trees and beyond the plain the mountains were brown and bare. There was fighting in the mountains and at night we could see the flashes from the artillery. In the dark it was like summer lightning, but the nights were cool and there was not the feeling of a storm coming.

"'A storm coming' . . . the war coming. And all that dust he talks about, and things falling. And you know those rich crops and fruit trees won't last long. You, too, might try out a beginning where you speak through the setting. Who knows where it might lead you?

"You all have heard of Mark Twain's *Huckleberry Finn* and how Huck speaks in a Southern, country-boy dialect about his adventures rafting the Mississippi River in the 1880s. Now, I don't read this stuff too well, so bear with me."

You don't know about me without you have read a book by the name of *The Adventures of Tom Sawyer*; but that ain't no matter. That book was made by Mr. Twain, and he told the truth, mainly. There was things which he stretched, but mainly he told the truth. That is nothing. I never seen anybody but lied one time or another, without it was Aunt Polly, or the widow, or maybe Mary. Aunt Polly—Tom's Aunt Polly, she is—and Mary, and the Widow Douglas is all told about in that book, which is mostly a true book, with some stretchers, as I said before.

"I have to admit that the first time I tried reading *Huck Finn* I had a hard time. But later on I sort fell into it, as I would with Shakespeare's writing. I like the way Huck talks to me, his unabashed, down-home voice, the way people in certain places actually do talk. I also like his honesty and humor and gumption.

"You've all heard and read a few local poems in pidgin—a creole, really. It's the language of the cradle. This next opening comes from Darrell H. Y. Lum's 'What School You Went?' which, as you know, is a common local question posed to new acquaintances, meaning, 'What high school did you go to?' And once the school is named, the next question might be, 'You know my cousin Kimo?' (or nephew Frank or friend Maile), asked in order to make some connection, since the islands are small and many families and friends are often tied to each other in some way."

My students know by now—or least know my opinion—that local pidgin is a dialect of standard American English, not something inferior to it, retaining its own virtues and its own poetry. And since they come from these islands, they should be able to at least understand the local way of speaking. For one thing, it is fun. "Now, folks, you gotta bear with me again."

Mrs. Wagnah was our kinnigarden teacha. She was one old haole lady wit gray hair and her glasses was tied to one string so dat she no lose um. I dunno how she could lose um cause she had big chi-chis and her glasses always stay dere j'like on top one shelf. And she had one nudda stuff, like one necklace dat clamp to her sweater, so da ting not fall off. She wear her sweater j'like one supahman cape. And when she put on her art apron wit her glasses stuff and her sweater stuff, she get all tangled up and den somebody gotta help her figgah out how fo take um all off.

Mrs. Wagnah one pretty nice teacha. Only ting, she made you sleep during nap time. She was strick about dat. You had to put on your eyeshades and lie down on your sleeping mat and no talk and no move around. Even if you wasn't tired, you couldn't move around and you had to shut your eyes cause she said she going check. But how she going check unless she get x-ray vision?

My kids enjoy this passage very much. They like hearing the local voice and seeing the world from the point of view of someone young. They like the honesty and the irony and humor of the speaker's observations. "Remember, your main character, too, will come from somewhere and speak in a certain way.

"The next opening is from Anthony Burgess' *A Clockwork Orange*, whose narrator employs a futuristic slang as musical as hip-hop or rap or the jazz talk among musicians. The story is about teenage violence and perhaps its more violent antidote of brainwashing. Listen."

"What's it going to be then, eh?"

There was me, that is Alex, and my three droogs, that is Pete, Georgie, and Dim, Dim being really dim, and we sat in the Korova Milkbar making up our rassodocks what to do with the evening, a flip dark chill winter bastard though dry. The Korova Milkbar was a milk plus mesto, and you may, O my brothers, have forgotten what these mestos were like, things changing so skorry these days and every body very quick to forget, newspapers not being read much neither. Well, what they sold there was milk plus something else. They had no license selling liquor, but there was no law yet against prodding some of the new veshches which they used to put into the old moloko, so you could peet it with vellocet or synthemesc or drencrom or one or two other veshches which would give you a nice quiet horrorshow fifteen minutes admiring Bog And All His Holy Angels And Saints in your left shoe with lights bursting all over your mozg. Or you could peet milk with knives in it, as we used to say, and this would sharpen you up and make you ready for a bit of dirty twenty-to-one, and that was what we were peeting this evening I'm starting off this story with.

"Pretty far out, no? But inventing language is not easy. Remember, it's the sound of words—and how they're yoked through the rhythm of your phrases and clauses and sentences—that results in gracefulness; that few ears are deaf to; that can draw us in of its own power.

"For character, let me mimic the narrator of Dostoevski's *Notes from the Underground*, a man who, at times, expresses perverse sentiments we might find similar to our own."

I am a sick man . . . I am a spiteful man. I am an unpleasant man. I think my liver is diseased. However, I don't know beans about my disease, and I am not sure what is bothering me. I don't treat it and never have, though I respect medicine and doctors. Besides, I am extremely superstitious, let's say sufficiently so to respect medicine. (I am educated enough to not be superstitious, but I am.) No, I refuse to treat it out of spite. You will probably not understand that. Well, but *I* understand it. Of course, I can't explain to you just whom I am annoying in this case by my spite. I am perfectly well aware that I cannot "get even" with the doctors by not consulting them. I know better than anyone that I thereby injure only myself and no one else. But still, if I don't treat it, it is out of spite. My liver is bad, well then—let it get even worse!

"People's perverseness, peculiarity, oddness, eccentricity arouse our curiosity. We want to know more, what it might lead to. This singular voice and these strange ideas grab us.

"Next I'll read the opening of Charles Dickens' *Hard Times* and his stylistic description of a square classroom and its square headmaster who spouts a square curriculum."

"Now, what I want is Facts. Teach these boys and girls nothing but Facts. Facts alone are wanted in life. Plant nothing else and root out everything else. You can only form the minds of reasoning animals upon Facts: nothing else will ever be of any service to them. This is the principle on which I bring up my own children, and this is the principle on which I bring up these children. Stick to Facts, sir!"

The scene was a plain, bare, monotonous vault of a schoolroom, the speaker's square forefinger emphasized his observations by underscoring every sentence with a line on the schoolmaster's sleeve. The emphasis was helped by the speaker's square wall of a forehead, which had its eyebrows for its base, while his eyes found commodious cellarage in two dark caves, overshadowed by the wall. The emphasis was helped by the speaker's mouth, which was wide, thin, and hard set. The emphasis was helped by the speaker's voice, which was inflexible, dry, and dictatorial. The emphasis was helped by the speaker's hair, which bristled on the skirts of his bald head, a plantation of firs to keep the wind from its shining surface, all covered with knobs, like the crust of a plum pie, as if the head had scarcely warehouse-room for the hard facts stored inside. The speaker's obstinate carriage, square coat, square legs, square shoulders—nay, his very neckcloth, trained to take him by the throat with an unaccommodating grasp, like a stubborn fact, as it was—all helped the emphasis.

"The repetition here, as in Hemingway's opening, is very effective, underscoring the emphasis—the squareness, the facts, the dictatorial oppressiveness made absurd. You can feel the writer's enjoyment as he makes fun of this self-righteous, puffed up know-it-all.

"How would you like someone like that as your principal? Who knows, maybe you've had a teacher like that? I know myself how school can be trying, with all those facts. For example, I'm sure it was part of the reason that the young narrator of the next piece, Holden Caulfield, dropped out of prep school. At the beginning of J. D. Salinger's *The Catcher in the Rye*, Holden tells us—or possibly a psychiatrist—"

> If you really want to hear about it, the first thing you'll probably want to know is where I was born, and what my lousy childhood was like, and how my parents were occupied and all before they had me, and all that David Copperfield kind of crap, but I don't feel like going into it, if you want to know the truth. In the first place, that stuff bores me, and in the second place, my parents would have about two hemorrhages apiece if I told anything pretty personal about them. They're quite touchy about anything like that, especially my father. They're nice and all—I'm not saying that—but they're also touchy as hell. Besides, I'm not going to tell you my whole goddam autobiography or anything. I'll just tell you about this madman stuff that happened to me around last Christmas just before I got pretty rundown and had to come out here and take it easy.

"Now here's a contemporary voice you're probably familiar with, of a teenager near your age, not without a little sass or irreverence, rich in colloquialisms and slang and sometime swearing. Though the voice seems typical, it is, at the same time, the vehicle that reveals the boy's psychology. That is, his voice and language are more than a manner of speaking. They are a way of seeing the world. Think: How will your characters speak the world?

"For plot I'll read the beginning of Franz Kafka's *Metamorphosis*, whose protagonist wakes one morning finding himself transformed into 'a monstrous vermin,' or cockroach."

> When Gregor Samsa woke up one morning from unsettling dreams, he found himself changed in his bed into a monstrous vermin. He was lying on his back as hard as armor plate, and when he lifted his head a little, he saw his vaulted brown belly, sectioned by arch-shaped ribs, to whose dome the cover, about to slide off completely, could barely cling. His many legs, pitifully thin compared to the size of the rest of him, were waving helplessly before his eyes.

"Yuck!"

"Like oddness of character, oddness of event also grabs. It is more often used in other media, like the movies.

"This next opening is from John Dominis Holt's *Waimea Summer*. It take place during the early part of this century, on the Big Island, up country, where some Hawaiians claim the presence of spirits remains the strongest. All the good and evil of their ancestral past seem as natural as some of the vindictive winds that visit these islands. Here, more than anywhere else I've visited, I remain sometimes wary, having heard stories from Big Island old-timers, my wife's uncle especially—and I know that you've heard them, too, maybe from your grandparents. Let me ask you this: How many of you or your relatives have had your house blessed by either a Hawaiian priest or a holy person of another faith—or both?" Many hands are raised. "They bless new hotels and other commercial buildings, too, don't they? And there are so many things that are sacred: stones, plots, walls, fishing and burial grounds . . . And the first generations of Chinese and Japanese immigrants, whose universe was populated with ancestors and gods and spirits of all sorts, were careful not to offend, having themselves witnessed the spiritual presences that shared the islands with them. Which makes me shiver. Anyway, let me read Holt's opening."

> At four in the morning, three days after I arrived on the Big Island to pay my first visit to Waimea, I awoke and was gripped by a sense of doom and apprehension, even before I could shake off the lingering remnants of sleep. All the things I'd heard said about Waimea being a place of ghosts and black magic seemed now to be true. Before this, the excitement of being at last in this place my father had so endlessly extolled, my explorations around the once handsome house and garden, and exhaustion had successfully kept back the age-old sensitivity Hawaiians have to the world of spirits. But this morning, in my darkened room, a chilling sense of portent and unseen things being everywhere had complete hold of me. The fourposter in which I'd felt quite comfortable for three nights now seemed forbidding. The handsome quilt of the breadfruit design, which had been specially granted, felt now like a shroud.

"I like this because of its subtlety: the possible presence of something malign or threatening, the premonition of evil, of something unknown and invisible yet palpable, which makes me afraid. As I said, you've heard some of these stories yourselves from relatives and friends, and some of them ring with a certain truth. Let's face it, people like scary stories, however difficult they may be to write.

"Shucks! We're running out of time. I wanted to read to you my two favorite beginnings, one from Herman Melville's *Moby-Dick* and the other from William Faulkner's novella 'The Bear.' Oh, well, next time . . . You know what. I've changed my mind. I'll tell you what to do when you come back from break."

"Okay. Now, look over all your writings and exercises and your other doodlings, and pick out the three pieces you find most interesting. As you go through your writings, keep in mind the possibility of combining some of the writings into one. You don't have to, of course. It's just another option. Once you've decided on your three, get together with another student and decide which of the three promises the best story. When you've decided, you can sketch out the rest of the story or work on your beginning. That's up to you. In any case, the first draft of your story or personal experience is due on Monday."

"MONDAY?!"

"Monday. *Capisce?*"

Day 9: Early Revision

On Monday, whether their first draft is complete or not—their word-processed drafts run from a page or so to three-and-a-half pages—I tell them the following:

> You will rewrite, by hand, the first page of your story.
>
> **First,** you will rewrite your story, beginning it at a new place and time.
>
> **Second,** if you wrote your original draft in the first person, you will write your revised version in the third person—and vice versa: if you wrote your original draft in the third person, you will rewrite your draft in the first person.
>
> **Third,** you may want to look over your original, because once you start, I want you to turn it over and focus your attention on your new draft.

These three revision strategies ensure in most cases that students will create a substantive alternative against which they can compare their original. It is not as important that their second and third versions be superior to the original as it is that they be different from the original—in the process of writing the new versions, students will generate new information, which they often use. And switching points of view and starting their story in a new way shows students the possibility of what else their story could be. Rewriting their work from memory helps them overcome the tyranny of the original draft.

The revision process focuses on things global, *what to write* and *how best to write it.*

When most of the students have written about three-fourths of a page, I tell them, "Stop writing. If you want to complete the page, that's up to you." And I give them these instructions:

> **First,** I want you to take out another page and rewrite your story from the *first-person-witness* point of view. That is, the person telling the story is *in* the story but is *not* the main character. The main character is the person the witness is writing about. You can choose another character in the story to be your narrator, or you can invent another character to tell the story.
>
> **Second,** I want you to start your story in a new way.

"There are innumerable ways to acquire information about people. You could start with a tombstone inscription, a criminal record, a report card, a résumé, a letter or diary that somehow falls into your hands, a health record, a newspaper article—almost any kind of document will do. Or you could be spying on a person; or hear about the person from a conversation at a restaurant; or bump into the person on the street or over the Internet or over the phone as a wrong number. Again, do not look at any of your previous drafts. I want you to start this page now. If you don't complete it in class, you may complete it for homework tonight."

Let me repeat: This early point-of-view revision not only offers students three different ways to tell a story, but the revisions also result in greater data, information, and possibilities, some of which students will use when concentrating on the draft they intend to flesh out.

There are four things I must constantly do, then: help students create story options for themselves; help them to recognize the various ways they can speak; expose them to the various ways stories can be told; and draw their attention to the tools that writers use in crafting their stories. To read as writers do is to learn about and appreciate literature.

Day 10: Group Work

On the tenth day, in small groups of three or four, the students read to each other the three versions of their first page, which are of equivalent length. Group members inform the writer which of the three versions they think promises the best story. At the end of this activity, about half-way through the period, I have the students expand and develop the version of their choice, using information from their other two pages. I tell them, "Keep us abreast of the physical setting. Make us see." This work is completed for homework.

Day 11: Feedback, and the Checklist

The next day, for three-quarters of the period, students exchange their second drafts with each other. When they are done with one paper, they stand and look around to see who else is done in order to exchange drafts again. They do not see their own drafts until I call an end to the activity. I have them respond to their classmates' papers by writing who, what, where, when, why, and how questions in the margin and by writing their final suggestions on the attached sheet to the drafts. The focus of this circle revision is on developing their pieces.

In the last part of the period, students look over the responses and begin making changes. Just before the period ends, I give them a checklist to help them work up their third drafts. I emphasize the first three items on the list especially:

1. The pace of the writing is too quick; you need to slow down and take your time at important parts.

2. Too much of the story seems to take place in the dark; you must keep the reader aware of the surroundings: light, air, climate, objects, people, time, smells, sounds, etc.
3. The problem or conflict is too easily resolved; you have to make the story more complex, perhaps add complications.
4. Who are these people? Is the main character a three-dimensional person?
5. You have no dialogue, or need more. People reveal themselves when they speak. Got an accent? A style?
6. Do you use similes and metaphors? Do you create sensory experiences?

Day 12: The Reading Code, and More Feedback

On the last day before Christmas break, for the first ten minutes, I repeat at the chalkboard the quick punctuation lesson I gave during the poetry unit.

"Remember, punctuation is a mutually agreed upon reading code: The various marks, the stops and pauses, help your audience read your story the way you want them to read it. Some of you have yet to try some of these. Now, you can look back in your marble notebook at your notes, or you can take notes again. Either way I'm going to be moving fast. Punctuation waits for no man."

First: The period, question mark, and exclamation point. These you know, but again, *one* exclamation point is always enough—Mia!
Second: The semicolon. This joins complete sentences; oftentimes the second sentence follows the first fairly quickly. The test is how you might speak the sentences aloud. [I write quick examples on the board.] The second use is when you make a list of items and one or more of the items contains internal punctuation, like a comma. So that the comma does not confuse your reader, separate the items with semicolons.
Third: The colon. Use the colon to signal the reader that one of the following is coming next: (1) a list, (2) a definition, (3) an explanation, or (4) an important or long quotation.
Fourth: Parentheses. Think of it this way: Whatever goes inside the parentheses is less important than what you say outside the parentheses. It's like talking from the side of your mouth.
Fifth: The dash. This is the opposite of the parentheses: whatever you say between dashes is more important than what's outside them. The dash is also used to show sudden changes of thought or when you want to show people interrupting each other in dialogue.
Sixth: The ellipsis. Three dots signal that words have been omitted or that there is a pause.
Seventh: Italics. You know, words that lean sideways? If you were handwriting, you'd show this through the use of an underline. Use italics to emphasize

the words and phrases you would by changing the pitch of your voice when speaking. That's the test: Say the sentence aloud. Also use italics when signifying the title of a book or magazine.

Eighth: The apostrophe. I won't say much here because it doesn't help. Use it, for the love of man, to show possession and to show that letters are missing in a contraction.

Ninth: The hyphen. Use it especially for compound adjectives and when breaking up a word by syllables when the whole word won't fit at the end of a line.

Tenth: The comma. As I have said before, command the comma and you rule the world. I won't go into all the uses for the comma—just the ones that bug me:

1. Use both a comma and a conjunction when joining two sentences. A lot of you, when connecting sentences, use one or the other, failing to use both, which causes a little hitch in our reading. In that instance, your use of the "and" or comma by itself tells us that what follows the "and" or the comma is part of the preceding sentence. But when we read what follows, we find out *you lie!* The words that follow make an entirely new sentence.

2. In a list of three or more items, they are separated by commas. Never use a comma when there are only two items.

3. Separate an appositive with commas. For example, the stuff after "John" is an appositive: "John, the ugliest guy in school, smiled." Think of the commas as an equals sign.

4. In dialogue, use commas to separate the names, nicknames, and labels people are addressed by.

5. Use commas to separate interjections like "hey" and transitional words like "however."

"Now, take out your third draft and write on the top of it what you want your reader to feel or think. Try to be as specific as you can. I want you to work with someone who you know has *not* read your work thus far.

"As a reader, respond to your partner by telling him or her *the degree you feel or think what the writer intends.* If you do not feel or think what the writer intends as strongly as the writer would like, talk about how the story could be changed to better fulfill the writer's goal. Any questions?"

Just before the period ends, I tell them, "Remember, final drafts are due upon your return from the holiday break. I also—*take this down, please*—I also want you to attach to the back of your story a sheet that lists the two or three things you want me to evaluate as I read and grade your paper.

"For those of you who still want feedback during the break—and that should be most of you—come up and get this handout":

Getting Outside Feedback from Friends, Family, and Others

Principles Validated by Class Experience

1. The most powerful revisionary force is other people.
2. All people are fallible and perceptive in their own ways.
3. The more feedback you receive from various people, the more options for change, development, and improvement are available to you.
4. The kind of feedback you want is often determined by how much you have worked on a piece and how you feel about the piece. After a while, you will know *when* to get feedback and *what* specifically to ask your readers.

Suggested Ways to Obtain Feedback

- Opening Up the Whole Piece
  When the work is not yet complete, say to your reader, "Please place dots next to sentences, lines, phrases, or words *that you have questions about or do not understand.*" After reviewing the response, you may or may not want to talk to your reader; that will depend on *your* understanding.
- Opening Up Parts
  When the work is not yet complete—yet you know what parts you feel uncomfortable about or suspect are weak—identify those parts for your reader beforehand and ask your reader, "How would you develop, re-work, or refine these parts if this piece were yours?"
- Clarifying the Whole
  After you feel generally comfortable about your piece, ask your reader, "What places make you stumble, hesitate, or stop in your reading? Please note those places with dots."

A Note to the Reader

Hopefully, you will have the time to give the writer what he or she needs. *Following the advice below will prevent you and the writer from entering into a teacher-student relationship, thus preserving your personal one.*

1. As a relative or helpful friend, allow yourself to be directed by the writer's wishes.
2. Simply respond with what you honestly think or feel, *confining* your responses to the question asked of you. Of course, if the writer queries you further, respond as you will.
3. That you are limited to reading the writer's piece in a particular way is precisely what the writer wants.
4. That your response is subjective and personal is *fine*.

6

Speech Writing

"Friends, Romans, countrymen . . ."
—*Mark Antony in* **Julius Caesar,** *W. Shakespeare*

One of the traditions at our school reaches back more than 120 years, to the death of graduate William Damon, who died at the age of twenty-two of typhoid fever in 1878. During his senior year in 1874, William was the single best speaker of his graduating class. To honor his son, his grief-stricken father, Reverend Samuel Damon, a Punahou trustee, donated $750 to the school for a scholarship in William's name. This was the origin of the Damon Speech Contest, which is held annually at both seventh- and eighth-grade assemblies in the spring.

This means that thirty classes of 25 students each, totaling 750 students, spend five to six weeks writing, rehearsing, and delivering speeches to their classes in a mini-contest to determine who will represent the class in the final contest. Although most students dread the performance—you can hear them groan—all the students profit from the experience: Seventh graders promise themselves they'll do better in eighth grade, and eighth graders demonstrate that they have indeed improved upon their seventh-grade performance.

"Please come up and get the guidelines for the Damon Speech."

"When do we have to do it?"

"Soon. As you read the guidelines with me, you'll notice that it's addressed to teachers. You might as well have the same thing."

Damon Speech Contest Guidelines

Topic: The Damon Speech will deal with a *problem, concern,* or *opinion,* and will have a *serious intent or goal.* A teacher may disqualify a speech from the finals if he or she deems the subject matter inappropriate for an assembly.

Length: The target length for speeches is *three minutes.* There may be some variations around this target length, but *no teacher will permit any student to go to the finals with a speech over four min-*

utes. Speeches over four minutes will be disqualified by the judges.

Humor:	Humor may be used to emphasize a point or points, but the speech shall not consist of a stand-up comedy routine.
Costumes:	Costumes are not permitted.
Props:	Props are not permitted.
3-by-5s:	Three- by five-inch note cards are optional. There shall be no reading of standard-size or larger papers.
Mic:	The microphone will be kept on its stand. Contestants will not be allowed to walk around the stage with the microphone.

Process of Selecting Finalists Within Each English Classroom:

Each teacher will make the selection process clear to students before deciding on the class finalist.

In-Class Presentation Dates:_____

[This year, you'll begin giving speeches in class on Monday, January 25th, during the second half of the double period, and end on the 29th, Friday. Write those dates in now, please.]

You Will Be Evaluated by the Teacher and Your Classmates:

[So please—*do not lose this sheet.* The front row and the back row will evaluate students by alternating Criteria I and Criteria II. Look, I'll repeat this later.]

Criteria I: *Quality of Presentation:*
[*Criteria* is the plural of *criterion,* which is like a standard against which we measure something—in this case, your speech performance. The first criterion is:]

1. *Projection/Pronunciation.* Separate consonants can be distinctly distinguished from the back of the room.

[What does this mean? EMPHASIZE YOUR LIP MOVEMENT! Not only that. Some of you soft-spoken folks will have to go home and practice screaming in your closets. You know who I mean.]

2. *Poise.* Your body is under control; it does not draw attention away from your speech.

[DiBella, you have to get that knee under control! You cannot give your speech in the same manner that you read your poetry. You can't pretend that this is a hoe-down.]

3. *Personality.* Your presence and voice give impact to your words.

[Some of you are so deadpan, so stone-faced, that you'll deaden the audience too. You must move more than just your lips. You have to animate the whole face—the chin, the cheeks, the nose, the eyes and the area around them, the eyebrows, the forehead. Maybe just before you give your speech, you can lubricate your face. *These three criteria are the most important.* If your speech is brilliant, containing significant ideas that might benefit the whole human race, but you deliver it so poorly that nobody can hear you or understand you or you are decidedly boring, what you offer amounts to nothing. You are the faulty wire between two telephones; the static on the radio that kills your music. On the other hand, let's say you've written a mediocre speech that really doesn't amount to much, yet you deliver it with such style and verve, with such a melodious voice, that it appears meaningful and people are swayed or impressed by your charisma, your confidence, your language, or your wit. You have seen examples of such performances given by local politicians—even by President Clinton. And you will see examples of this later in a video I will show you of former contestants at the Damon Speech assembly.]

Criteria II: Quality of Substance

1. The *thesis* is significant.

[The *thesis* is the opinion you assert to be true, or the claim that you make about the way to solve a problem, or a statement about how something ought or ought not be. And that thesis is somehow important to the rest of us.]

2. The *argument* is easy to follow.

[What I mean by *argument* is not the combat you wage in the battlefield of the kitchen over whose turn it is to do the dishes. What I mean is the reasoning in your speech or paper. The question is this: Is the argument easy to follow from one point to the next? Does the whole body seem connected? Think of it this way: The thesis is the hook that hangs on the wall, and the rest of the paper is the coat that hangs on the hook. In some way, everything is somehow connected to the hook.]

3. The *argument* is *persuasive* or you make the audience *care*.

[You provide compelling evidence via personal experience, testimony from experts, statistics, historical facts, other sources of research, and logical reasoning. And you present your findings in a vivid manner, making us see through your verbal pictures, through your use of images, similes, metaphors, analogies, examples, anecdotes, etc.]

"Just as you used what you learned in poetry writing for narrative writing, you can use what you learned from poetry and narrative for argumentative writing.

"Okay, everyone take out a piece of paper and brainstorm topics you might like to give a speech on. In a little while we'll stick some of them up on the blackboard." I give them maybe five minutes. "Ready? Everyone will give the class at least one topic. Malia? Rob? Could you two write the topics on the board? Just alternate as you hear them read by the students. But let me give you two to start with." And the board begins to grow crowded:

The Homeless in Downtown Honolulu
Why My Parents Don't Put a Punahou School Sticker on Our Rear Window
Make Foreign Language Optional
Eliminate Grading in Bishop Hall
Anorexia Nervosa
Capital Punishment

"Ugh."
"These last two will require some library research. By the way, do you mean here in Hawaii?"

Banning the Dress Code
Child Abuse
False Advertising
Gay Rights
Hawaiian Sovereignty

"You for it?"
"Yes."

Cafeteria Food
Banning the Giving of Christmas Presents in Bishop Hall
Zits
Mililani Trask

"What about her?"
"You know, what she said about Senator Inouye, calling him a one-armed bandit."

Lower Tuition at Punahou
Rush-Hour Traffic
Year-Round School for Punahou
Abortion Rights
Designer Clothes
How Cliques Are Good
Lower the Voting Age
Sibling Rivalry
Drop P.E.
Parental Pressure
Pornography
Legalizing Marijuana
Professional Wrestling
Dating

"What about it?"
"Eighth graders should be allowed to."
"You're not allowed to?"
"No. And neither are a lot of kids."

The Importance of Flowers in the Home
Video Games
Swearing
Dealing with Death
Overpaid Athletes

"Underpaid teachers."

Divorce
Pidgin English
What You Have to Do to Be Popular
Assigning Less Homework

"Mr. Holbrook, a former math teacher, called it HomeFun."

Cheating in School
Tourists
Tattoos

Student Abuse
The Movie Rating System
Dirty Bathrooms
Raising a Parrot
Backpacks
Rap
Picking on the Portuguese
Hate Crimes
Clinton
Eliminate Study Hall
TV Violence
The Problem with the Internet
Chapel Should Be Optional
Teenage Killers
Rumors
The Importance of Travel
The Dangers of Deodorant

"Really?"

Candy

"That's enough for now. I know you have other topics on your list that you haven't volunteered. Another thing: no one *owns* a topic. If you see something on the board that interests you, put it on your list.

"Now, take out your marble notebooks and freewrite on three topics, say, for three-quarters of a page each. Just freewrite everything that comes to mind, everything you know. At the end of each writing, construct a thesis statement that begins 'I think that' or 'I believe that.' And make sure your thesis is a complete sentence and not a question. Lastly, beware of absolute statements that contain *all, everyone, no one, always, all the time,* or words that imply the same thing. Rarely will such statements be true.

"Begin now and—what time is it?—complete it for homework. In the second half of the double period we'll do something else."

After the bell rings, signaling the end of the break, I show a video of past contestants in the speech contest. We rate them according to the criteria on the handout, focusing primarily on delivery. For the most part, their delivery is polished; students' criticism is directed at the quality and substance of some of the speeches. Though the students can't agree on who gave the best speech, they can agree that all contestants delivered their speeches in an effective manner.

For the remainder of the period, we focus on the speech "It's a Date!" written by Inga Earle, an eighth grader.

These personal ads are so weird! Look at this one: "Macho man seeks attractive, crazy lady for sharing, caring, and daring."

Or how about this one: "Divorced White female, 38, blonde, wants loving relationship. 200 pounds and losing."

Or even this one: "Sassy grandma says, take me out to romantic dinners, shows, and the beach."

All of these are from the column in the newspaper called "It's a Date!" Sure, these ads are entertaining to read, but I think if you take a closer look, they're also a gold mine of information about what adult Americans are looking for in a relationship.

"Yes, that's her thesis. Now, what do you expect the writer will do in the rest of her paper? Melissa?"

"She'll tell us what adults are looking for."

"Do you believe that she can tell us for sure, just by reading these particular ads?"

"Sure, why not? They're adults."

"Well, let's hope she gives us a wide enough sampling. Adam?"

"I like the way she begins."

"Why?"

"It captures your attention."

"Yes, it does. Right away. Journalists call this the *lead*. I'll give you a handout later that lists several kinds."

Bishop Hall girls are always saying things like, "Oh, he's soo cute!" But mature women write ads that say: *D W F enjoys beach, movies and sunsets. Wanting tall, financially secure male for romance and a lasting relationship.*

"What is the writer doing in these two sentences? Beth?"

"She's comparing Bishop girls to mature women."

"Right. She connects her topic to her classmates—to her audience—involving them in her talk. She makes them use themselves as a reference point."

As I see it, the three key words are *financial*, *romance*, and *lasting*. Notice that money comes first. Then comes romance. Women are still looking for love, as long as he's got the bucks.

"By the way, is money an important consideration for you folks in choosing a girl- or boyfriend? . . . No takers, I see. Liane?"

"Well, it is important."

"*How* important? I mean, where would it come in your list of traits if you were to go steady with someone? . . .Okay, let me put it this way: What traits would come before it?"

"A nice bod!" says Mike.

"Very funny," says Liane. "He has to be kind. He has to be smart and have a sense of humor. Someone thoughtful and good looking, too."

"As I said: A good bod!"

"Well, that eliminates you, Michael," I say.

"*Oh, please,*" says Liane.

"Let's go on."

The third key word is *lasting* relationship. Women want sincere men who are willing to commit to them, not ones just out for casual sex. It's interesting that the age and looks of a man do not seem to be very important to adult women.

On the other hand, a typical ad for men is: *Tall, dark, divorced Polynesian male seeking attractive, fun-loving young pussycat.* Focus on the words *attractive* and *young.* Men want looks, youth, and sexiness in a woman. They also frequently ask for ones who have a good sense of humor and who love sports and thrilling times.

"Right on," says Mike.

"Let me ask you, Mike. Would you, as an eighth grader, go out with a seventh grader?"

"Sure, why not?"

"A sixth grader?"

"A *sixth* grader? No way!"

"How about a ninth grader?"

"Maybe."

"A tenth grader?"

"I don't know."

"What about a senior?" He shakes his head.

"In the next paragraph, the writer analyzes the ads for gays. So how has she organized the body of her paper?"

"By gender," says Nicole.

"And gender preference," adds Natalie.

"Good. Everybody see that?"

And finally, how about gays? "It's a Date!" has columns named: Men looking for Women, and Women looking for Men. But they don't call it the gay and lesbian column: Gays looking for Gays: They smooth it over by calling it: Alternative Lifestyles.

Here's a typical ad: *Local Asian Male seeking straight acting, feminine Single Male. Must be adventurous and clean. No drugs or kids.* Think about "straight acting" and "no drugs." Obviously, many gays still feel they have to hide their sexual orientation. Also, this shows us that gays are very scared of getting AIDS from partners who use intravenous drugs.

I have a friend who was recently telling me that she is depressed about her nonexistent love life.

"Note how the writer brings us back to kids her age in her final paragraph."

Well, if we had a similar column in Bishop Hall's newspaper, her troubles would be over. I might even consider putting in an ad myself. How about: *14 year old, single, white female, no kids, non-smoker, seeks cute financially secure male, 13–15, to take her to the 8th grade dance. Sincere only. Call Inga. I'll be waiting!*

{Time: 3:15}

"What do you think of her concluding paragraph?"

"I think it's fun and pretty cool," says Adam.

Yeah," says Tia. "She sticks in some of the stuff that mature women want and what she wants, too, and repeats stuff like *no kids*."

"Note also that, at the end, she includes the time. She had her sister time her as she practiced it. Though her speech may look short, her pace of delivery matched her manner of speaking. And considering her topic and audience and her *intention*, her manner of speaking was very much conversational. There is no mistake that she was speaking to us and wanted to amuse us, while offering us a few insights on the way adults think. That is, what you *intend* for your speech will help you determine the *manner* in which you speak to us. Obviously, if your message is a more serious one than Inga's, and you want us to take action on it—like petition the government—your manner of speaking would probably be more formal and intense.

"Finally, you can use Inga's paper as an approximate measure of how long your speech should be, so as not to exceed the four-minute limit. As a general rule, do not go beyond two and a half pages, typed.

"Now, what is the homework again? Rachel?"

"Ah . . . let me look . . . to freewrite on three topics."

"Kainoa?"

"And write a thesis statement at the end of each."

"I have that, too," says Rachel. "And three-quarters of a page for each."

"You got it. Michael! Your face tells me you *don't*. You better hook up with either Kainoa or Rachel before you go to your next class. *Capisce?*"

"*Yeah*, I got it."

The next day, I put the students into small groups to share their three theses. Most, favoring only two, will read only those. Group members say which thesis seems to promise the most interesting speech. Students who come to a decision and feel confident in the phrasing of their thesis begin fleshing out the speech at their desks or at the classroom computers. If those three computers are taken, students head to the computer center, where they can access the Internet, or to the library; or they use the school telephone to connect with agents, officers, experts, or others in the know; or they simply bounce from one student or another to begin their research through a survey. I tell them this before they begin:

> Before anyone makes a move, you might want to take down some of what I have to say. You all have a thesis, or a thesis you want to revise. With either, you can begin to develop your paper, or begin to search for data, or do both. But, first, you must look over what you already have—a thesis *and* a freewrite (however short it may be)—and question what you have written. Remember: The hints to how to develop your paper exist in what you have already written. The questions you pose will probably point you in the right directions.

For the remainder of the period and the next two classes, I respond to students who are uncertain about their theses. This can be time-consuming, especially with students who don't like their thesis and find little interest in the other topics they copied from the board. This means sitting down with the kids and helping them think of another thesis by asking them about their interests, difficulties, problems, achievements, and concerns—their life, really.

Students must also search for another thesis when they discover that theirs is not a thesis at all, but an assertion of a fact: "I think that cigarette smoking is bad for your health." Other times, given the time limit, the thesis is unrealistic: "I think that God exists." Sometimes the thesis is of questionable significance: "I feel that alarm clocks are disturbing."

More frequently a thesis is too broad: "I think that people are cruel to animals."

"All people?" I can help them qualify the numbers.

". . . . ."

"Most people?"

"A lot."

"A lot of people are cruel to animals," I repeat. "Where? In Scotland? In Nigeria? Where?" I can help them narrow their thesis in terms of space.

"In America."

"Where? In Vermont? New Mexico? How do you know?"

"In Hawaii. You hear stories on the news about cockfighting and how they put knives on the chicken's feet. And stories about abused pets, dogs especially."

"Do you have pets?"

"Three dogs, a rabbit, fish, two turtles, two finches, and a cockatiel," she says, smiling.

"Wow. I suppose you help take care of them, too. Let me ask you: Do you think, because of what you've heard on the news, that cruelty to animals is increasing in Hawaii, or has remained the same?" I can help them narrow their thesis in terms of time.

"I don't know. I've just been hearing a lot of it on the news recently."

"You could call the Hawaii Humane Society. They might know."

"Can I use the phone now?"

"In a sec. What do you mean by 'cruelty'? If you forget to feed your pets, is that cruelty? What if you don't play with them? By the way, are there laws against animal cruelty?" *I can help them define the pivotal terms of their thesis.*

"I think so."

"Okay, why don't you write down some of the questions before you call."

Two days later, after the students have accumulated some data or typed up at least a half-page, I go over the following handout with them or have them do the exercise alone at their seats, depending on the schedule and how far along the students are in their writing.

Principles in Developing a Point

The following uses hypothetical or inaccurate facts, but this, for our purposes, is unimportant. Our problem is this: What general principles can we discover in our analysis of how a single point may be developed? Specifically:

A. How can we move from Step 1 (below) to Step 2, from Step 2 to Step 3, and so forth?

B. Is the movement from one step to another similar?

C. If so, what principle seems to govern that movement?

1. Cram school students do well in school.

2. Most cram school students succeed academically in school.

3a. Most cram school students succeed academically in school, having accumulated grade point averages of 3.1 or better in courses recognized by major universities.

OR (=many possible strategies)

3b. Most cram school students succeed academically in school because only the best students are selected by the admissions committee.

4a. Most cram school students succeed academically in school, having accumulated grade point averages of 3.1 or better in courses recognized by major universities. That is, the student has earned a B or better in English, math, science, social studies, and foreign language.

4b. Most cram school students succeed academically in school because only the best students are selected by the admissions committee. The committee—composed of school officers and faculty representing the various academic disciplines—evaluates the student applicants according to their academic records, standardized test scores, diversity of interests, and contributions to their schools.

5a. Most cram school students succeed academically in school, having accumulated grade point averages of 3.1 or better in courses recognized by major universities. That is, the student has earned a B or better in English, math, science, social studies, and foreign language. What the B means in any course is that the student has good command of the intellectual skills demanded by the discipline and is aware of its principle ideas and theories; and, therefore, is able to demonstrate better-than-average mastery over the subject.

In English, this means that the student is able to . . . and knows . . .

In math, this student can . . .

In science, . . .

(Etc.)

5b. Most cram school students succeed academically in school because only the best students are selected by the admissions committee. The committee—composed of school officers and faculty representing the various academic disciplines—evaluates the student applicants according to their academic records, standardized test scores, diversity of interests, and contributions to their schools. Ideally, the committee is looking for students who have acquired a B+ average or better in their academic subjects and scored in the eighty-fifth percentile in both the verbal and math portions on the SSAT; who have a range of serious interests, from playing a musical instrument and participating in organized sports to participating on the debate team, the dance program, the computer club, and so forth; and who have performed volunteer service to the school in some capacity, from fund raising and work in student government, to monitoring, tutoring, campus clean-up, and so forth.

However, since most students are stronger in one area than another . . .

This goes fairly quickly when I read it aloud and we tackle the given problem as a class, underscoring the idea of questioning what one has already written in order to discover what more can be said, or needs to be said, in order for the writing to be sufficiently clear. The rest of the period, the students continue to write as they try to complete a first draft. They consult with each other as much as they consult with me.

The next day, the fourth day, I dictate the following points on complexity:

- You have considered the counterarguments to your thesis and show their weaknesses.
- You have considered various situations wherein your ideas are not valid.
- You have considered alternative ideas, variations that result from omitting or changing a part of an idea or from adding to the idea.
- You have considered how your ideas, if true or valid, may affect larger or lesser ideas.

Just before the bell rings, I tell the students, "Tomorrow, Friday, we'll begin hearing the leads to your speeches." I then give them a handout I've used since being a teaching assistant at the University of Hawaii, something I adapted from a handout given to me by a fellow TA.

Writing the Lead

Question: How do you write the introduction to your piece of writing?
Answer: Focus on an intriguing angle of your subject, the one you intend to develop in your story.

The *lead* serves four functions: It captures the audience's attention; it introduces the subject; it shows the direction and focus of your piece or your talk; and it sets the tone and tempo for the details to follow.

There are many different types of leads, sometimes found in combination. Here are ten of the most widely used types found in newspapers, magazines, and other publications:

News Lead

Found in straight news stories when the basic facts of an event must be given quickly. Contains at least some of the "5Ws and H": who, what, where, when, why, and how.

Example: Sandra Day O'Connor today won overwhelming approval from the Senate Judiciary Committee for her nomination to become the first woman on the Supreme Court. The vote was 17–0.

Direct Address

You talk to us using "you," trying to establish intimacy or community or identity with your audience.

Example: We've all been there. You know what I mean: The Hot Seat. When either Mom or Dad or both, in their not so subtle way, question you about the broken vase or the broken window or little Johnny's broken nose.

Question

One or more questions that lead naturally into your thesis.

Example: What I want to know is this: How many of you girls have ever taken the initiative and asked a boy to go steady? Not many. And how many of you were rejected? Again, not many. So most of you girls have no idea of the trauma boys go through and the courage it takes to approach you. Nor do you treat us very well when you turn us down—*by laughing in our faces!* I think Punahou should require classes on social training, making kids more sensitive to each other's feelings.

Striking Statement

Designed to startle the audience with an arresting fact or idea.

Example: Only God knows whether the new president of Chaminade's student body will get through his term, because 22-year-old Bob Frigault is dying of cancer.

Quotation Lead

Use when a person has said something colorful or striking. You could also begin by quoting someone famous or from a well-known book.

Example: The day after everyone had rested and eaten their fill, God said, "Let there be rock 'n' roll."

Anecdote Lead

This is a brief story, usually with a point. This lead is especially effective in personality sketches or personal experience accounts.

Example: A teacher at Waipahu Intermediate School was assigned a class of 17 boys, all of whom had told their school adviser that they were unable to read. Within a week, the teacher discovered that they all read the surfing news in the daily newspaper, and she built an entire reading program around it.

Narrative Lead

This differs from the anecdote lead in that it may not contain a punch line. It eases the audience into the piece by way of storytelling.

Example: Once upon a time there was a mild-mannered college professor who taught microbiology. He occasionally lectured to his students in pidgin, but on tests he was merciless about things like subject-verb agreement. "This might be Micro 101," he'd say. "But it is still a university." An observant student might have noticed a glint of mischief in the prof's eyes, behind black-rimmed glasses, a hint that Ozzie Bushnell wasn't just a college professor.

Descriptive Lead

The old saying "I'll draw you a picture" makes sense when applied to the lead. Vivid description makes the audience feel they are there with the writer. Specific facts, concrete details, and exact images help readers visualize what is happening.

Example: Almost every afternoon, after my mom backs the Toyota into the carport, I like to lean back against the warm hood and pause for a while, my book bag at my feet. Down our driveway lined with jasmine bushes and sprinkled with the white petals from the overhanging plumeria tree, I can see the ocean and the horizon and all the mingling pastels of dusk: blues, greens, apricots, and pale-red apples, pinks, lavenders, purples. And as usual everything seems to stop. The breeze. The sounds of birds and insects. Even the clouds and the ocean. And though it's been a long day, I feel happy.

Summary Statement

One or two sentences that summarize what the rest of the piece develops.

Example: What every household needs is an Amy Bowlen—a 14-year-old who is not only willing but able to put together a dinner party for 18 or take over the stove at mealtime.

Analogy

A comparison—often an image—used as description.

Example: A French philosopher once said that American society was like a glass of beer: foam on top, dregs on the bottom, but clear, settled brew in the middle.

We hear leads through class on Monday. I give the students feedback and begin working on their voices. By Thursday, most of the students have settled on their second or third drafts as their final. They come to class that day with three-by-five note cards on which they have transcribed their speeches, writing down key phrases from each paragraph to help them remember the substance. From here on out, to the middle of the third week, our attention focuses on performance.

As they rehearse together in the hall, focusing especially on body control, I work with individual students, showing them where they should stand and how they must take in the entire semicircle of their audience, moving their heads and making eye contact. But most of all I focus on their voices and the personality they project, because many seem to lack emotion. I tell them this:

Many of you need to know your speeches better. How in the world can you make eye contact with the audience when your eyeballs are locked at the tops of your eyes, or when you have that distant inward look because you're so consumed in trying to remember what to say that you forget us? Such behavior distracts us from your words and what you want to communicate. In fact, we come to feel the strain that you feel, when we should be feeling as bitter as you do about the unfair rules, or as sympathetic as you do for the boy who lost his sister, or as elated as you do after winning the soccer game.

Another thing, go home and put yourself on tape and follow along with your final draft. And every time you stumble or slur or rush certain words, put a dot on top of the word or phrase to remind you to take extra care with it. Then tape yourself again, as many times as necessary, until you have mastered those words. I did this myself when I had to give a speech a number of years ago. But it was easier for me, as it will be for our winner, because, when you are on stage before a large audience, the faces become a blur. But here in the classroom you'll have to make eye contact and contend with some faces that are funny looking.

On that Friday and for the rest of the following week, students deliver their speeches, while the rest of the class and I evaluate them according to the given criteria.

The front row will focus on Criteria I; the back row on Criteria II. You will switch criteria with each speaker. In addition to rating the speaker from first through fourth, with fourth being the highest, I want you to comment on one thing you found effective and on one thing you wished the speaker had done. At the end of the class, give your slips to the right speaker. The day after you give your speech, submit to me a learning log with the average grade for each criterion and your overall average. Also, write up your feelings about the entire process and the overall experience, from brainstorming topics to delivering your speech to hearing the speeches of your classmates. Do you think it was worthwhile?

According to their logs, the most difficult part of the experience is, of course, delivering their speeches in front of their classmates. Otherwise, they are very positive about their experience (many mentioning how they enjoyed hearing the speeches of others), and they are generally pleased about their individual performance. Most important, it becomes clearer to them what they have to work on in the future in order to improve as speakers.

7

The Function Paper

Perception is imagination here.
—Jordan Harrison (Grade 8)

The function paper is basically a thesis paper. Individual students present to the class a first draft on an assigned chapter of *To Kill a Mockingbird*, asserting why the writer included the chapter in the novel and arguing the validity of the assertion. A student might claim, "One of the functions of Chapter 1 is to introduce readers to the community of Maycomb. This is important because, through its people, we can understand what they value and how they judge others, like Boo Radley, the principal object of the children's fascination." The student would then, in the rest of the paper, argue the claim's validity, drawing on the text and other means of persuasion and elucidation. The class and I give each student feedback to improve the paper before submitting a final draft.

On the first day, I tell my students the following:

Never again will you experience a novel at such a leisurely pace—a chapter or two per class. High school English classes and college classes, too, won't have the time to examine every chapter of a book. They don't meet as a class as often as we do, and there are just too many books you're required to read to have time to do that. But those teachers *will* expect you to read with some sensitivity.

And they will expect you to know at least the rudiments of writing a thesis paper, where—as in your Damon Speech—you assert an opinion and argue its truth or validity. It's the kind of paper that you'll be asked to write for the rest of your academic life.

Others—your boss, your coworkers, your clients—will expect you, an educated, intelligent adult, to produce clear and concise letters, explanations, memoranda, and proposals, especially if the substance of your writing is new, complicated, or controversial. And you must be able to do this as both a speaker and a writer. So what you are practicing here is important.

I then give them each a reading and paper schedule for *Mockingbird*. The first few entries for the entire class look like this:

Date	Chapter	Paper
M, 19	3	Malia
T, 20	4	Jay
W, 21	5	Jason

On any given date, the assigned student comes to class with the first draft of a function paper and delivers that paper to the class; the class and I give that student feedback. I tell them this:

> This is one day of school you cannot miss. You need the feedback. More important, not only is your responsibility to yourself in trying to write a good first draft, but you are also a kind of expert on the chapter, having studied it, so the class will need and appreciate your input.

To move the class along through Part One of the novel, I assign function papers to my most reliable and most skilled students first, using both them and their papers as examples for the rest of the class. That gives the others more time to grasp the paper expectations as well as the particular world of Maycomb County and its characters. On days that students are not assigned a paper, they must come to class with a thesis on the given chapter, so that, if the student who's giving a paper is working with a thesis that is of questionable value, the class will have at hand alternative theses from which the writer may choose a substitute.

However, whatever our initial misgivings, we don't give up on a student's thesis prematurely. The class—and this is *their* primary responsibility—"tests" the student's thesis by trying to support it through textual evidence and reasoning. At the end of the class, I give everyone, as an additional example, a copy of a relatively accomplished function paper on the chapter just discussed. In general, these example papers, written by former students, contain theses that are similar to those asserted by the current students.

On the back of the reading schedule is an explanation of the function paper and the form I expect them to follow. I read and talk about expectations using an example student paper written on another book, which I hand out next.

Function Paper
1. Your *title*:

   The Function of Chapter ___ in *To Kill a Mockingbird*
   Note that book titles are italicized. Skip four lines.

2. *Thesis* (your first two sentences):

>   One of the functions of Chapter ___ is to . . . . This is important because . . .

Your thesis (like your Damon Speech thesis) is an opinion statement that tells us what you will discuss and defend in your paper. The thesis—if you are clear and specific—will give you focus in your writing; it will guide you in what to include and exclude and suggest how best to organize your ideas and evidence. [I repeat orally: "As I said before, the thesis is the hook on the wall, and the rest of your paper is the coat that hangs on the hook. Everything in one way or another is connected to the hook."]

Ask: What is the purpose for including this chapter in the book? Is it to show something? Emphasize something? Provide something? Introduce a new character? Raise another problem or issue? Think of the function of a hammer: it is to pound nails and, at other times, to extract them. Chapters (and other kinds of writing or parts of writing) often serve several functions. Your job is to pick one and prove that it is true or that it is likely to be true. As a way to choose a function, ask yourself, What seems the major concern or conflict? What seems the dominant feeling or mood? What new things are established? What do most of the words center on? But you also might find some relatively small part in the chapter that seems significant to you and that you can talk about at some depth and length.

3. *Providing Textual Evidence*: You will need to quote from the chapter to support your claims or to show how you arrived at certain interpretations. When you do, you need to prepare your readers by telling them who is speaking to whom, and when, in terms of events. ["Saying that such-and-such happened on page 87 does not orient us; we don't remember numbers; we remember events."] For example, when the kid is peering out at the street from his cell, he sees Judge Holden, for the second time, and says to his prison-mate, "'_____,'" (p. 46).

>   Note that, in the example, when quoting dialogue (what the kid or another character says), you use quotations *within* quotations. Note also the end comma inside the quotation marks and, in parentheses, the page where the quotation is found (so that others may look it up for themselves). When quoting the narrator, just use regular quotation marks.
>
>   As a general rule: When quoting thirty words or more, set the entire passage off (see the example paper).

4. Write your paper in the present tense as though the characters are alive and what they do is occurring now. For example, "At the beginning of the chapter, Black Dog is wondering . . . He is sick of the life he is leading . . . We know that he is . . ." Use past tense when referring to events that occur

in earlier chapters. For example, "In the previous chapter, when he cursed his . . . , he did not . . . "

5. After you read your first draft to the class and receive feedback, submit a final draft to me within two school days.

The following function paper was written by Jessica Hui, a precocious seventh grader (who herself was inspired by an earlier seventh-grade example). Not wanting to prejudice my eighth graders, I always choose my first example from texts other than the one they will be studying and writing about. Although some of her diction and phrasing could be refined and be more precise (and though she doesn't follow all the advice set forth in the guideline), Jessica's accomplishment is exceptional, setting a high standard for my eighth graders. (For one thing, though she uses 14-point type, her paper is three and a half pages, single-spaced. So, for the sake of economy, both here and with my students, I cut portions to emphasize her use of quotation conventions.)

One of the functions of Chapter 3 in Robert Lipsyte's *The Contender* is to introduce Mr. Donatelli and the way of life he expects from everyone who enters into his management.

The dialogue between Donatelli and Alfred that ends Chapter 2 continues as Donatelli "grabbed one of Alfred's hands, studying first the knuckles, then the palms. 'Big hands. You'll grow some more,' he said. His voice was cold and rasping. He pointed at a battered white medical scale against a wall. 'Get on,'" (p. 21). From this quote, Donatelli seems to be a man of few words . . . never saying much more than what is essential. Donatelli continues to judge Alfred's physicality, as the narrator says, "as if he were inspecting a slab of meat in a butcher store," (p. 21). He seems to calculate every aspect that has to do with his profession, portraying him as very businesslike. I also find this simile fitting, as boxing is a punishing and bloody sport. Many descriptions of Donatelli emphasize his "pale blue eyes" and "square, boxlike body," (p. 22). I think that his having pale blue eyes suggests a colder personality, and his square stature hints at him being kind of conventional. A secondary definition for "square" is also a person who is old fashioned or conservative. Donatelli isn't the Generation X type trainer who goes for money and fame and all that. His goal is to teach his kids to be a contender. The narrator also tells us that Donatelli speaks with "no expression in his voice," (p. 210). This, once again paints him as cold, businesslike, and to the point. There is no superfluous emotion when he addresses Alfred.

She further builds upon Donatelli's character through Alfred's point of view, foregrounding a rich personality.

The second part of my thesis is that one of the functions of Chapter 3 is to describe the kind of life that is required from all who venture into Donatelli's world.

She then talks about three questions that Donatelli asks Alfred and what they imply about the world of boxing. Donatelli shows Alfred around the gym and some of the equipment, then rattles off all the things Alfred must do in his daily routine if he is serious about becoming a boxer.

Close to the end of the chapter, Alfred says, in reply to Donatelli's question on why he thinks he won't quit here like he quit school, "I want to be somebody . . . somebody special. A champion," (p. 25). As the narrator describes,

> Donatelli's thin lips tightened. "Everybody wants to be a champion. That's not enough. You have to start by wanting to be a contender, the man coming up, the man who knows there's a good chance he'll never get to the top, the man who's willing to sweat and bleed to get up as high as his legs and his brains and his heart will take him," (p. 25).

After reading this example paper, I wrap up the class: "For tomorrow, two things. First, read Chapter 1 and research whatever needs researching on the pages I assign you. Let's see: Chapter 1 has thirteen pages and it begins on . . . page 7. Okay, count off by sixes. You first, Melanie. Those who are ones have pages 7 and 8. Those who are twos have pages 9 and 10." And so forth.

The next two days of the *Mockingbird* unit are devoted to Chapter 1, the most difficult chapter of the book, since the bulk of it is told in summary fashion or exposition. It's about the Finch family and its history, the town, and Boo Radley, Maycomb's resident "monster." I also spend two days on this chapter in order to show students how *I* read a novel. But I tell them, too, that the way I read is but one model. In addition, I try to connect the students to the book's young protagonists by questioning them about their own childhood.

"The first thing I look at with a book this thick is the end—as many of you probably do—to see how many pages I have to read. Wow, this one has 284 pages. I say 'wow' because I am a slow reader. Then I look at the title again: *To Kill a Mockingbird*. I had to look up 'mockingbird.' It's a bird that imitates the songs of other birds and is found in the South. *To Kill a Mockingbird*—why would anyone want to do that? I open the book and find out it was published in 1960, before you folks were born . . . that it is dedicated to so-and-so; that it— follow me now—has an *epigraph*. An epigraph is a quotation at the beginning of the book that relates in some way to the book's subject. This one says, 'Lawyers, I suppose, were children once. —Charles Lamb.' This is kind of funny to me. Lamb says 'I suppose,' as if lawyers, by the way they behave as adults—they're stereotyped as serious wheeler-dealers out to hustle a buck— were never innocent."

"Atticus, Scout's father, is a lawyer," says Adam.

"Children are in the story, too," says Melanie.

"Good points. The next page says 'Part One,' so I flip through the pages and find 'Part Two,' but no parts after that. Why is the book in two parts? I keep that in mind. The first sentence of the book reads, 'When he was nearly thirteen, my brother Jem got his arm badly broken at the elbow.' The narrator goes on for a paragraph about Jem's arm, and I'm thinking, 284 pages—it can't just be about Jem's breaking his arm. In the next paragraph we find out the narrator's age: Scout says that Jem was 'four years my senior.' That makes her eight at the time Jem broke his arm. But I find out on the bottom of page 10 that, when the forward action of the story begins, Scout is five and Jem is nine—meaning the book spans three years.

"The second paragraph begins, 'When enough years had gone by to enable us to look back on them, we sometimes discussed the events leading to his accident.' I wonder, how old is the narrator *now* who will tell us the events that lead up to Jem's breaking his arm? She doesn't tell us.

"Let me stop for a moment. This story is told from the first-person, *retrospective* point of view. The author invents Scout-the-Adult, who looks back at events as they occurred to Scout-the-Child. We live out the story through Scout-the-Child's experiences and through her observations and judgments." I try to explain this through a simple diagram on the blackboard:

AUTHOR invents
The narrator "I": Scout-the-Adult
who tells the story of
Scout-the-Child in <u>Mockingbird</u>

"However, because of the adult language that we take as the child's, not only do we experience irony and humor—through the incongruity between the sophisticated language of an adult and the mind of a five-year-old—but, through the author's manipulations, we also get to know more than what Scout-the-Child knows.

"And sometimes more than what Scout-the-Adult knows. For example, to Scout-the-Adult, the names—Scout, Jem, Dill, Boo, Calpurnia, and Atticus—are simply the names of people she knows. The author, however, seems to have selected the names for other intentions, just as Saki did in 'The Open Window.' Remember Nuttel?

"Jem is a homophone for *gem*, suggesting something precious. Scout reminds me of the guy you send out ahead who comes back with information about the enemy or the right trail to follow. So a scout leads the main body of the army in the right direction—like what Scout might do for us, the readers. By the way, I was surprised to discover that Scout was a girl, when Jem tells Dill, on page 11, that Scout has been reading since *she* was born. I guess I've watched too many cowboy movies. Yet it stands to reason: The author, Harper Lee, is female, too.

That's another thing I forget, maybe because to me Harper sounds like a boy's name. Dill, too, has a name that connects to his character. Dill is a spice. One of its uses is in pickling vegetables. It gives a nice kick to things. And Dill sort of spices things up, too. He's the one that inspires Scout and Jem to fixate on Boo. You might say he's a *dilly*, someone or something remarkable. Dill is not only an instigator, but he's also a good talker and storyteller, with lots of imagination."

"And Boo is the monster that everyone fears."

"Boo!" says Andrew.

" And Calpurnia, where have we—"

"*Julius Caesar*. She was Caesar's wife," says Kim. "She had nightmare visions of what would happen to her husband. She was very worried for him. Remember? I had to paraphrase her lines. She loved Caesar, too. As much as Portia loved Brutus."

"And what characteristics, besides loving and caring, might you give her?"

"Wise," says Kenji.

"And how many of you knew that Calpurnia is black?" A number of students raise their hands. "How do you know?" Only three hands remain raised. "Nicole?"

"At the bottom of page 16, when Calpurnia says, after Boo's father dies of sickness and they're taking him away, 'There goes the meanest man ever God blew breath into,' and Scout is surprised because it was rare for her to hear Cal make comments about white people."

"Terrific. You had pages 15 and 16 for research, right? No? Wow. Then that's doubly terrific. Okay. Now Atticus comes from the Greek word *attikos*, meaning an Athenian or upstanding citizen, someone who is marked by purity, humility, and refinement. Now my belief, like the belief of many writers—poets especially—is that, even if you are not conscious of other intentions and meanings, they nevertheless have an impact on the reader's psyche.

"I just want to give you one example to keep in mind, that you might want to return to after you finish the book. On page 9, to explain her father's dislike for handling criminal cases, Scout tells us of Atticus' first two clients, the last to be hanged in the Maycomb County jail. The Haverfords (a name that Scout tells us is synonymous with *jackass*) had killed the town's main blacksmith in front of three witnesses, then insisted that 'the-son- of-a-bitch-had-it-coming-to-him was a good enough defense for anybody.'

"In addition to the absurdity and humor of the account, the author also *foreshadows*—that is, hints at—events to come later on in the book."

I usually take the tack of leading students to these conclusions by asking them questions. I've abbreviated the process here.

Before returning to the text, I ask the kids if any of them call their parents by their first names, as Scout and Jem do with Atticus. None do. I ask them to try an experiment: Go home tonight and, at dinner or in the kitchen or living room, address either parent by first name, as naturally as they can, and see how they react, then quickly tell the parent what they are doing. The following day, we hear some interesting stories and compare the reactions to Atticus' permissiveness.

"In the second paragraph of page 7, Scout says that 'the Ewells started it all.' What does the 'it' refer to, I wonder? Then she says that Jem claims it all began when Dill came up with the idea of making Boo Radley come out of his house. Four pages later, we find out that Scout has deferred to Jem's opinion, because the first scene of the novel introduces Dill, who is staying with his aunt, Rachel Haverford. And the Haverfords are synonymous with what, class?"

"JACKASS!"

"The traditional definition of a *scene* is a specific action occurring in *a specific place at a specific time.* Everything leading up to the novel's first scene is summary; the narrator is in no identifiable place, and the time of her telling the story is uncertain. In their little dispute about when things first began, Scout says that, in 'the broad view,' the story began with Andrew Jackson, because Simon Finch 'paddled up the Alabama' after Jackson sent 'the Creeks up the creek.' This is a clever way, I think, for the author to have Scout talk about her ancestry and her family. What is a finch? Researchers?"

"A bird," says Keith.

"And who was Andrew Jackson?"

"He was an American general in the War of 1812 against the British and was president from 1829 to 1837," says Rachel.

"Scout goes on to describe how some members of the Finch family were ashamed that their ancestors weren't more important. She says that Simon Finch was more stingy than he was pious, and that because he was a Methodist from England, and the Methodists were persecuted at the time, he emigrated to America. What's a Methodist?"

"It's a denomination of Protestantism," says Keith. "Its leader was a guy named John Wesley. Scout says that Simon forgot Wesley's ideas and bought some slaves after he got rich selling medicine. He was an *apothecary*, which is like a pharmacist."

"Good stuff, Keith. How ironic. He buys slaves after being persecuted himself. In the middle of the second page, Scout says that, because the Civil War left the Finch family with nothing but land, 'Simon would have regarded with impotent fury the disturbance between the North and South." And I think, *disturbance*— HA! I mean, the Civil War was *devastating!* When did the Civil War occur?"

"It went from 1861 to 1865."

"Okay. Scout says some things that describe how much a part of Maycomb County the Finches are, including a reference to Simon Finch being a philanderer. Then she talks about what a hot, tired old town Maycomb is, and how narrow its residents' lives are. But, she says, some townspeople had a 'vague optimism' because they had been told that they 'had nothing to fear but fear itself.'"

"Anybody research that—'We have nothing to fear but fear itself'? Anybody know who said that?"

"Roosevelt?"

"Which one? Theodore?"

"No. F. D. R."

"Franklin Delano Roosevelt. And when did he say this? Because, if we find that out, we know when this novel is taking place. No one? He said it in his 1933 inaugural speech to the nation, which was sinking under the Great Depression.

"Then we get some information about Calpurnia, who acts like a mother to Scout, since Scout's mother died of a heart attack when Scout was two. Calpurnia teaches, disciplines, and cares for the two kids and sets their summertime boundaries, which are in calling distance of Calpurnia. Scout says that the children never disobeyed Cal's boundaries—they were frightened by both the Radley place, which housed 'an unknown entity,' and the neighbors two houses away in the other direction.

I stop here and ask the kids if they remember the neighborhood boundaries that *their* parents set for *them* when they were young. And I ask if there were certain houses in their neighborhood that they stayed away from. The kids trade stories for about five minutes before I continue.

"As we move into the first scene of the book, I need a narrator and three people to read the parts of Scout, Jem, and Dill." I pick the volunteers and tell them they have to use a Southern accent. They think this is fun, woeful as they sound in their attempts. "Being from Meridian, Mississippi, Dill has been to the picture show a number of times. The narrator tells us that Dill had seen *Dracula* and tells Jem and Scout the story of the blood-sucking ghoul, setting us up for the rest of the chapter, which centers on Boo Radley. From the bottom of page 12 until the end of the chapter on page 19, more than half the chapter focuses on Boo and his curious family. So if I were writing a function paper on this chapter my thesis would read something like, 'The function of Chapter 1 is to introduce the mystery of Boo Radley. This is important because, more than anything else we are given, it draws us into the story.' Of course, you could also write a thesis on Atticus or on any of the kids, or even on the kind of place Maycomb seems to be. Let's finish off the dialogue before we go. Narrator?"

When Dill reduced Dracula to dust, and Jem said the show sounded better than the book—

"Which says two things," I say, interrupting. "One, that Dill is a good storyteller and, two, that Jem is an advanced reader for a nine year old, since Bram Stoker's *Dracula* is a long, dry, difficult book. Please continue."

—I asked Dill where his father was: "You ain't said anything about him."
   "I haven't got one."
   "Is he dead?"
   "No . . ."
   "Then if he's not dead you've got one, haven't you?"
   Dill blushed and Jem told me to hush—

"Stop. Why does Jem tell Scout to hush? Lauren?"

"Because Jem sees that Dill doesn't want to talk about his father and is embarrassed by Scout's . . . "

"Persistence," adds Natalie.

"Yeah, that's the word," says Lauren. "Maybe his parents are separated or divorced. Maybe back then that was something shameful."

"Maybe he's a criminal or something," says Mike.

"Or he abuses Dill," adds Nicole.

"Right now, we don't know. Why is it," I ask, "that Scout can't see what Jem can: that Dill feels uncomfortable being asked about his father? Anu?"

"Well, she's only five, right?"

"So?"

"She's still very young and just says what comes into her head without thinking. My brother is like that. He just opens his mouth about anything."

"And Jem?"

"Jem," says Anu, "is more mature. He's more sensitive to other people's feelings. He's nine, right? and goes to school."

"You mean, *you have to go to school* to be sensitive about—"

"There's a lot of people in school you have to deal with," says Nicole. "I mean, if you want to get along."

"That's right," says Peter. "Scout doesn't go to school until the next chapter, and on the first day she gets into trouble with—"

"Hold on, Peter. Some of us haven't read that far yet."

"I read the whole book," says Adam.

"Good for you," I say. "One of the things you might want to watch is the intellectual difference between Scout and Jem, who is four years her senior. Much of this story is also about their growing up together and, at times, apart. And there's the bell."

The next day, I continue: "At the bottom of page 12, Scout says that 'Dill gave us the idea of making Boo Radley come out.' On the next page she describes where the Radleys live, a dark house with 'rain-rotted shingles,' a deteriorated picket fence, and an unkempt yard.

"And I'm thinking, these people don't care. Through neglect, the place has gone to pot. But then again, I've seen front yards in a lot of neighborhoods in similar ruin or disarray, some looking like junkyards. Then I think of my son's bedroom and sigh. Scout continues, describing the 'malevolent phantom' who people say lives in the house and who they claim is not only a Peeping Tom and a petty criminal, but freezes azalea bushes just by breathing on them.

"And so forth. People said this and people said that: sounds like rumors or tales adults like to tell children in order to humor them, sounding so believeable that, as Scout admits, no one would even think of retrieving a ball from the Radley yard.

"This reminds me of some of the stories I heard from old-timers when I first came to Hawaii, about neighbors or distant kin or even strangers who experienced sometimes grave misfortunes. One story was about a tourist who took home with her a rock from Kilauea Volcano; I was told she grew seriously ill, her husband lost his job, and her dog died. Things didn't improve until she sent the rock back to Hawaii. My wife's uncles told me of another uncle's house—really his daughter's bedroom—being haunted by a disturbed or evil Hawaiian spirit. It seems the daughter's bed would start shaking at odd hours of the night, even after she got out of it. The father, who was three-quarters Hawaiian, called in a Kahuna to bless the room and pray for the family, and in the next few days the bed stopped rocking. The point is, the tales were told with such conviction that I was convinced that the storytellers themselves believed in their causes. I wonder if that's true about the people of Maycomb, however goofy or irrational their thinking might be in blaming Boo for the slightest irregularity in nature or personal misfortune. I mean, born and bred in New York as a skeptic, especially wary of other people's motives, I nevertheless gotta keep an open mind to the possibility of things out there that science or psychiatrists can't account for.

"Scout informs us that many years earlier the Radleys had rejected the people of Macomb by keeping to themselves, which the townsfolk held against them. I guess if you don't behave as others do, especially in a small town where everyone tends to know what everyone else is doing, people will look down on you or think you're odd. Scout gives us more details about how the Radleys were odd: They didn't attend church and they kept their house closed up on Sundays. And I'm thinking, I'd keep my doors and shutters shut, too, if I didn't like Maycomb's ways or the people's nosiness.

"Scout then tells us of the time when Boo was a teenager hanging out with some of the Cunninghams his age, cutting up as teenage boys tend to do. But they raised worries and the hackles of the old fogies who ran the churches and the town. What did they do that was so bad? They hung out, went to the movies on Sunday, danced at a gambling den, and experimented with whiskey. One night, Scout continues, 'in an excessive spurt of high spirits, the boys backed around the square in a borrowed flivver—an old car.' They resisted arrest and Boo was locked in the courthouse outhouse. The judge sent the boys—except Boo—to the state industrial school, where they received an excellent education. Boo, on the other hand, was given over to his father, who felt that going to such a school would be a disgrace and promised the judge that Arthur (Boo) would cause Maycomb no further trouble. After Mr. Radley took Boo home, Scout says that Boo was kept out of sight for fifteen years. FIFTEEN YEARS! He hasn't come out of his house for fifteen years. My lord! What unutterable sin did Boo commit to deserve such a fate? What's going on here? And with the oak trees keeping the sun out and the doors and shutters always closed he must be paler than a ghost. And what of his mind?

"Scout tells us another story about Boo, the details of which are related to Jem by Stephanie Crawford, a neighborhood busybody. Apparently it occurred when Jem was very young. It seems that, as Boo was cutting out items from the newspaper, his father walked by, whereupon Boo stabbed his father with the scissors, then wiped the scissors off and acted like nothing had happened. It was suggested that Boo, who was thirty-three at the time, be put into an asylum, but Mr. Radley said that Boo wasn't crazy, that he was just high-strung at times. So Boo ended up back at home. Now I'm thinking, if the story was true, and maybe even if it wasn't, Boo would probably have received some help in a sanitarium—away from Mr. Radley. I'm also thinking that, if I were Boo, maybe I would have stabbed Mr. Radley in the leg, too. Boo didn't harm his mother . . . though she must have played a role in his confinement, too.

"After Mr. Radley dies of some unnamed sickness—remember how mean Calpurnia said he was?—Boo's brother, Nathan Radley, returns to the house, taking Mr. Radley's place, and for all intents and purposes is identical to his father. How nice for Boo, I think. And, here, I'd probably amend my original function paper thesis to read, 'One of the functions of Chapter 1 is to introduce the character of Mr. Radley, Boo Radley's father, who has confined Boo to their house for fifteen years. This is important because, like for the rest of the people of Maycomb, Boo remains a mystery to the reader. Like the kids, we, too, want to know what Boo is like now.'"

We finish off the chapter with volunteers reading from near bottom of page 17, including Jem's "reasonable description," as Scount calls it, of Boo as an unnaturally tall, malformed beast who has permanently bloodstained hands as a result of eating raw squirrels and "any cats he could catch."

"Yeah, that's a *reasonable* description," says Mark.

Dill challenges Jem to knock on the Radley's door, betting three Gray Ghosts to two Tom Swifts (comic books) that Jem won't get any further than the gate. Jem thinks about this for three days, until Dill says the folks in Meridian weren't as afraid as the folks in Maycomb. As Jem hesitates, Dill says, "You gonna run out on a dare?" When Jem continues to stall, Dill lightens the challenge by saying that all he has to do is touch the Radley house. At this, Jem brightens, but hesitates nevertheless.

The two boys dramatizing the scene, as Dill and Jem, do it very well, no doubt experienced at taunting others about their "manhood," as well as feeling the pressure themselves. A few boys in the class share quick stories of how they were on the giving or receiving end of a challenge to their courage. "What about girls," I ask. "Do they go at each other in the same way that boys do? Lauren?"

"No. We aren't so crude," she says in mock superiority, which gets a rise from the boys. "We use more *sophisticated* means."

"Oh, give me a break," says Mike.

"Yeah, right," says Josh. "You just stab each other in the back."

"See what I mean about being crude?"

"Lauren's right," says Nicole. "Girls prey on other kinds of vulnerabilities."

"Woooo! Fancy word," says Josh.

"Like what?" says Mike. "The need to be liked?"

"Wouldn't you like to know," says Lauren, turning her face away.

I wrap up the discussion: "So Jem rushes through the gate, touches the house, and flees the vicinity, with Dill and Scout, as scared as Jem is, bringing up the rear. Looking back at the house from safely down the street, the children see that it's unchanged by Jem's touch—except for what may be a tiny flicker of movement inside.

"For tomorrow, Thursday, read Chapter 2 and come in with a function thesis. We'll pick one to defend as a class. Also, mark up the chapter in places you find interesting. Remember, David, you'll be reading your function paper on Friday. See me if you need help. Aloha."

The next day, after I check to see if students have marked up Chapter 2 (most have), the class hears individual thesis statements about the chapter that recounts Scout's first day at school. Most of the theses center on Miss Caroline, Scout's first-grade teacher; Walter Cunningham, one of the students in Scout's class; and Scout, who seems to be the only child in the class who can read and write. Two other theses touch upon the Depression and its effect on the people of Maycomb. Another focuses on Jem.

As a class, we settle on Walter Cunningham. "Jennifer, could you read your thesis again?"

"'One of the functions of Chapter 2 is to introduce Walter Cunningham, a poor, barefoot, farmer's boy.' I had trouble with this second part: 'This is important because Walter and the class get Scout in trouble with the teacher'?"

"Is that a question?"

"No."

"Why do you feel uneasy about it?"

"I don't know. It just doesn't seem important enough."

"Well, maybe by the end of class, you can revise it. Okay, class, what's Walter like? By the way, weren't the Cunninghams mentioned in Chapter 1? Kai?"

"Yeah. Boo used to hang around with some of them when he got in trouble."

"But," says Adam, "there're a lot of Cunninghams. It says—"

"*The narrator* says—"

"*The narrator* says—"

"What page?"

"On the top of page 14 . . . that they were an 'enormous and confusing tribe,' which means there're a lot of them and it's hard to figure out their family relationships."

"Good. Now, Kai, were those Cunninghams you talked about bad?"

"Not really. They were just acting like teenagers. When they were sent to that industrial school, they did all right."

"Do you think we ought to add to our paper by saying something about what we already know about the Cunninghams?"

"Yes," says Natalie. "That way we can provide a little background info."

"What is the first thing we notice about Walter?"

"That he's got hookworms from going barefoot in barnyards," says Rachel. "Scout says he doesn't own a pair of shoes. But on page 24 she says, 'He did have on a clean shirt and neatly mended overalls.'"

"Rachel, who cleans and mends your clothes?"

"My mother, mostly."

"Why?"

"*Why?* So I'll look presentable in public . . . though my mom complains sometimes about the kind of clothes I wear."

"You mean breaking the dress code?" says Tia.

"Talk about the pot calling the kettle black," is Rachel's retort.

"Beef! Beef!" says David.

"You gonna take that, Tia?" says Mike.

"Oh, be quiet," says Rachel.

"What? You want me?" Mike smiles and holds up his fists like an uncoordinated boxer.

"You're such a child," says Tia.

"*Enough.* So Walter's parents care about how Walter looks in public?"

"I guess," says Rachel in a huff.

"What I want to know is why he lies to Miss Caroline about forgetting his lunch, when Scout informs her he never brings lunch?"

"'Cause he's ashamed of being poor," says Tia.

Rory joins in: "Scout says to Miss Caroline, at the top of page 25, 'The Cunninghams never took anything they can't pay back.'"

"So they scrape by and refuse charity—why?"

"Because they're proud people," says Rory. "Walter refuses Miss Caroline's quarter because he's been taught to."

"So Walter is a reflection of—"

"His family," Rory says.

"And maybe *all* the Cunninghams," adds Stephanie. "Or most of them anyway. And maybe most of the farm families in Maycomb because, when Scout asks Atticus if they're poor, Atticus says yes, because the farmers are, and they all pay the lawyers and doctors with goods, since they have no money. That's how Walter's father paid Atticus for his legal services, right?"

"Jennifer?"

"Can I read my new thesis?"

"Please."

"'One of the functions of Chapter 2 is to introduce Walter Cunningham, a poor, barefoot, farmer's boy. This is important because Walter represents, not only his family, but also the farmers of Maycomb County.' How's that?"

"Very good. Since we have some time left, let me read from the middle of page 20 near the beginning of the chapter. By the way, when Scout complains to Jem about Miss Caroline, on whom he has a crush—you know?—that used to happen to me when I was teaching high school at Seabury Hall."

Choke, cough-cough, guffaw, and, "Yeah, right."

"I was a lot younger then, and trimmer," I add.

From the side of the room, Scooter says, "YOU LIE!"

Laughter.

"Anyway, Jem explains to Scout that Miss Caroline is introducing a new teaching method in the school, called—what?"

"The Dewey decimal system," says Keith.

"You know what that is?"

"I do," says Rory. "It's a library system for organizing books."

"So what's Jem doing?"

"Giving Scout the bull," says Mike.

"Why?"

"Because he's the older sibling," says Mike, "someone who's supposed to know more. Jem's a kick. He does the same thing when Scout asks him what an *entailment* is, and he tells her that it means having your tail in a crack." Laughter.

"He *is* funny," I agree. "When Jem shows Scout where her classroom is, he warns her not to embarrass or bother him in any way.

"How many of you have younger siblings?" Many hands go up. "Now most of you are twelve, right, so—"

"THIRTEEN!"

"And a few of us are FOURTEEN."

"I know that," I say coyly. It's so easy to get them riled. "Now let's say your younger sibling is five or six. Would you want him or her to hang out with you?"

"No way," says Mike.

"It'd be embarrassing," says Tia. "They do such stupid things."

"As Jem said," adds Josh, "they'd probably blab about what you do at home."

"What do you do at home that's so bad? Sleep with your teddy bear?"

"Just private stuff," says Josh.

"My sister would try to get all the attention," adds Tia.

"And," says Keith, "you don't want them going home to your parents and telling them all that me and my friends do."

"Or say," says Nicole.

"You know: who so-and-so likes, that kind of stuff."

"Anything else?"

No answer.

"Well, this might be speculation on my part," I say, "but I think there are things that you and your friends might say and do that you don't want your younger sibling to know, not because of telling tales on you, but because they are still young and generally innocent. Whether you know it or not, many of you might want to protect them, perhaps to preserve their childhood, which, as you know, passes too quickly. Maybe it's the paternal part in you that contributes to your wanting them to be at a distance. And I'm sure you *do* love them. And that's one of the things that disarms me about this book. The people of Maycomb, both black and white, are very protective of children. And . . . there's the bell. Aloha."

After they read their drafts to the class and we give them feedback, I give students example papers that address the same chapters. This one was written by Natalie Watanabe, an eighth grader:

> One of the functions of Chapter 3 is to show how Calpurnia acts as the mother figure in Scout's life. This is important because, although Calpurnia is a hired housekeeper, she plays a big role in raising Scout.
>
> Love and affection are the greatest gifts any mother can give a child. These gifts of love to the child are essential for positive emotional growth. Scout grows up without her real mother because she dies when Scout is two years old. This causes Calpurnia to step in, assuming the role of mother. She cares for Scout as if she were her own, showing affection and being very protective. We see this when Scout returns home from her first day of first grade. Calpurnia greets her by saying, "'I missed you today . . . one of you's always in callin' distance. I wonder how much of the day I spend just callin' after you.' Calpurnia bent down and kissed me," (p. 29). Calpurnia saying she misses Scout when she is gone shows she is emotionally attached to her. Also, making sure either one of them is in calling distance proves she is concerned about their health and welfare.
>
> Usually it is a parent who is protective like this, but Scout describes her father Atticus in Chapter 1 as, " . . . satisfactory: he played with us, read to us and treated us with courteous detachment," (p. 6). This shows that Atticus tries to be a good father, but his ability to do so is hindered by his other priorities. Calpurnia is the only adult left in Scout's life who is able to devote her time to caring for her. My own mother did the same thing for me. She gave up her career as a teacher so she could be at home when I returned from school.
>
> It is only natural for a mother to want her child to be the best he/she can. One of the ways she can accomplish this is by teaching her child everything good in her power. In Chapter 2, we find out that Scout learned to read from Atticus. However, after Miss Caroline reprimands Scout for knowing how to write, we learn that it is Calpurnia, and not Atticus, who teaches her how to write. One would think, since Atticus is the father and he is the one who teaches Scout to read, he would also teach her to write. But this is not the case. Instead, Calpurnia again acts as a mother figure by teaching Scout such a crucial skill which she will put to use throughout her life.
>
> In addition to teaching Scout a skill that will help her intellectually, Calpurnia teaches her a lesson about life as well. A good mother tries to teach her child manners so he/she can be as successful with people as possible. Calpurnia displays this characteristic when Walter Cunningham comes over for lunch. When Scout is very rude in commenting about his manner

of eating, Calpurnia is upset and takes Scout into the kitchen to scold her. Calpurnia is very clear in getting her point across that everyone deserves to be treated with equal respect. She also tells Scout that guests are to be treated politely. This is an important lesson for Scout to learn because it will improve her social skills. If she is taught to never look down on anyone, she will begin to believe it herself, acting that way all the time. Mutual respect will result from this because others will admire her for the maturity she shows in doing so. Once again, Calpurnia acts as a mother figure by teaching Scout a skill which will be useful when associating with others, an inevitable part of life she will have to face as she gets older.

From this passage, we can also see that Calpurnia is the disciplinarian in Scout's life. When Scout acts out of line, Calpurnia is the one who scolds and disciplines her. Although Atticus also hears Scout's remarks, it is Calpurnia who takes action. When I act inappropriately at home, my mother corrects me. She says she is doing it because she loves me. Though I don't agree with her at the time, I see now that her discipline serves in my favor. If I am not disciplined, I will continue to act inappropriately, possibly leading me to later grief. The same thing is true for Scout. Calpurnia's disciplining her shows that she cares about Scout. She cares so much that she is willing to put her effort into teaching Scout the appropriate way to act, even if she risks being disliked and unappreciated.

Throughout the chapters we have read so far, it is obvious Scout does not like Calpurnia very much. In fact, we get the feeling that Scout almost resents her. Scout does not realize all that Calpurnia does for her, therefore leading her to be unappreciative of Calpurnia. However, Atticus notices the need for Calpurnia. When Scout complains that Calpurnia likes Jem better than her, Atticus simply says, "We couldn't operate a single day without Cal . . ." (p. 25). This is very true. Without the motherly influence of Calpurnia, the Finches could be exactly like the Ewells.

We find out late in the chapter more about the Ewell family. When Scout asks about them, Atticus explains that, " . . . the Ewells had been the disgrace of Maycomb," (p. 30). Earlier that day in school we learn that all the Ewell children only come on the first day. When Miss Caroline asks why, all the children in the classroom answer, "Ain't got no mother," (p. 27). Because the Ewells have no mother, the children have no sense of respect or cleanliness. This shows the importance of a mother in a household.

It is very apparent that Calpurnia is the mother-figure in Scout's life. She supplies her with love, guidance, and discipline. To me, those three things are what an ideal mother would give her children. Calpurnia also gives the Finches the sense of a "normal" family. Without Calpurnia's influence, Jem and Scout would probably be just like Burris Ewell. Although Calpurnia is not Scout's real mother, she is the closest to one that Scout will ever have.

After reading example papers, at the end of Part One we pause for three days to consider some of the works of three notable black writers—to view history and *Mockingbird* from the perspective of black people. This, in part, prepares the way for Part Two and the Tom Robinson trial, and the rancorous, bitter behavior of Lula in the first chapter of Part Two, when Calpurnia takes Jem and Scout, two white children, to her black church.

First, I read to the students from *The Life and Times of Frederick Douglass.* "This book," I tell the students, "is an adaptation of *The Narrative of Frederick Douglass, An American Slave*, which was published before the Civil War in 1845. Douglass had escaped slavery in the South and come North, where he became an abolitionist, an influential orator, and a writer. He worked with the Underground Railroad, which transported escaped slaves to the North; supported Abraham Lincoln for president; and, among other deeds, organized two black regiments from Massachusetts to fight against the South in the Civil War.

"But before I read, I just want to say something.

"Imagine what it must have felt like to be sold into slavery by your king, ripped away from your family and friends and home; shorn of your roots, your country, all that you know and are familiar with; then shipped like cattle to the other side of the world. If you survive the trip, you'll work in a white man's field for the rest of your life, fetch and carry with hat in hand, resigned to your master's will, at the threat of your life. You retain no rights whatsoever over yourself, your loved ones, or your children; like you, they are property, little more than mules whose fate is not in their hands, who may be whipped at the master's whim or to appease his choler. You teach your children, for their own good, for their suvival, the proper way to behave in front of white folks: what they expect, what pleases them, what offends them, how to humble your head, how to speak in servile tones. For the fact is, you are nothing but a slave, only a percentage of a man or a woman. And your children will teach their children, just as generation after generation of white folks will teach their children the superiority of their race, 'that different from you and me, black people, in the natural order of living things, and by God's will, do not share the same faculties or sensibilities or qualities that you and I have.'

"The following, from Chapter 5, 'Miss Sophia,' recounts Douglass' learning how to read from his mistress. At the time, during the early 1800s, Douglass is a young house slave owned by Sophia and Hugh Auld of Baltimore, Maryland. Douglass begins by telling us that when Sophia Auld came to consider him as property, their relationship deteriorated. The second paragraph begins:

> The frequent hearing of my mistress reading the Bible aloud awakened my curiosity in respect to this *mystery* of reading, and emboldened me to ask her to teach me to read. With an unconsciousness and inexperience equal to my own, she readily consented, and in an incredibly short time, by her kind assistance, I had mastered the alphabet and could spell words of three or four letters.

"Proud of Douglass' progress, Sophia Auld exultingly told her husband of the aptness of her student. Whereupon Hugh Auld was astounded and 'proceeded to unfold to his wife the true philosophy of the slave system' and

> . . . forbade her to give me any further instruction, telling her in the first place that to do so was unlawful, as it was also unsafe; "for," he said, "if you give a nigger an inch he will take an ell. Learning will spoil the best nigger in the world. If he learns to read the Bible it will forever unfit him to be a slave. He should know nothing but the will of his master, and learn to obey it."

"Why would Douglass' learning how to read the Bible, as Hugh Auld says, make him an unfit slave? Doug?"

"Because God loves everyone equally."

"And because," says Kara, "Douglass would not see his master like a god. Which the master wants to be for his slave."

"Interesting. Ryan?"

"And there is someone higher than the master to obey."

"What about the very fact that Douglass is learning to read? What does reading have to do with any of this?"

"Well, when you read," says Kara, "you get exposed to all kinds of ideas. And you start to think."

"Douglass didn't think before?"

"Not that. But ideas can make you start to think differently—"

"From what?"

"From being a slave," says Walter.

"Let me go on. Hugh Auld then says":

> "As to himself, learning will do him no good, but a great deal of harm, making him disconsolate and unhappy. If you teach him how to read, he'll want to learn how to write, and this accomplished, he'll be running away with himself."

"Why would learning make Douglass unhappy?" I ask.

"Well," says Ryan, "learning means you learn something, right? And one of the things he'll probably learn is how other people live free and say what they want. And he might even read the Constitution."

"So?"

"So he'll see that the way he is living, being a slave," says Amanda, "is not right."

"Yeah," says Justine, "he's a man. Not an animal or a piece of property. It makes me sick."

"What about when Hugh Auld says that, if Douglass learns how to read, 'he'll want to learn how to write, and this accomplished, he'll be running away with himself. What's he talking about?"

"I know," says Doug. "He'll start thinking his own thoughts as we do when we write. And he'll start thinking that his thoughts are as good as anyone's."

"So one way to keep the system of slavery in place," I add, "is to keep your slaves ignorant—especially of ideas that contradict your own. As Jefferson said, in order to maintain a free, democratic society you have to make sure you have an educated public who can tell when their liberty is at stake. In a slave state, the last thing you want is an educated slave whose ambitions might transcend menial labor, for then who would work the land?

"When Douglas is thirteen, after earning some money through bootblacking, he buys a popular school book called *The Columbian Orator* and reads again and again a short dialogue between a slave and his master, in which the slave vanquishes his master at every turn in an argument. So impressed is the master that he emancipates the slave. Douglass wishes that the same fate might befall him. He also says, about reading *The Columbian Orator*:

> From the speeches of Sheridan I got a bold and powerful denunciation of oppression and a most brilliant vindication of the rights of man. Here was indeed a noble acquisition. If I had ever wavered under the consideration that the Almighty, in some way, had ordained slavery and willed my enslavement for His own glory, I wavered no longer.
>
> With a book in my hand so redolent of the principles of liberty, and with a perception of my own human nature and of the facts of my past and present experience, I was equal to the contest with the religious advocates of slavery, whether black or white; for blindness was not confined to the white people.

"Then, after expressing his loathing for slaveholders as the meanest and most wicked of men, Douglass ends the chapter with great generosity of feeling for his former mistress:

> Nature made us friends, but slavery had made us enemies. She had changed, and I, too, had changed. We were both victims to the same overshadowing evil, *she* as mistress, I as slave. I will not censure her harshly.

"Under such an evil system, no one goes untouched: Lives are warped, hearts are broken, minds are perverted, but, as Douglass would agree, not to the same degree—not equally."

I give the next two pieces to students for homework on consecutive nights. The first is from Richard Wright's *Black Boy*.

"This book was published in 1945, eighty years after the Civil War and the freeing of the slaves. But over that length of time, and for the next ten years, blacks were denied participation in democratic America. They were discouraged from voting through poll taxes and registration requirements, forestalling the exercise of their political power and economic growth. They were also denied the use of many public institutions, especially public schools. The 1896 'separate but equal' ruling handed down by the Supreme Court supported not only separate water fountains for whites and blacks, but also separate accommodations; means of transportation and education; and places to work, eat, live, and frequent. That meant, because of lack of government support and lack of money, blacks got third-rate facsimiles of the things established for white people. Otherwise, there was no black accommodation or counterpart at all. Black people had to make do without.

"For example, there were no black libraries. How do you learn, broaden your mind, and deepen your intellect without books? How do you educate yourself and improve your economic condition, even rise into the ranks of the professional world? Put another way, in addition to denying black people the right to an equal education and denying them access to books, what better way can you keep a people down? Frederick Douglass knew this, and Richard Wright did, too. The piece you'll be reading tonight is a chapter from Wright's autobiographical fiction.

"The chapter opens with Richard coming to work early and stepping into the lobby of a bank to read the *Memphis Commercial Appeal*. He is stunned by an editorial attacking H. L. Mencken. Richard says:

> I wondered what on earth this Mencken had done to call down upon him the scorn of the South. The only people I ever heard denounced in the South were Negroes, and this man was not a Negro. Then what ideas did Mencken hold that made a newspaper like the *Commercial Appeal* castigate him publicly?

"His curiosity aroused, and feeling a vague sympathy for Mencken, Richard figures that the only way he can learn more about Mencken is to read some of his books. To that end, he asks one of his colleagues at work, at the M—— Optical Company, to help him obtain some from the public library. He decides upon an Irish Catholic whom the white men called a "pope lover." When the man consents, holding Richard to secrecy, Richard forges a note and the man's signature to protect him if Richard is caught. Despite some suspicion on the part of the librarian, Richard acquires the books he wants, and later that night in his rented room, with hot water running—

> . . . over my can of pork and beans in the sink, I opened *A Book of Prefaces* and began to read. I was jarred and shocked by the style, the clear, clean, sweeping sentences. Why did he write like that? I pictured the man as a raging demon, slashing with his pen, consumed with hate, denouncing everything American, extolling everything European or German, laughing at the weaknesses of people, mocking God, authority.

"Richard is stunned by Mencken's fearless, combative voice, recognizing that words could be used as weapons, as one might use a cudgel or a bat. For here was Mencken fighting with words. What amazes Richard is not so much what Mencken says, but that anybody would have the audacity and courage to say it.

"Richard then gives us an expansive list of writers whom Mencken had mentioned in his writing, from Conrad to Zola, from Balzac to T. S. Eliot, from Dostoevski to Dreiser, and scores of others.

"Richard, thus inspired, forges more notes, visits the library more, and reads more books, whereupon reading becomes like a drug for him. But he feels guilty and suspects his colleagues sense that he is changing. He says:

> I knew what being a Negro meant. I could endure the hunger. I had learned to deal with hate. But to feel that there were feelings denied me, that the very breath of life itself was beyond my reach, that more than anything else hurt, wounded me. I had a new hunger.
>   In buoying me up, reading also cast me down, made me see what was possible, what I had missed.

"He struggles hard to maintain his former appearance, his former behavior, to mask his new sensibilities and understanding: 'I laughed in the way [my boss] expected me to laugh, but I resolved to be more conscious of myself, to watch my every act, to guard and hide the new knowledge that was dawning within me,' which surely must wear on Richard's nerves.

"The chapter ends with this:

> My reading had created a vast sense of distance between me and the world in which I lived and tried to make a living, and that sense of distance was increasing each day. My days and nights were one long, quiet continuously contained dream of terror, tension, and anxiety. I wondered how long I could bear it.

The class and I talk about the similarities of experience between Frederick Douglass, during the era of slavery, and Richard Wright, eighty years after emancipation and living in the South. We find little difference between being a slave and being free when being free meant, as one student says, "Surviving, just getting by on the crumbs doled out by the white people who own all the businesses. Without making waves for the white people." Or, "Constantly being afraid of what you say or do in front of them," fearing a baseless, mindless retribution "because of the color of their skin"; having still to defer to white people as the master race; having, as their "inferiors," to endure disrespect and ill treatment, always enduring hatred and humiliation. Both Douglass and Wright became changed people after learning to read, and because what they read made their lives unendurable, fled those lives.

"The second homework reading is from James Baldwin's *The Fire Next Time*, which was published in 1963, nine years after the 'separate but equal ruling' was reversed, which led to the hard-fought integration of public schools and the beginning of the Civil Rights movement. At the time of Baldwin's writing, racial discrimination had not much abated, and it didn't even after the Civil Rights Act of 1964, which prohibited discrimination in public accommodations and by employers, unions, and voting registrars. In the late '60s and early '70s, race riots ensued across the country. The following piece is called 'My Dungeon Shook: Letter to My Nephew on the One Hundreth Anniversary of the Emancipation.' Baldwin begins by comparing his nephew, James, to James' father:

> Like him, you are tough, dark, vulnerable, moody—with a very definite tendency to sound truculent because you want no one to think you are soft.

"Then he says how, physically, James resembles his dead grandfather, saying that his grandfather had a terrible life, feeling forever defeated 'because, at the bottom of his heart, he really believed what the white man said about him.' At the end of the paragraph, Baldwin says:

> You can only be destroyed by believing that you really are what the white world calls a *nigger*.

"Then Baldwin spells out for James the crime their country has perpetrated, and continues to perpetrate, on James' father and on the hundreds of thousands like him. The subtlety of the crime is that their countrymen do not know of it and do not want to be made aware of it.

> But it is not permissible that the authors of destruction should also be innocent. It is the innocence which constitutes the crime.

"Baldwin then says that their country put black people in a ghetto to live out their lives, *because* they were black—'and for no other reason'—establishing the boundaries of their ambition. They were expected to accept mediocrity as their way of life, told where they could and could not go and in what manner, told where they could and could not live, and even whom they could marry. But, Baldwin says to James, 'If you know whence you came, there is really no limit to where you can go.' He ends his letter to James:

> Please try to remember that what they believe, as well as what they do and cause you to endure, does not testify to your inferiority but to their inhumanity and fear. Please try to be clear, dear James, through the storm which rages about your youthful head today, about the reality which lies behind the words *acceptance* and *integration*. There is no reason for you to try to become like white people and there is no basis whatever for their impertinent

assumption that *they* must accept *you*. The really terrible thing, old buddy, is that *you* must accept *them*. And I mean that very seriously. You must accept them and accept them with love. For these innocent people have no other hope. They are, in effect, still trapped in a history which they do not understand; and until they understand it, they cannot be released from it.

Although my students experience much difficulty in following Baldwin, one of the first things that they remark on is Baldwin's Christian tone of voice. It reminds them of Dr. Martin Luther King Jr. and his mission of establishing social justice for black people in his attempt to gain civil rights for all people. I tell the students that I also recognize in the letter—in Baldwin's effort to encourage his nephew—a foreshadowing of Malcolm X, that fiery orator of the Black Muslims, who instilled pride in his people in being black and *fearless*. After his trip to Mecca and meeting hosts of many-colored Muslims, Malcolm X recanted his theory that all white people were evil, and in 1965 he was shot to death by black assassins.

The other thing my students mention is that African Americans are not as bad off today "as they were back then"; that many blacks are successful in professional sports, in the movie and music industries, and in politics; and that blacks are more and more in the middle class. I add that by group comparison, however, the proportion of blacks at economic risk exceeds that of other groups, and that many black people retain little hope.

"Why," asks Randal, "is James Baldwin writing to his nephew anyway?"

"Anyone? Nicole?"

"Because he doesn't want James to believe what the white people say about him. Mostly, you know, through the way they maybe treat black people—"

"Also," says Natalie, "I looked up the word *truculent* and it means 'feeling or displaying ferocity: cruel, savage.' Baldwin says his nephew sounds that way. Maybe he *is* that way."

"Can't blame him," says Mike. "I feel that way when store folks look at me like I'm some sort of thief. Makes me angry."

"But the writer also tells James not to be afraid. So he's scared, too?"

"Wouldn't you feel scared if you saw no way out of the ghetto?" I ask. "If you could see no future? So James has all these feelings—anger, fear, rage, frustration—probably all pent up, too. Do you think he can do what his uncle says, '*you* must accept *them*,' and with love?"

"No," says Scooter, echoing some of the other voices.

"Maybe," says Natalie.

"Could you, if you were in a similar position?"

"No way," says Mike.

"So there's no other way but explode? Baldwin says, on the top of the last page, 'that we, with love, shall force our brothers to see themselves as they are.' Isn't that what Dr. King tried to do? And he says, 'our brothers, our countrymen, our country.'"

For this is your home, my friend, do not be driven from it; great men have done great things here, and will again, and we can make America what America must become.

"Think about this. And think about all you've read these past three days as we enter Chapter 12, the first chapter of Part Two, where Calpurnia takes Jem and Scout to her church. There, we get our first glimpse of the black community of the rural South in the early 1930s. Also, we begin hearing function papers again. Aloha."

Contrary to general belief, I think that teaching kids how to write thesis papers is easier than teaching them how to write stories and personal narratives. That may sound strange when we consider all the stories their parents read to them when they're young, all the stories they hear from relatives and friends, all the stories that they themselves tell others, and all the stories they write in elementary school. I mean, they know the basic structure of a story. Yet writing a good story is very, very difficult. Although the writer must follow certain dictates of time, which the story must necessarily span, the good writer also operates according to other kinds of "logic," for which, many times, we have no name and which we cannot easily explain.

On the other hand, thesis writing, like the function paper, is grounded on logical reasoning, and there are certain limitations, governed by the conventions of writing such a paper and by the literature their writing addresses, which the writer must follow. This is unlike the unlimited freedom granted the story writer, which can cripple a writer. Thesis writing is easier to teach—and theses are easier to write—because the patterns are more easily identifiable and are, for the most part, universal, predictable, and repeatable. Out of this basic structure, good papers can continually emerge, whereas a good story, to be distinguished at all, must be a singular, one-time creation. That's a formidable challenge, to say the least, for anyone.

The point of this short reflection is to remind myself that I sometimes place unrealistic demands on my eighth graders when they write stories. I must remember, also, all the writing they practice in the rest of the year, all their reading, and all the classroom talk that helps them in the struggle to learn thesis writing. How, exactly, things work together still puzzles me. All that I know for sure is that kids just do it, and sometimes their achievements astonish me.

8

Exam Writing

Dare you see a soul at the White Heat?
—Emily Dickinson

We learned how to howl at the moon.
—Keli Sato (Grade 7)

At the beginning of class, I say, "I don't know why it is that every time I assign the take-home exam on *Mockingbird*, I end up assigning it on a Friday—"

"Right on!" says Reid.

"How do you like *them* apples?" says Dane.

"Hold on. That extra day won't make that much of a difference. It won't make the assignment any easier, believe me, though it sounds simple enough: Write a paper in response to *To Kill a Mockingbird*—"

"But on what?" asks Kelly.

"That's a question only you can answer. Think of poetry. Did I tell you what to write for your Memory Poem, or your Family Poem, or your Holiness Poem? Like most of your poetry assignments, this one is open-ended. You must define the assignment yourself: You must find a specific topic and choose the genre you want to write it in. And the expectation, like for all your writing, is that it will be original, that you will write from your gut."

I read them the following handout:

First [*as I said*], your *Mockingbird* exam will be a take-home exam due on Monday. As with all your other writings, let me encourage you to seek feedback from people you trust and to submit drafts with your final. And [*Please!*] proofread your final aloud.

Second, different from other exams you have taken, I will not specify your task except in the broadest terms. [*As I said*] You will write your response to your reading *Mockingbird*. What topic you choose to write on and what genre you choose to write in are things that only you can decide.

Third [*Right after this*], I will give you options and read you example papers by former students that will suggest to you the range of possible papers that you may write. Further, as in poetry writing, the examples will establish for you the standard of excellence that you yourself can equal or even exceed, the standard of excellence against which both you and I can measure the quality of your writing.

Fourth, the purpose of this exam is to encourage you to respond in your own unique way to *your* reading of *Mockingbird*. You can ask yourself, How can I *apply* my understanding (say, of a character or any part of the book)? Or, How does my life or my own understanding of the world *connect* with the book? How you might apply your knowledge or how strong or weak your connection to the book should be will also be suggested by the student examples I will read.

"Any questions? Yes?"
"How long should it be?"
"The example writings will suggest this. Again, use 14-point type and double-space. Anything else?"
"Mr. T? I'm not exactly sure—"
"Trust me, you will be . . . ready?"

It has been said that one of the purposes of reading is to inspire in the reader the desire to write his or her own words. Of course, the quality or intensity of inspiration will, in great part, be determined by the reading experience and by the book and the book talk the teacher and students share in the classroom. *To Kill a Mockingbird,* in addition to being a great teaching machine, is also a richly enjoyable novel, especially for young adolescents, who are caught up in puberty and are in the process of growing up in a multicolored America. *Mockingbird* is ripe for and begs individual response, an *open* response, whose substance and form the teacher cannot anticipate.

It can be argued that students need lots of practice in writing traditional essay exams—that is, explanatory or argumentative writing—and that students do not get, or cannot get, enough practice.

I wonder: These kinds of writings, timed or not, increasingly dominate students' writing experience from junior high to postgraduate school. They don't get enough? I sometimes wonder if I require too much of this kind of writing, through learning logs, literary journals, speeches, and function papers.

Traditional timed writings generally test students' understanding of what they've read and their ability to communicate their knowledge clearly. Usually all students are given the same questions to answer or the same passages to interpret. Most often they are required to complete the exams within a class period. Their writings, then, under the illusion of fairness, are compared against each other and are ranked or grouped for grading.

In the past, I have assigned such exams myself too often. And, too often, the results drove me to distraction ("After *all* we've been through?!"). Not only were most of the writings repetitive from paper to paper—and tritely so, often regurgitating what had been said in class discussion, but most were also immensely boring, couched in the stalest expressions, and lacked genuine conviction. Where was their sense of poetry and grace? Or humor? Or their sense of *human* talk? I mean, it was wholesale reversion to the beginning of the year.

But why complain, I would ask myself. The questions were not the students', and rarely were the questions I concocted for them of striking interest.

All of which amounted to what?

I mean, what *truly* is achieved?

My knowing that they have read the novel? That they have good memories? That they have paid attention in class? That they take good notes? That they can read metaphorically, as in class discussion? All worthy things, I know. But what about our students? I realize that practicing timed writing is a benefit to them—for test-taking in the future? *I guess.*

And what of the writings themselves? How meaningful might they be to the students? How important? How close to their hearts and their understanding of the world?

Might they have worked things out—memories, vague feelings, questionable values—broadening their consciousness or modifying their vision *had they been given the opportunity?* Might they have made sense of the ways people and society operate—creating order, form, and meaning where none existed before— *had they been allowed to write on what they wanted?* Those possible achievements, for me, far outweighed the purposes of traditional exams. That is, those possible achievements, *those* ends, presented a higher justification.

In an open exam, because the teacher dictates little, the teacher cannot anticipate anything: not the subject, not the theme, not the form or genre that any student may use. Which raises the teacher's curiosity and, more often than not, leads to interesting and fresh-minded reading. Our definition of "exam writing" can be broadened to include other kinds of writing in addition to those required by traditional exams—and broadening our definition benefits everyone.

"But, my little ones, I won't thrust you out into the cruel world naked. I'll give you some options, which you may consider in your own way for your own purposes.

"The first is this: You may write another function paper, especially if you feel you want more practice with this type of writing. Here are some topics:

What is the function of Part One of *TKM?*
What is the function of Scout, Jem, Dill, Boo, or Atticus?
What is the function of Scout's description of the Maycomb
County Court House or any other public building?
What is the function of any passage that you find significant?

"The other option will become plain to you as I read the following student examples. The first was written by Maile Gresham in a single hour-and-a-half sitting for NCTE's Promising Young Writer's contest. The rest are take-home exams written by eighth graders who have passed through this class in previous years."

I think my grandmother was one of the more influential people in my life. She was, as they say, a tough old bird. She lived in Florida, and I remember each time I used to visit her we would (we being my father and I and anyone that was already there) do things like play cards for nickels, or have swearing matches that always ended quite colorfully. What brought Grandma to mind was the book *To Kill a Mockingbird* that we're reading in English. I guess Grandma was my first lesson in prejudice.

There was a black family that lived across the road (dirt lane, my mother called it the one and only time she came), and I used to go over and play with the boys there. I would leave, wait around until they finished eating breakfast, and on our father's consent (usually), we would go romping through what is now a parking lot and resort near the edge of Orlando. There were all sorts of things to do, and my dad's only cautionary advice was to "stay away from the neighbors across the stream." Why, I had no idea, until later.

We would go through what seemed to be miles of brush until we reached some pond or brook of some sort. There was always the smell of dying weeds that hurt my always bloody nose; I wasn't used to Florida winters, no matter how mild. We'd climb the orange trees, and it was possible to go from one end of the orchard to the other without touching the ground more than once. The fire ant bites were the worst part about our adventures, although we would sit and watch a pond for crocodiles for maybe an hour.

Well, we cut back through the neighbors across the stream's backyards one day because we were late, and I not remembering my father's warning, thought nothing of it. So off we trundled, sneakers squelching that dirty mud all through people's yards. We ducked under a bush and found ourselves looking at an angry flowered dress flapping wildly in a sudden gust of wind. Thinking for an instant it was an occupant (instead of a clothesline) of one of the bungalo-type houses, we screamed and jumped down the embankment getting deliciously dirty in the process. Shambling and laughing, we crossed the shallow stream and were in my backyard. I ran up to the house and flung open the back door and found my grandmother standing there glaring fiercely over my shoulder. I turned, expecting to see the dog that always fertilized Grandma's lawn, or perhaps a few squirrels stealing her nuts. But all I saw were my three companions. Grandma yelled, "Niggers" and various other names at them, and shooed them out. Then she pushed me rather roughly in the house and told me to stay put while she got her favorite past-time food to eat while lecturing me, a tangerine.

She sat me in the living room and told me in the dusty dark not to *ever again* play with "them nigger boys." She spat her whole speech out in two minutes, and found herself short of breath and went to take a nap. I, on the other hand, was not tired, but just sat there petting Albert, her German Shepherd. I couldn't understand why I couldn't play with my colored friends, as I was brought up not to care about such mundane things as color, because in Hawaii you wouldn't have any friends if you stuck solely to your own tone. So I sat there, unbelieving. I can remember every little detail. There was a low ticking from the air conditioner and the TV. Albert was quiet, just a large ball of heat next to me. There were jelly stains on the old weathered piano that was never played because only Grandma knew how and her arthritis was too bad. But the smell of a lot of dust and a sharp acid smell from the tangerine skin filled my once-again bleeding nose. It wasn't such a horrible smell, I guess. But I'll never forget how seriously Grandma took the "evilness" of the niggers next door.

"This was Maile's first experience of prejudice against black people and, unfortunately, was rooted in her family. She can't forget it, nor all the persuasive little details surrounding the incident, especially the ones that impinge upon her senses as she is left alone at the end with Albert the dog, the jelly stains, and the smell of the tangerine skin.

"The next is by Jon Arakawa, a boy who likes history."

Of Late I Think of Maycomb

I read recently that the "South," as we know it in America, is disappearing. I don't remember where I read it or who wrote it but the article was about changes that occurred in the South since World War II (1941–1945). Blacks such as Jackie Robinson broke into sports in the early 1950s; Rosa Parks sat in front of the bus in 1956; Sidney Poitier won the Oscar in 1960; Malcolm X expressed civil rights in 1965 through violence, while Martin Luther King Jr. expressed it through peace in 1968. The author of the article went on to say that the South had also grown immensely by adapting to technological changes, industrializing and blending in with intercontinental commerce, such that today, you can hardly distinguish Florida, which was once a Confederate state, from California. Though there are isolated spots in the South that are slow to change, the author of the article said that there is generally little difference in the South with the rest of America. In politics, it is mentioned that more blacks hold office in the South than in the rest of America.

I was born in 1977 and grew up in a time when blacks had sitcoms on T.V., Afro hairdo's were "in," Alex Haley was finding his "Roots," and Vanessa Williams was crowned Miss America. I don't know about the "South" as much as my uncle George, who was stationed in Alabama in 1958, but through Harper Lee's novel, *To Kill a Mockingbird*, I made my own travel back in time to a place whose meaning is defined by the peculiarities of its people.

In her novel, Ms. Lee took me to a South that consisted predominantly of small towns with people whose thinking was no more expansive than the boundaries of their verandas. These people perpetuated caste systems and tradition from the time of their ancestors. Ms. Stephanie with her genteel background looked down upon white outcasts such as the Ewells who lived in surroundings almost as shabby as Kurdish camps. The Ewells, in turn, and just about everyone else who was white thought colored people were even lower in the caste. Blacks lived in their own communities.

There was more than a difference in social standing. People like Atticus and Miss Stephanie were educated. The Ewells are what is known as "white trash" or whites who could barely read or write their names. Blacks were forbidden an education. Economically, people like Atticus held professions. People like the Ewells either did menial jobs or were unemployed. Blacks did the most humiliating type of jobs such as Zeebo, Calpurnia's son, who shoveled dead dogs off the road.

It was a treat to be invited onto the porch of a Southern house and to listen to the conversation. Words like *chillun, nome, reckon,* and *nigger* are not familiar to my vocabulary. Peeping in on the missionary circle and hearing what Southern ladies discuss over lane cake and dewberry tarts wasn't particularly exciting. But standing before a lynch mob and witnessing the trial from nigger heaven were hair-raising and nail-chewing experiences.

These are memorable experiences and at the same time those that make me glad that I was not living then and down "South."

"What Jon tries to do is place the world of Maycomb—its peculiarities, its social hierarchy—into the context of his own study and limited knowledge of black America. The writing, at least for me, seems to promise deeper, longer meditations on this or similar topics in the future.

"The next piece, by Carrie Ching, is an example of point-of-view writing, which you yourself had practiced in the story-writing unit. It's a popular option."

Daddy

Once I dreamt that I was lookin' through a dirty window, the streaks of foul, brown water raked across my vision like drops of blood. I watched as all the little white chillun' frolicked and giggled and skipped 'cross a field o' daisies toward a crystal clear pool. They beckoned me to follow 'em.

I pressed my nose against the glass, its cold, hard surface chillin' me to the bone. I ran to the door which was wide open, I could almost smell the flowers. Then, suddenly a huge, fat man blocked the doorway. I smelt beer an' dirty, sweaty skin. I stepped back. He laughed and pointed at me, backin' out the doorway into the sunlight. He says, "You don't belong here, nigger," and slams the door in my face. I was left alone in the dark.

Momma tol' me it was just a dream, an' that everthin' was alright. But soon she had to leave an' go to work for Mr. Link Deas, and I was all alone.

I looked around for Daddy so he could comfort me and call me his little butterfly. So I could climb into his lap an' he could put his one good arm 'round me and love me. But he was gone.

Momma said he was killed by a disease, she never tol' me what it was, but now I know. My daddy was killed by a lie. He was a hardworking man, a kind man, and an honest man. He was, in fact, the only man in Maycomb who paid any attention to Miss Mayella Ewell. She was a lonely woman, and he was nice to her, but he was black. And according to society, no black man ever touched no white woman, it ain't right. She was so lonely, she didn't care. Miss Ewell loved my daddy, though he could never love her back. For that he would pay, and he did pay, pay with his life. She may have been white trash, but even white trash is above the nobles o' blacks, at least in Maycomb. I guess the jury was too blinded by society to see the truth.

After a while, I realized Daddy wasn't comin' back, and my poor family had to pay for that too. Are us poor blacks always gonna pay for the mistakes of everybody else? I pushed open the screen door and stepped outside. A cool spring breeze comforted my achin' heart. I listened to the wind whistlin' through the trees, the leaves rattling like the rusty iron chains that once bound the wrists of my ancestors. A dog barked in the distance, an' I heard the sweet sounds o' my brothers and sisters playin'.

> The itsy bitsy spider climbed up the water spout,
> down came the rain an' washed the spider out,
> out came the sun n' dried up all the rain,
> but the itsy bitsy spider would never live again . . .

"Carrie, through her imaginative identification, opens us up to the feelings of loss experienced by Tom Robinson's innocent daughter. Carrie gives us what the novel does not: Tom Robinson's family and personal grief. If you choose point-of-view writing, ask yourself what new understanding you bring to the table.

"The next piece, by Wendy Ikemoto, who is part Hawaiian, blasts a short-lived network TV program, set in the islands, that distorts the reality of the Hawaiian people."

Byrds of Paradise?

All local Hawaiians speak pidgin. They live in rundown houses and sleep on the floor. They drink, smoke, and have sex all the time. They are constantly fighting with each other. They have either a poor education or no education at all.

This is the impression which I received after watching one episode of "Byrds of Paradise." "Byrds of Paradise" is a fairly new television show and is filmed in Hawaii. The show uses many local people as actors and extras. I was astonished at the way the producers of this show portrayed Hawaiians. It denigrates the native Hawaiians and portrays them as bumpkins who are inferior to mainlanders. I was almost as astonished at this as I was at the prejudice against Blacks displayed in *To Kill a Mockingbird*. Southerners looked down at Blacks the same way that some mainlanders seem to look down on Hawaiians.

In the episode of "Byrds of Paradise" that I watched, Zeke is invited to sleep over at Nikki's house. Zeke is a young Haole boy [Caucasian] who moved from the mainland to Hawaii with his family. Nikki is a young, part-Hawaiian girl, the same age as Zeke. She is a tomboy and Zeke's classmate. She grew up in Hawaii. If Nikki were Black instead of Hawaiian, this show could have been entitled "The Byrds of Maycomb County."

This episode shows Nikki's mother driving her daughter and Zeke to her house. They own an extremely old, beat up, rust blue car. When Zeke tries to get out of the car, Nikki's mother tells him to use the other door. His door is broken and won't open. Nikki's yard is almost completely red dirt. There are farm animals scattered all over their property. When Zeke asks to drop his bag off in Nikki's room, Nikki explains that she doesn't have a room. She sleeps on the floor with her grandparents. At dinner, everyone has one slice of cold pizza on their plastic plates.

This suggests that all Hawaiians are poor people who scrape up just enough money to feed the family. This lifestyle may pertain to a few Hawaiians, but it definitely does not pertain to all Hawaiians. Many Southern Whites also stereotype Blacks in this fashion. They believe that all Blacks are poor and live in rundown houses.

Zeke doesn't feel comfortable at Nikki's house because his family is much wealthier. Zeke isn't accustomed to Nikki's lifestyle so he complains about an imaginary stomach ache. When he asks to use the phone, Nikki's father explains that they don't own a phone. The closest phone is miles away.

In another part of the episode, Zeke's older sister, Frannie, plans a huge birthday party. Approximately forty people show up. When the party is over, the Local people don't want to leave. One boy is willing to fight Frannie's brother to stay, until another Local boy tells him to leave "before I gonna bust your legs." After the party, two Local seniors steal two cases of wine which belong to Frannie's father. Again, the Local people are portrayed as violent trouble makers and thieves, just as many Blacks are stereotyped as people who constantly steal from the White people. Many Blacks have even been falsely blamed for the crimes that White people committed.

In another instance, Frannie's older brother, Harry, is planning the menu for a special date. He asks his housekeeper for a suggestion. Harry's family has two housekeepers, a middle aged, married, Hawaiian couple. Both are overweight. The male housekeeper suggests that Harry make his favorite Hawaiian food—fried pork fat. This implies that Hawaiians are unhealthy eaters and that most of them are overweight.

Harry goes out with his girlfriend, Crystal. While they are in the car, Crystal announces that she is pregnant. It is her previous boyfriend's baby. Harry gets angry and asks her if she had even thought about the diseases she could catch and how irresponsible she was. Harry also confronts Crystal's previous boyfriend, Junior, and demands to know what he is going to do now that Crystal is pregnant. Junior replies that it isn't his problem that Crystal is pregnant. In this scene, Hawaiians are portrayed as promiscuous and irresponsible. Blacks have also been stereotyped as being promiscuous and irresponsible. This is shown in *To Kill a Mockingbird* when Mr. Ewell charges Tom Robinson for raping Mayella Ewell.

Ever since Harry's family came to Hawaii, he has been called, "Hey, Haole boy!" He has been teased and beat up by the Local kids just because he is Haole and has orange hair. All people who live in Hawaii know that Haole kids aren't usually beat up just because they're Haole. This suggests that Hawaiians are prejudiced and violent. It also suggests that Hawaiians hate those who are higher on the economic ladder.

Harry's father, Mr. Byrd, goes out to get a drink with a friend. At the bar, Mr. Byrd accidentally bumps into a tough, Local Hawaiian. He apologizes, but the Hawaiian man doesn't forgive him. Mr. Byrd gets punched out; and when his friend tries to help him, he gets punched out too. This scene gives the impression that Hawaiians are violent people who drink too much. Also, it suggests that Hawaiians solve all their problems by fighting. Blacks have also been thought to be violent. Many people picture them as gang members.

After watching this episode of "Byrds of Paradise," I never watched it again. However, my sister has. I asked her if Hawaiians were ever portrayed as having an education. She replied, "No, except for one lady. But I think they also mentioned that she was educated on the mainland."

People who live in Hawaii know that most of these stereotypes are false. I fear that people who live on the mainland and have never visited Hawaii may blindly accept these stereotypes. This negative image could cause some not to visit Hawaii. As a part-Hawaiian, I deeply resent the negative image created by this show.

As in *To Kill a Mockingbird*, the "Byrds of Paradise" demonstrates the maliciousness of negatively stereotyping an entire group of people. In *To Kill a Mockingbird*, Southerners subjugate and mistreat Blacks and excuse this behavior by stereotyping the Blacks as lazy, stupid farmhands or servants. I don't know what the goal of the writers and producers of "Byrds of Paradise" is but the net result is outrageous racism.

"Wendy's biting argument is well crafted, presenting persuasive evidence and reasonable judgments, and it is heartfelt. We can understand her indignance at the producers' insensitivity for and ignorance of Hawaiian people, which project to the rest of the world, as Wendy says, negative stereotypes.

"This next piece, by Lopa Shaw, is another personal experience story on prejudice."

My Childhood Monster

I spent many months of my childhood living in a poor village in western India with my grandparents. During that time, the caste system was taken very seriously. There were the priests, who were the highest, the farmers and merchants, and the untouchables. The untouchables lived on the outskirts of the village in tiny dry-grass huts. They lived in filth; the dirt roads were their beds; they never bathed; they had hardly any food. Religion is a major part of Indian culture and was taken very seriously. All the Indian children were told to never ever come into contact with one of these untouchables because, if they did, their spirits would become contaminated. Since I was a child from America I had no idea that the caste system existed.

One day as I was playing outside, I accidentally bumped into one of the maids, who was on her way home. Immediately my grandmother grabbed my hand and rushed me to the front door. She ran into the house and came out with a clay pot filled to the brim with water. She began to sprinkle water on my forehead and began to chant. She was doing a ritual to repurify my spirit which had been touched by the maid, who was an untouchable. She then, in a panicking voice, ordered me to take a shower. As I disappeared into the house I could hear her yelling in the background at the young girl. She told the girl that she should have watched where she was going and that she should know better than to stay near us. The young girl took on the look of fear and sadness. She turned around and quickly walked out of the gate and down the dirt road back to her home.

I can still remember the look on her face as she walked away. It was the look of helplessness. The look of confusion and frustration. I never really understood what she must have felt like until I came back to America and started my first year of school in kindergarten.

From the first day I was called names pertaining to my skin color, beaten, and ignored just because I was different by color. I was very lonely. I did not have any friends to play with, so I kept myself busy at school by counting down the hours until my mom would come and pick me up from school and take me home. I sat in the stone-cold sandbox in the corner of the playground. I would watch slugs creep across the sidewalk, leaving behind their slimy trail, and it was during this time in my life that I was confused. I was very frustrated. There was no one I could talk to because all of the other children were white.

Now I look back and I realize that those children did what they did because it was how they were brought up. They were ignorant. They believed that everyone who had a dark skin color was stupid and less than they. Prejudice is disgusting and unfair, but it exists. Many people have stories of how they were free and careless as a child, but for me, my story is that I was trapped in a world of hatred. In a place where I was not wanted. I was one of my only companions. Prejudice is the one thing that destroyed my childhood and made it a living nightmare.

"Different from Maile Gresham's experience with her grandmother, this time the writer herself becomes, because of the tint of her skin, the object of scorn. It is similar to what she witnessed in India, where an entire nation may scorn the *untouchables*, those who, by accident of birth, occupy the lowest caste in their social system, where discrimination and prejudice are acceptable by tradition.

"The next piece, by Mark Hoffman, is a function paper."

A Characterization of Atticus Finch

Atticus Finch serves a major purpose in the novel *To Kill a Mockingbird*, both as the father and only parent of Jem and Scout and as the defending attorney in the Tom Robinson case. In both instances, he consistently shows respect to everyone he deals with, no matter race or social class.

Most of the Finch family feels he is failing as a parent. Aunt Alexandra especially has trouble accepting such abnormalities as Scout wearing trousers and swearing. She doesn't believe the children will ever turn out right without her "proper guidance."

However, we see that Atticus' way is in fact best. Attempts by other family members to discipline or communicate with the children only serve to confuse them. For example, Uncle Jack punishes Scout for fighting with and swearing at Francis before even giving her a chance to tell her side. Then, later on when Scout asks Uncle Jack what a "whore-lady" is, he gives her an answer that makes no sense.

Talking down to the children or hiding them from the reality of life causes more harm than good in the long run, and Atticus realizes this. He therefore treats his children as adults and individuals, always showing them respect and not brushing off their questions as unimportant. This is, in fact, a reflection of the way in which he treats everyone, no matter what race or class of society.

This respect toward all others is shown in the way in which he handles the trial. Although he was appointed to the defense of the Negro Tom Robinson and realizes he has no hope of winning, he is determined to do his best and prove Tom's innocence on principle alone. He knows this will cause most of the town to torment him and his children, yet still gives it his total effort, because he is a strong believer in equal justice for all. In fact, he believes that there is nothing worse than a white man taking advantage of a black man; these whites are the worst kind of trash. This differs greatly from Aunt Alexandra's definition of trash, which is based on social standing.

During the trial, he treated all witnesses with respect—even Bob and Mayella Ewell. In fact, when Mayella gets upset about Atticus addressing her as ma'am, Judge Taylor explains that addressing people as ma'am and sir was simply Atticus' way of being courteous to everyone. That was just Atticus' way.

Throughout the novel, Atticus serves as a voice of reason amongst a crowd of very emotional and prejudiced people. He is continually telling Scout to see things from another perspective, to step into their shoes and try to see things from their point of view. Atticus is the one constant in an ocean of flowing tides, the one light that never goes out, the one rock that will always be there, immobile. Not to say that he is unopen to change, just that he will not yield ground on the things he believes in, that he will not give into social pressure, and that he will not compromise his values no matter what. That takes a special, a rare kind of courage.

"I like that. Atticus constantly maintains the high moral ground, which he will never yield. And the way he behaves with his children is indicative of the way he behaves with everyone. A succinct piece of writing.

"This next piece, by Virginia Loo, switches back and forth between analytical prose and poetry, and I think successfully so—even though the challenge she presents herself is hugely ambitious: making us feel sympathy for Mayella Ewell, the primary witness against Tom Robinson, who lies and initiates the events that bring about his death."

Mayella Ewell

Mayella Ewell seemed to be a constant victim—victim of society, time, and circumstance. She was an enemy, not hated, but felt sorry for. Mayella was born into a family whose provider was a man with little concern for his family, reputation, and his own future. Mayella seemed pushed into the role of homemaker and forgotten. She received the responsibility of the job, but the respect to come with it was lacking.

Society considered Bob Ewell and his family white trash. This was the lowest of the white social classes. It wasn't just that they were poor, but that Bob Ewell was a drunk and wasted his money on that evil. Mayella's father wasn't hardworking like Mr. Cunningham, and there was no maternal figure to support the family. Mayella tried to make her family a unit instead of just a group of people with the same name. I think she failed because she had to do it alone. Her father didn't care much and the other children had been hurt too many times to trust her. Mayella wanted better than what she had, but society made it almost impossible. Society felt pity for the children of Bob Ewell and made sure they had spam at Christmas. Actually accepting them as equals was unheard of because nobody wanted to lower themselves to that level. So Mayella's social experiences were put downs, phony smiles, and charity baskets. If she tried to climb higher, her fingers would be stepped on.

Encased
by a sleek Mercedes,
going down smooth highways.
Inhaling
new fish-smelling leather,
Hearing
clear soothing music,
Cooled
by manmade breezes,
inside a bubble,
oblivious to outside
your mausoleum "world"
      not
Encrusted
by the dirt and trash,
lining rutty streets.
Breathing
pungent black tar,
Listening
to angry, frustrated groans
of everyday survival.
Beaten
by sun
and whipping winds,
Ignored
by what you want to be,
Locked out,
echoes off walls.

I think that Mayella needed to be loved and accepted by someone. Her family and society had both rejected her. She seemed to feel inferior to others—not an equal. She was still a child who wanted to please. Then came Tom Robinson, the only person who was nice to her. He did things for her and wanted nothing in return. I think that is why she tried to kiss him. He was black, somebody in the world that was lower than she was. He couldn't possibly reject her, but he did. I think that hurt her more than any of her father's abuse.

After kissing Tom Robinson, Mayella must have felt so alone. The friend she could have had in Tom Robinson was gone. When society heard what happened they just had pity for her. They didn't give her personal support—it was just another case, an unfortunate thing to happen, at least it didn't happen to one of us. The only person left was her father. She tried to make her father love her by doing what he wanted. I think she was afraid of losing her father, so she testified the way he wanted her to. It was too bad that Bob Ewell only cared that he "wasn't getting into no trouble 'cause what Ma'ella did." Mayella would probably live and die in her home—never marry, never be somebody. Mayella needed somebody, but nobody was there.

Sitting alone
on a green, flaking bench,
Indian style.
baloney for lunch
(eaten a lot of it),
Blowing bubbles
between munches.
Blue glass bubbles
reflecting the sun,
each one bigger than the last.
Just before
reaching the clouds,
they pop.
Blowing them anyway,
one had to make it.
Some pop
in my face,
the taste of soap
in my mouth.

Throwing
leftover baloney
to the birds.
Change jingles
in my pocket.
No dimes or nickels
to pay people.
Only pennies
from others.
two pennies,
two thoughts,
85 &
Sitting alone.

I think it was then when the hate exploded from her. She was angry at her father for being a drunk, society for treating her as trash, and Tom Robinson for rejecting her. When Atticus began to rip holes in her testimony she was angry because she realized that society might not believe her. She knew how little society thought of her, but she did not think they would trust a black man over her. Her one comfort in life might have been the knowledge that she was still better than any black person, and now society would rip that away from her, too. Putting her below a black man was the ultimate insult, because prejudice slaps the bottom the hardest.

"Though Virginia makes me pity Mayella, I can never condone what she did, nor can I forgive her, except maybe, *maybe* on my death bed. What you've heard suggests the possible exams you might write, and may suggest to you what has yet to be written. I will evaluate your work against the standard established by these writings *and* the degree to which your writing shows individual growth, which to me, is more important. Finally, though this is an exam, you may, as you have practiced throughout the year, seek feedback from others—but this time not from your classmates, for I don't want you to prejudice each other's thinking as you try, perhaps, to anticipate mine. Look into your heart and write! Aloha."

The student examples I read to the class set the standard for student achievement and suggest the range of possible themes, modes, and methods that they can emulate in their own writing, through their own variations.

Through reading a fine book, through chapter-by-chapter study (via function papers), and through critical class discussions, the students will be well prepared to write personally meaningful responses that are worthy of reader interest. And that's good for us teachers, for, though we cannot flee the number of exams we must read, our reading will not be a tedious chore. In fact, we will often be pleasantly surprised and sometimes even stunned by students' accomplishment. And that's what makes us realize that we're in the right business.

9

The Teacher's Persona

It is such examples of passion and exhilaration that
students need in their teachers . . .

Yet there is no single, ideal character for teachers.
Human types being infinitely varied, many different types of
character can "work" in the classroom.
—*Banner and Cannon,* Elements of Teaching

One definition for *personality* is this: the totality of an individual's character traits. It is who we are—all that we do and feel and know, all that we desire, all that we dislike; it is all our flaws and prejudices, as well as all our virtues and strengths—it is a unique, complex mix. It's enough to boggle the mind. Humanity is rich. Some personalities appear *larger*, more memorable, or more charismatic than others, while some of us feel overlooked by nature or God. There is nothing more to say about the matter.

But, of course, there is much to say, especially when this belief impinges on teaching and the nature of the teacher, which is the subject of this chapter.

There have been, and are today, great teachers, people we admire and revere because of their dedication and passion, like the biologist Louis Agassiz, who, on the surface, did little more than screw up his face, point to the fish, and say, "Look again!" People who have awed and elevated us through their vast knowledge and vision, like Harvard's George Lyman Kittredge, whose legendary lectures were experienced as "events." People who have touched something deep within us, inspiring us, like my teacher, Lardas, whose honesty and compassion and resonant voice made the classroom and his students tremble. But there are many great teachers, and a host of very good ones—many more, I think, than we tend to believe—who go about their work anonymously and quietly, enlarging the characters, spirits, and minds of their students in their own inimitable ways.

The truth is that many teachers have had to work very hard over many years (albeit through self-flagellation and trial and error and, most times, unconsciously) to become the selves who students benefit from in the classroom, the selves that stem from and are shaped by their own—and no one else's—personality. This second self we call the *persona*. By definition, as a self-created thing, it can be cultivated, developed, grown. I dare say that those who have stayed in the profession any meaningful length of time know intuitively that the difference between being a so-so teacher and a good one is *nine times the space of heaven*, and that becoming a good teacher is dependent upon the growth of the persona.

This kind of growth is rarely talked about in education. Instead, discussion tends toward, as my astute colleague puts it, "the mystique of personality" of the teacher, toward awe and mystery and myth, as some talk of poetry.

The teacher's persona is a professional facade. It is the character the teacher presents to the classroom. It is the teacher's genuine personality shorn of the characteristics that detract from or are irrelevant to effective teaching and learning. The persona is made notable through the distillation and emphasis of the characteristics that help the teacher communicate with unquestioned confidence and memorable intensity. It is like the ideal self the writer creates when telling a story: The writer excises utterances that may bore or offend while foregrounding strengths through the use of her finest words, filling her audience with light and heat, broadening its consciousness and deepening its care.

Among my colleagues at school, the person whose classroom persona comes closest to the way he is with other teachers and friends is Mr. Otagaki, or Mr. O, as his students fondly address him. But differences can be seen. For example, when explaining a chemical reaction or preparing students for a lab or lecturing them on their behavior, Mr. O's eyes narrow as though in anger, and he seems to speak through gritted teeth (which are very white because they're not his own). His voice, already loud (you can hear him through the wall), becomes sharper, especially the consonants, especially when he karate-chops the air or his left palm. His whole bearing seems made of steel, and he communicates with a zeal that is commensurate with his understanding that the stakes are large and that the purpose of teaching and learning is deadly serious.

Otherwise, Mr. O is a stand-up comedian, entertaining his kids with jokes and comments or images that he might exploit for his teaching even though other teachers would not dare. Almost like a kid himself, he echoes students' interests. He treads, some would say, a dangerous edge, as one who is accepted as both mentor and pal. But he's an expert at walking the tightrope. You can see him in the corridor lecturing or disciplining a kid, or hugging a kid with abandon.

When he explains something scientific to his colleagues, on the other hand, Mr. O's teacherly traits are muted, while his joking becomes racier or more risqué. Through his many years of teaching, he has learned which knobs to turn up and which to turn down in order to fine-tune his persona as an aid to his students' learning. However slight the difference seems between Mr. O's persona and his larger self, it is of huge significance—it accounts, in fact, for his excellence as a teacher.

Another former Teacher of the Year from our state is Mrs. Nishimoto, for whom this poem was written:

Mrs. Nish

A clown
Standing in front of the classroom
Making funny faces.

Enthusiastic,
With creative
And insane
Ways of teaching.

We played with sand,
measured the density
Of a gummy worm,
And dropped eggs and marbles off
The third floor of Bishop.

She is obsessed with
Albert Einstein.
Pictures of him
Are hung all over the room
Like a museum.
She even names folders and books
Albert or Alberto.

An animal lover,
With a photo of her dog and bird
On her desk,
Two beanie babies
Jenny and Ken
Sit on her computer,
And a chinchilla
Named Pookie
Lives in the back of her classroom.

She names all her sections
After fruits,
Says nail polish causes brain damage,
And believes that
Correcting in red makes
Students angry.

Sometimes,
She becomes very excited

And yells during class
"Oh! Oh! Oh!"
When she thinks of a
New way to teach or explain something.

Her ideas always keep coming,
Brightening the light
Shining over her head.
                    —Jenny Maehara (Grade 8)

Mrs. Nishimoto's persona is dramatically different from the larger self that she is at home with her professor husband, who also teaches science. No, she does not have Beanie Babies draped over her living room lamp shade or cutely tucked in the corners of her bookcase (there's no room). But she does share with her husband her enthusiasm for teaching and learning, and shares, from time to time, a science project or a brilliant lab report that bowls her husband over. She shows both her husband and her students ("Oh! Oh! Oh!") her great love for learning and teaching, which is plainly manifest in everything she does.

This brings to mind a small group session with English teachers from our high school during a recent Curriculum Day, where the subject was passionate teaching. I remember one teacher saying: "What I tell my own children is that I hope they find a job that they love, that they enjoy going to, day after day. Good teachers give them a good example of that."

Funny. Of all my grade-school teachers, only a handful come to mind, and then only as caricatures without names. Like my ninth-grade English teacher in L.A., who taught us Shakespeare's *Julius Caesar*, an experience I don't recall at all. What I do remember is him calling us up to the front of the room to retrieve our papers or tests. One time, as he handed back a paper to me, he wouldn't let go of it. I was stuck short holding my end, which forced me to raise my head and look into this face with its U-shaped grin that, like Bert Lahr's (the Cowardly Lion in the *Wizard of Oz*), reached nearly to his ears. It was the most mobile face I had ever seen. Surely, had it little feet, it would dance like Jim Carey across the podium.

He'd bring us up short in other ways, too. For example, a girl would raise her hand and ask, "May I go to the restroom?" and he'd respond, "No. You may go to the restroom." Or to another question, he'd nod his head vigorously up and down and say, "No." What was the purpose of befuddling us this way? So we'd remember his face? Even then, I knew that humor and oddness and bewilderment had their place in the classroom, and that they were part of me, too. In fact, this peculiar teacher and I, despite the great difference in our ages, shared a similar spirit.

The math teachers I've had, on the other hand, were on the whole a humorless lot, high on discipline, all business, like the numbers they cuddle up to.

One who comes to mind (who in all probability helped set the standard when the Earth first cooled) was my calculus teacher, who was no bigger than a broomstick. With no iron-gray strand out of place, meticulously dressed in dark business suits, she brooked no arguments, no excuses, gave no quarter, had no time. I was forced to act the robot she wanted me to be.

One day, she seemed to receive input from some invisible source, crossing her wires. The most remarkable thing happened. In the middle of a review session, her face softened and her eyes took on a distant look. Her voice changed and she spoke, almost to herself, of a young mathematician, speaking in tones we had never heard before, in tones of admiration and reverence. She praised his genius and his intellectual achievements, emphasizing his youth, the poignancy of his age at his premature death, mourning the loss, the waste, what more he could have shared with the world—speaking in tones almost like love.

We were stunned, fixed in our seats until, breaking from her reverie, the teacher dismissed her vision with the back of her hand and turned back to the blackboard, drawing most of the students with her. But I tarried in the moment, for, through an accident, an unaccountable breach in her usual character, I was permitted a glimpse of what she felt was sacred—and what was possibly the motive behind her endeavor to be a pure mathematician, one who would chart the heartbeat of the cosmos.

What intrigued me was the single moment that revealed my teacher as a human being—revealed her humanity, her desires, her regrets, her vulnerability, which made her a figure both tragic and noble. These were the moments I waited for, you might say hungered for. But never again did she permit her inner voice such passionate freedom. Had she done so, many more of us might have pursued different careers. Perhaps our teacher's persona as it usually was appealed to those already committed to math.

Professor Yao Shen, on the other hand, held nothing back. She was nearing her seventies at the time, her head bobbing atop a long, narrow, Chinese dress as if she were Hawaii's version of Popeye's Olive Oyl. She taught a graduate course on the history of English, teaching us as if we were children, babies even. She particularly taught us with the grandmotherly machinations of her narrow, rubbery face. There never was a moment we didn't know what she felt, especially if our answers were right or, even better, if we said something original. Her face would tell us if we were wrong, or if she felt doubtful about our conclusion, or felt disappointed, or was comically shocked when a bizarre speculation appeared just left of Mars. There, too, just left of Mars, we'd find her face. She drove my desk mate Wyndnagle nuts. Once every session she'd refer to the poet Keats as "my Johnny," as if he were her next-door neighbor or a nephew or her boyfriend. Wyndnagle would roll his eyes, as if losing consciousness, and drop his bushy head into the frying pan of his hands. "I can't stand it!" he'd say after class. "John Keats!" Wyndnagle held Keats in the highest esteem, seating him between Socrates and Shakespeare on the frieze of his personal pantheon. "My God, Joe," he'd say, his face twisted in genuine agony. "My *Johnny!*"

Shen's passion was just too positive for me. She was always up, always jolly, always grandmotherly sweet. That can wear on your nerves. Which shows that, no matter how true and "shapely" one's persona may be, it will not resonate with everyone. Nevertheless, I liked Shen tremendously.

I was looking for a different kind of passion, something akin to the hard-edged cynicism, resignation, and compassion of someone like Professor Kriegel, my first writing teacher, whose fine pen was also his cudgel. I ran across a personal essay of his in *Harper's* a few years back, a strong narrative argument against handguns. Toward the end, Kriegel described a time when, had there been a gun readily at hand, he would have used it, having been pushed to the wall. I wasn't surprised, for he would shoot from the hip when responding to my short story characters, who, for the most part, tended toward loud, ignorant pronouncements on famous writers. ("One would wonder why that ass Fitzgerald bothered to write at all.")

That Kriegel was intolerant of mediocrity was evidenced not so much in his words as in his voice, in the streetfighter's grimace that was his smile, and in his thick upper body, which served to challenge you and to hope that you would do your best—and to say that to do otherwise was dishonesty.

On one particular day, after setting his battered briefcase on the desk at the head of the class and propping his crutches against the chalk rail, after bending to shift his steel-braced legs beneath the desk, Kriegel withdrew from his briefcase a book—his book, which had been recently published. He remarked, without raising his eyes, that there were a few sentences that he didn't recall writing. His talk was short, and we returned to our own work, though I'm sure others watched him as I did, fascinated.

Oblivious to us, Kriegel seemed to fondle the book with his large, powerful hands, feeling the spine, tracing its edges, testing the thickness and the quality of the paper. Cradling the book in one hand, he flipped through the pages with the other, his eyes glazed with a fiercely possessive, fiercely proud light.

Passion is who you are, what you teach, and the way you teach it that—at different moments, to different degrees—dissolves into a single, luminous sound, tumultuous or tremulous, that signals like a pulsating light at the roof of your students' skulls. At its most intense, the signal reads, "Here is something important, here is something powerful and fine, here is something that I ought to look into more closely." Students are infected, suddenly or gradually, by a teacher's dementia—for all the right reasons that the teacher shows. And students tremble with truth.

Good English teachers possess five common passions: love of language, love of teaching, love of learning, love of witnessing growth in their students, and love of showing their passions through their voice and manner—through their persona. One of the reasons I wrote this book was to remind my fellow teachers of our first love—our passion for language—which drew us into the discipline in the first place. This love became a great part of who we are, defining us, and, whether students know it or not, they crave to hear and see and know this love.

More important, I think, than "individualized learning" is "individualizing teachers," helping them to modify themselves in the crafting and shaping of their own personas. We can point out to teachers the strong and wonderful traits that reveal their humanity, "to which," according to Banner and Cannon (1997, p. 2), "contents and methods are adjunct." As teachers, in our efforts to continually master knowledge and means, we must not overlook the never-ending development and refinement of our singular classroom selves. From the standpoint of our students, we are both the instrument of learning and the subject to be learned.

To quote Sizer again, "We win or lose with kids to some considerable measure with our personalities. Good teachers use their personas even at the risk of being characters."

Put it this way: Who else is there? *What* else is there?

It is an old story told again and again. And it is about teachers, about us. Like Prometheus, we bring fire.

Works Cited

"All worked up . . ." 1998. From "Korean Figures" in *East Window: The Asian Translations*. Edited by W. S. Merwin. Port Townsend, WA: Copper Canyon Press.

Baldwin, James. 1963. "My Dungeon Shook: Letter to My Nephew on the Hundredth Anniversary of Emancipation." In *The Fire Next Time*. New York: Dial Press.

Banner, James M., and Arnold C. Cannon. 1997. *Elements of Teaching*. New Haven: Yale University Press.

Bashō, Matsuo. 1991. "Four temple gates . . ." In *Beneath a Single Moon: Buddhism in Contemporary Poetry*. Edited by Kent Johnson and Craig Paulenich. Boston: Shambhala.

Borges, Jorge Luis. 1964. "Everything and Nothing." In *Labryrinths: Selected Short Stories and Other Writings*. Edited by Donald A. Yates and James E. Irby. New York: New Directions.

Burgess, Anthony. 1965. *A Clockwork Orange*. New York: Ballantine Books.

Dickens, Charles. 1961. *Hard Times*. New York: Signet Classics.

Dostoevski, Fyodor. 1960. "Notes from the Underground." In *Notes from the Underground and the Grand Inquisitor*. Translated by Ralph E. Matlow. New York: E. P. Dutton

Douglass, Frederick, 1966. "5. Miss Sophia." In *The Life and Times of Frederick Douglass*. Adapted by Barbara Ritchie, Ann Arbor, MI: T. Y. Crowell.

Forster, E. M. 1924. *A Passage to India*. New York: Harcourt, Brace and World.

Fuentes, Gregorio Lopez y. 1999. "A Letter to God." In *Reading and All That Jazz*. Edited by Peter Mather and Rita McCarthy. Translated by Donald A. Yates. New York: McGraw-Hill.

Hara, Marie. 1994. "Old Kimono." In *Bananaheart and Other Stories*. Honolulu, HI: Bamboo Ridge Press.

Hemingway, Ernest. 1957. *A Farewell to Arms*. New York: Scribner.

"The Historic Fart." 1973. In *The Tale from the Thousand and One Nights*. Translated by N. J. Dawood. Baltimore, MD: Penguin Books.

Holt, John Dominis. 1976. *Waiamea Summer*. Honolulu, HI: Topgallant.

Huysmans, Joris Karl. 19–? *Against the Grain (A rebours)*. London: Fortune Press.

Joyce, James. 1964. *A Portrait of the Artist As a Young Man*. New York: Viking Press.

Kafka, Franz. 1972. *The Metamorphosis*. Translated by Stanley Corngold. New York: Bantam Books.

Kaneshiro, Wayne. 1983. "Sandcastles." Honolulu, HI.

Lee, Harper. 1960. *To Kill a Mockingbird*. Philadelphia, PA: Lippincott.

Lorca, Garcia. 1955. "The Duende: Theory and Divertissement." In *Poet in New York*. Translated by Ben Bulitt. New York: Grove Press Inc.

Lum, Darrell H. Y. 1995. "What School You Went?" In *The Best of Honolulu Fiction: Stories from the Honolulu Magazine Fiction Contest*. Edited by Eric Chock and Darrell Lum. Honolulu, HI: Bamboo Ridge Press.

Munro, H. H. 1930. "The Open Window." In *The Stories of Saki*. New York: Viking Press.

Nunez, Susan. 1962. "The Grandmother." In *A Small Obligation and Other Stories of Hilo*. Honolulu, HI: Bamboo Ridge Press.

Salinger, J. D. 1946. *The Catcher in the Rye*. Boston: Bantam Books.

Sizer, Theodore. 1988. "Introduction: Kids Differ." In *The Teacher's Journal* (Spring).

Tsujimoto, Joseph I. 1988. *Teaching Poetry Writing to Adolescents*. Urbana, IL: National Council Teachers of English and ERIC Clearinghouse on Reading and Communication Skills.

———. 1989/90. "Mantis." *Hawaii Review* 28 (Winter)

———. 1990. "The Affective Teacher." Keynote address to the annual meeting of the teacher-consultants and site directors of the National Writing Project, Baltimore, Maryland, November 1989. Published in *The Teacher's Journal* (Spring).

Twain, Mark, 1958. *The Adventures of Huckelberry Finn*. New York: Harper and Row.

Updike, John. 1962. "A & P." In *Pigeon Feathers and Other Stories*. New York: Alfred A. Knopf, Inc.

Williams, John. 1988. *Stoner*. Fayetteville, AK: University of Arkansas Press.

Wright, Richard. 1937. *Black Boy*. New York: Harper and Row.